Psychology and the Cross

THE EARLY HISTORY OF FULLER SEMINARY'S SCHOOL OF PSYCHOLOGY

by
H. NEWTON MALONY
(in collaboration with HENDRIKA VANDE KEMP)

Copies of this book are available from
FULLER SEMINARY BOOKSTORE
135 North Oakland Avenue
Pasadena, California 91182

©Copyright 1995 by Fuller Theological Seminary.
All rights reserved.

Published by Fuller Seminary Press, 135 North Oakland Avenue
Pasadena, California 91182

Printed in U.S.A.

ISBN 0-9650740-0-5

Table of Contents

PREFACE iii

CHAPTER 1
   A School Is What We Need 1

CHAPTER 2
   How Firm Was the Foundation 19

CHAPTER 3
   Two Steps Forward, One Step Back 30

CHAPTER 4
   School Objectives Debated—The Clinic Is Opened . . . 39

CHAPTER 5
   A Dean Is Chosen 56

CHAPTER 6
   Students Come—Classes Begin 74

CHAPTER 7
   Travis Builds a Faculty 88

CHAPTER 8
   Attaining APA Accreditation 105

CHAPTER 9
   Integration 122

CHAPTER 10
   Travis Retires—Warren Becomes Dean 140

APPENDICES 157
   The Importance of a View of Man—John F. Finch 158
   Freud and the Dissenters—John G. Finch 173
   Spirit and Psyche—John G. Finch 188
   A Proposed Graduate School of Christian Psychology—
      John G. Finch and Paul D. Fairweather 201
   A Christian Approach to Psychology—Paul D. Fairweather 206
   Man: In Search of Him—Lee Edward Travis 219
   The Graduate School of Psychology: A Faculty Genealogy
      for the Travis Years—Hendrika Vande Kemp 228

PSYCHOLOGY AND THE CROSS

In appreciation of
CLIFFORD L. PENNER,
early graduate, loyal trustee,
notable clinician, faithful Christian

Preface

To write the history of times through which one has lived comes close to being an autobiography. I have been a part of Fuller Theological Seminary's Graduate School of Psychology for all but four years of its life. Without question, these have been the most important decades of my career. Thus, I am not an unbiased writer. While my intent would be to recount the events of these years in a fair manner, I look at this story through tinted spectacles.

I am proud of the school. I judge its record positively. Two years away, one on sabbatical and another on a visiting professorship, have convinced me even more of the importance of this effort to train mental health professionals who take seriously the integration of their Christian faith with their practice of counseling and psychotherapy.

When asked to undertake this project, I wrote my dean, Archibald D. Hart, "I am pleased to work alongside you in this grand and glorious project." For me, as I approach retirement, this feeling is colored by few, if any, doubts or misgivings.

Fuller's Graduate School of Psychology was the first of several, serious attempts to train psychologists who are Christian in their personal lives, in the principles they espouse, and in the professional help that they offer. While no history is spotless and all institutional records are uneven, the Graduate School of Psychology has accomplished its mission as the ancestor of a unique genre of religious professionals. However, the place to judge the Graduate School of Psychology's effectiveness is not in what I write. If one would judge effectiveness, it would be better to look out there in the world where our graduates have taken their place as Christian professionals—faithful in belief and in practice.

I am grateful for the help I have been given. Fuller Seminary trustees supported this project financially but set no limits on its content. I owe a special debt to Bert Jacklitch, the School of Psychology's administrative assistant to the dean, who made the skill and helpfulness of departmental secretaries available whenever I needed them. She was a constant cheerleader, a reliable source of information, and a very good friend. Her assistants Kim Roth and Caroline Beatley, as well as my secretary Greg Poland, were always there to assist me, as well as to goad me on occasion. Our director of Communication, Marilyn Thomsen, was the one who transformed these thoughts on computer disk into a "real" book, complete with cover and printed pages. She and her staff are miracle workers, especially Janice Ryder who formatted the photos and Esther Brinkley who did the copy editing.

Many of those who preceded me, or were my early colleagues, spent time in telling me the story of those years from their perspective. These persons include R. Donald Weber, Donald F. Tweedie, Neil C. Warren, Paul W. Clement, Paul F. Barkman, and Adrin Sylling. Professors Emeriti Daniel Fuller and Geoffrey Bromiley reminisced about the discussions that went into establishing the School of Psychology from the School of Theology's point of view. Annette Weyerhaeuser was most gracious in sharing her personal story with me—a story that became central in making the idea of a school become a reality.

Paul Fairweather, John Finch, C. Davis Weyerhaeuser, and David Hubbard, the "four horsemen" who gave legs to the dream, spent many hours with me. Lysa Travis, wife of the school's founding dean, and Marnie Frederickson, first of the school's able executive secretaries, recounted their memory of the events that took place under the deanship of Lee Edward Travis. A group of graduates, many of whom were here at the beginning, shared their stories—often serious, sometimes hilarious. These included John Fry, Clifford Penner, Sam Lo, David Condiff, Al Hess, Don Roberts, Bill Weyerhaeuser, Bill Evans, Gary Reese, Tom Malcolm, and David Bock. I am especially grateful to Dagi Finch, whose records proved invaluable. She turned out to be a "pack rat" par excellence.

To each and all of these advisors I owe a deep debt. However, I alone take responsibility for the final printed interpretation of all these consultations. As the project came to an end, I had concerns that I had made mistakes. My impulse was to give each of the persons who made the Graduate School of Psychology what it was, is, and has become, "one last look" at the document. I certainly wanted to present them fairly.

However, I decided to resist that urge and to go to press without their final approval. There are mistakes here. I acknowledge them in advance. This "history" is probably more an interpretation than an objective account. Yet, of one thing I am sure, the mistakes and misrepresentations were unintentional. They are my own fault. They cannot be blamed on my sources or my consultations.

Most of the written materials upon which I base this account are stored in the institutional archives of Fuller Theological Seminary. Thanks to Archive Director Russell Spittler, these documents have now become part of the official history of the seminary and are available to scholars for further research.

The title I have given to these pages is *Psychology and the Cross: The Early History of Fuller Theological Seminary's School of Psychology*. "Planting the cross in the heart of psychology" are the words emblazoned below the Greek *psi* out of which emerges a cross on a steel symbol that graces the courtyard of the School of Psychology's magnificent and functional building at 180 North Oakland Avenue in Pasadena, California. These words are attributed to John Geoffrey Finch, the Tacoma, Washington, psychologist whose inspiration led to the establishment of the School of Psychology at Fuller Theological Seminary and in whose honor the building was originally named. My title is an adaptation of that lofty ideal.

Although expressed in a variety of ways in the years since these words were first spoken, putting "the cross in the heart of psychology" remains the goal of all the school's endeavors. We boldly declare that our lives and our training are grounded in the mighty act of God in Christ Jesus, our Lord. His life, his death, and his resurrection are at the center of who we are and what we do. We do, indeed, intend to "plant the cross in the heart of psychology." While no institution ever wholly fulfills its dreams, these words still stand as a beacon which has guided the over three decades of the School of Psychology's efforts. I feel certain they will continue to serve as its aspirational magnet in the years yet to come.

My account will focus on early years and Pasadena events. Yet, limiting myself to Pasadena and to this first decade may provide only minor clues for the continuing story of the School of Psychology. The real history is written in the offices, laboratories, classrooms, and lives of the over 500-plus graduates spread throughout all 50 states and several foreign countries.

Of special interest to academic historians will be the Appendix which includes an essay on the intellectual histories of those who served the School of Psychology as its faculty through the tenure of the school's first dean, Lee Edward Travis. My colleague, Hendrika

Vande Kemp, has chronicled these foundations in a masterful way. She and I have worked together before.[1] Our thoughts complement each other and it is an honor to include her survey here. It gives depth to an otherwise somewhat sterile report of faculty who came and went. Readers will appreciate the substantive directions the Graduate School of Psychology has taken after reading this intellectual history of its professors. Further, she has assisted me in many other ways by copy editing the manuscript and adding the wealth of her historical knowledge at many instances in which my background was deficient.

Once again, while I hope that my references to these events of the past will be accurate and moderate, I acknowledge I am biased. Overall, I have little doubt that these events exemplify genuine and valid attempts to integrate the Christian faith into the practice of clinical psychology. It is to our graduates that I pay most tribute, nevertheless. We who have remained behind to train new students would have no story to tell had our graduates not entrusted to us their talent and their lives. Hopefully they hold their alma mater in as high esteem as we hold them.

Histories can be dry and boring to read. I have tried to avoid this all-too-common vocational hazard by writing in a quasi-novelistic fashion. It is left to you, the reader, to judge whether I have succeeded.

A final word regarding syntax: I am aware that the correct title of the school is the "Graduate School of Psychology" of Fuller Theological Seminary. Almost from the beginning this title was used interchangeably with the "School of Psychology." I will follow the practice of using both titles interchangeably.

ENDNOTES

1. Hendrika Vande Kemp. *Psychology and Theology in Western Thought (1672-1965): A Historical and Annotated Bibliography.* In collaboration with H. Newton Malony (Millwood, NY: Kraus International Publications, 1984).

H. Newton Malony
Pasadena, California
Epiphany Season 1995

Psychology and the Cross

THE EARLY HISTORY OF FULLER SEMINARY'S
SCHOOL OF PSYCHOLOGY

Chapter 1

A School Is What We Need

Three men leaned against the railing of the outdoor hallway bordering the classrooms on the third floor of Payton Hall, the main building on the campus of Fuller Theological Seminary. Below them lay the Garth—that grassy quadrangle which tied McAlister Library with the auditorium, food services, administration and faculty offices of the seminary.

It was the late spring of 1961 and one of the men, John G. Finch, had just finished delivering the last of three invited lectures to the seminary faculty and student body. Finch was a Tacoma, Washington, psychologist who had been invited to Fuller by R. Donald Weber, the seminary's director of development, at the suggestion of C. Davis Weyerhaeuser, soon-to-be chairman of Fuller's Board of Trustees.

The lectures had ended and the three men, Finch, Weber, and Weyerhaeuser, were reflecting on the events of the last three days. Weber, always a man with a vision on his mind, was still thinking of the project which had led him to Tacoma earlier that year, namely, a desire to see the seminary strengthen its program in pastoral counseling. Weber had hoped that the Weyerhaeusers, Davis and his wife, Annette, would catch his vision and contribute $30,000 to the endeavor.

In Weber's mind, he had just the man to head up such an expanded program, Lars Granberg. Granberg was Fuller's well-liked dean of students who had been at Fuller for eight years. He was a trained psychologist who was being wooed away by Hope College. Weber thought that it would be a real loss to the seminary if Granberg left, and he had divined a plan to entice him to stay.

Weber thought that the time had come for Granberg to play a significant role in the training of pastors to meet the needs of troubled persons. Training in "pastoral counseling" had become prominent in the curricula of many theological seminaries in the late 1950s and early 1960s.[1] Weber wanted Fuller to play a central role in this movement. He hoped that the Weyerhaeusers would help him design a plan that would entice Granberg to stay and to join with Paul Fairweather, the current professor of pastoral counseling and psychology, in a program that would become the best in the evangelical world.

In addition to these institutional concerns, Weber had seen the emotional struggles of his brother-in-law and Fuller's former president, Edward John Carnell. Carnell was becoming increasingly disturbed emotionally in that spring of 1961. A brilliant scholar who had sought to make evangelicalism credible to the wider theological community, Carnell, by this time, was undergoing psychiatric treatment for depression and anxiety which had overwhelmed him "with the force of a terrible tidal wave,"[2] Don Weber was keenly aware of Carnell's travail and yearned for him to experience relief from his distress. He also knew that Carnell was but one among several colleagues in the Fuller community who had suffered from emotional disturbance.

So, the time was ripe for the lectures of John G. Finch. Weber, in trying to nurture trustee involvement and investment, had, quite naturally, responded positively to the suggestion of the Weyerhaeusers that John Finch be invited to lecture at the seminary. He thought that Fuller needed a strong training program in pastoral counseling, and he knew that several faculty at the seminary were experiencing stress in their lives. As he looked down on the seminary Garth and talked with John Finch and Davis Weyerhaeuser that spring afternoon in 1961, this plan for a pastoral counseling program was at the forefront of Don Weber's mind. Little did he guess the direction the conversation was to take.

The Finch Lectures

Weber knew that Finch's lectures had been well received. The auditorium in Payton Hall had been packed each day with students and faculty to hear Finch talk on "The Importance of a View of Man," "Freud and the Dissenters," and "Spirit and Psyche."[3] Charles Fuller, the seminary founder, had attended every lecture. He sat on the front row and responded warmly to Finch's call for a type of counseling that called for meeting emotional conflict with the teachings of the Christian faith and existential insight. "This is what we need," Fuller had stated enthusiastically to Finch.

Weber thought that the approval of Charles Fuller and the approbation of those who attended the lectures bode well for his

Chapter 1 – A School Is What We Need

interest in strengthening pastoral counseling at the seminary. "Davis, don't you think that now is the time to underwrite enhanced training in pastoral counseling here at the seminary?" Weber asked. Before Weyerhaeuser could react, Finch responded, "We don't need a stronger program, we need an entirely new school."[4] Weber knew his vision had taken a right turn He could tell by the piqued interest in Davis Weyerhaeuser's face that a new and bigger idea had entered the picture. Weber was witnessing the birth of a dream!

History would prove just how far right Weber's hopes for training had turned.[5] Only recently has the seminary initiated a doctoral program in practical theology which includes Weber's long-hoped-for emphasis in pastoral counseling among its options. Up to this point, seminarians were only afforded one or two introductory courses in the field. Such courses have been overshadowed by master's and doctoral programs in marriage and family counseling and clinical psychology. It has been training of these kinds of mental health professionals, rather than pastoral counselors, that has earned Fuller Theological Seminary a noteworthy reputation over the last three decades.

Unfortunately, Granberg left for Hope College, but John Finch returned to Tacoma and, during June and July of 1961, his dream for a new school at Fuller began to unfold in his mind. In August of that year, Finch wrote a letter to Paul Fairweather in which he stated, "I hope you will keep this in confidence, but I have been thinking that we should start a school of Christian psychology, and it should be located there are Fuller Theological Seminary."[6] Finch had become greatly enthused by the reception he received when he delivered his lectures. "The whole experience was thrilling,"[7] Finch wrote to Weber after he got home. The idea of a new school grew out of that experience.

Neither Weber nor Weyerhaeuser shared Finch's late-spring statement about the need for a new school with anyone at the seminary. As the weeks went by, they may have even thought Finch was making an off-hand, only half-serious remark. Finch's letter to Fairweather corrected any such impression. Paul Fairweather responded that he would, indeed, not tell anyone about Finch's thoughts.[8] It was probably the first he had heard about such an idea. Certainly no one at the seminary had these plans in mind—before or after John Finch's lectures that spring.[9] In his response to Finch, Fairweather said that the idea of such a school was exciting to him also. This mutual enthusiasm became the motivation that propelled

Fairweather and Finch into more than two years of intense activity directed toward convincing the seminary faculty and trustees that a new school was indeed needed.

The Weyerhaeuser/Finch Relationship

Finch was a Methodist minister who had become a psychological counselor. After college and seminary, Finch had been a pastor for a number of years in his native India. He came to the United States for study and successfully defended a doctoral dissertation critiquing current psychological theories under Stanley Hopper at Drew University. He returned to live in the Northwest after a stint as chaplain in the U.S. Army at Fort Lewis, Washington. He resided in Tacoma and attended the First Presbyterian Church where he met the Weyerhaeusers.

Finch espoused a view of Christian counseling grounded in the thinking of Søren Kierkegaard and in existential philosophy. He had not anticipated that he would be welcomed at a conservative, evangelical, reformed seminary, such as Fuller. Yet he had been warmly received. Although being on the wane by the early 1960s, existential theory, in both theology and psychology, was still enjoying a marked influence, even at Fuller.[10] Finch did not know that Carnell's writing reflected a deep appreciation for existential philosophy[11] and Paul K. Jewett had titled his installation address, as Fuller's associate professor of systematic and historical theology, "What Is Right About Existentialism?"

In the weeks after returning to Tacoma, Finch relived again and again the enthusiasm with which students engaged him both at the lectures and in Paul Fairweather's classes afterwards. Finch had received a letter in which an ebullient Fairweather wrote:

I trust that the lectures will be made available on a broad-scale basis, somehow or other, within the near future. Certainly it would be desirable if students and other interested persons could have access to this very fine presentation.[12]

The idea of a school had not occurred to Finch before the lectures, but, after his experience at Fuller, this possibility began to germinate in his mind. People seemed hungry for what he had to say. He believed there was a great need for Christian psychologists. "I

Chapter 1 – A School Is What We Need

know of no place where students can get this sort of training," he had said to Annette Weyerhaeuser, the wife of the chair of Fuller's Board of Trustees. "We will have to grow our own." "Why not Fuller? Why not now?" Finch thought to himself. Annette Weyerhaeuser also became excited about this possibility and shared it with her husband.

In reacting to the suggestion of a new school, Don Weber could have predicted that Davis Weyerhaeuser would pay close attention to what John Finch was thinking. After all, Finch's counsel had been extremely beneficial to Annette Weyerhaeuser, his wife, when she was struggling with height phobia. Her account of these events went like this:

> In the late 1950s they began to build the Narrows Bridge connecting Tacoma with Gig Harbor. We had a summer house there where I loved to go for retreat and relaxation. Before the bridge was built, I always crossed Puget Sound on a ferry. I felt very comfortable on the ferry but, because of my fear of heights, I knew I could never go over that bridge which was designed to be built very high above the water. I might not be able to get to our summer home anymore. I needed help. One Sunday morning at First Presbyterian Church, Tacoma, where we were members, I shared my fear with a friend. I asked her if she knew of a Christian counselor who might help me. For me, it was important that whoever helped me be Christian. I knew a bit about the antireligious bias of many psychologists and I did not want to go to anyone who did not share my faith. My friend responded, "As a matter of fact, there is a new counselor in town who is Christian and who has been attending our church; I think he is just the sort of person who might be of help."[13]

This counselor was John Finch. Annette and Davis Weyerhaeuser were deeply grateful for the therapy she received from John Finch. As has been proven true of much successful psychotherapy, what Mrs. Weyerhaeuser took away from her therapy was a profound new way of thinking about herself, along with a decided alleviation of her fear of heights. Even before the idea of a school was conceived, the Weyerhaeusers were firmly convinced that Finch's blending of the Christian faith with psychotherapy was an approach about which they wanted the rest of the evangelical world to know.

Some years later, Annette Weyerhaeuser wrote this account of the process of her healing:

> Many hours were spent in therapy—open-ended sessions in which the depths of my heart and life were plumbed. . . . The anxiety and agony were the voice of my true self, struggling desperately for its very life. It

*was the voice of the Spirit, calling me back to truth in the inward parts.
. . . It was a call to authenticity. There was pain—the pain of realizing
that neither my life, nor my person, nor my environment were really all
that ideal. . . . (The experience) was painful, bewildering, elated, deep,
insightful, colorful and vital. The deeper I went into myself, the more I
was amazed to find a clearer and fuller inner concept and experience of
God—not as "Someone-out-there" but as an inner presence; one who
understands, loves, and knows already my falseness and forgives, who is
not a dictator to be pleased, but a presence who longs for cooperation.
Who is Christ? He is my inner brother, my Savior who has gone before,
the expression of God's love, my model. Who is Spirit? He is the inner
voice, the friendly enemy, the inimical friend, who will not let me rest in
falseness, but struggles with me to the end that I may emerge more and
more the unique person God created me to be—in his image. What are
the Scriptures? They are vital and colorful, speaking to me where I am.
Each new insight about myself and others enlightens them and they
enliven every insight.*[14]

Her life was profoundly changed. She was thrilled that Finch's ideas were shared and received so enthusiastically at Fuller.

The Finch Proposal

After Finch shared his idea for a school where the ideas that impacted Annette Weyerhaeuser so profoundly could be taught with Don Weber and Paul Fairweather, he spent much of the summer thinking about the possibility. He sent a proposal, which he called "a pre-pre-preliminary draft,"[15] to Davis Weyerhaeuser in August. In this draft, Finch spoke of the need for a "Christian psychotherapy." He criticized both Freudian and behavioristic approaches as ineffective and inadequate because they were based on a two-dimensional view that human beings were only composed of bodies and minds. Finch called for reasserting that persons were three-dimensional: They had "spirits," in addition to bodies and minds. He noted that humanistic and existential viewpoints confirmed this model, yet the Christian gospel had affirmed this three-dimensional structure long before there was such a thing as psychology.

Feeling that the time was ripe for the church to take the lead in guiding the world out of the confusion into which two-dimensional

Chapter 1 – A School Is What We Need

theories had led psychology, Finch called for someone to think through and compose an essay detailing the content of a genuinely "Christian" psychology. He suggested that such a report should be presented to a conservative seminary, such as Fuller, with the following recommendation: "That they constitute and form a school of psychology in courses affiliated with the School of Theology."[16]

Finch's recommendations also suggested that only applicants with seminary training be admitted and that students work toward a doctoral degree. He ended his proposal by stating:

> *This is a far-reaching plan; nothing like this exists in the United States, or in the world, for that matter. Departments of pastoral counseling in seminaries do not meet the needs that have been felt throughout the country; to wit, to have a Christian psychologist to whom Christians may go.*[17]

It was Finch's hope that such a training program could provide a trained Christian psychologist to work near every single pastor in the nation!

Davis Weyerhaeuser sent the proposal to the seminary president, Harold John Ockenga. In the meantime, Paul Fairweather had suggested that Finch come down to discuss the proposal with the trustee Executive Committee in late September 1961. President Ockenga suggested that they not move the idea too quickly to the trustees. He advised slowing down and discussing the idea with the faculty in order to involve them in the planning before asking Finch to come back and appear before the trustees.[18] He wisely noted that establishing a new school might change the character of the seminary which, heretofore, had only been concerned with theological training.

The Weyerhaeuser Grant

During the interval between September and the trustee/faculty meetings in early December 1961, the Weyerhaeusers advanced the idea of a school of psychology one step further. At John Finch's request, they offered to support the new school with a yearly gift of $65,000. Originally, the Weyerhaeusers conceived of this gift to be for 10 years. However, it was to last for 15 years. This led John Finch in the years to come to say that the Weyerhaeusers gave a million dollars to help the school. And this was true in the final analysis, but the Weyerhaeusers did not realize this in the beginning. This offer of help from the Weyerhaeusers caused the new school idea to be taken with greater seriousness than it might have been otherwise.

Sometime in that fall of 1961, President Ockenga appointed a faculty Fact-Finding Committee under the chairmanship of Everett Harrison, professor of New Testament. The committee was assigned the task of formulating a psychology school presentation for faculty consideration. As a member of that committee, Paul Fairweather began a correspondence with the American Psychological Association as to what kind of training they recommended for psychologists.

The December 1961 Meeting of the Faculty and Trustees

The faculty and trustees of the seminary met together on December 4 in Santa Barbara. Finch had been invited to attend and was present. The faculty Fact-Finding Committee made its report. The possibility of a new school of psychology was discussed. Some faculty were supportive and some were not.

Geoffrey Bromiley, professor of historical theology, expressed strong reservation. He felt that a seminary, any seminary, should focus its energy on training persons for the ordained ministry of word and sacrament. In his opinion, lay or diaconal ministers, such as psychologists, should be trained elsewhere. He was not against counselors. He was convinced, however, that the seminary should not set up a school to train them any more than it should train Christian social workers, nurses, or geologists.[19]

Although he was later outvoted, Bromiley remained convinced that energy put into a school of psychology siphoned off efforts that should have been put into the seminary's prime task. Further, as a Barthian scholar, he doubted that the social/behavioral sciences could ever have much to add to the truths of faith. While Bromiley resigned himself to the inevitability of a school of psychology and participated on several occasions in team-teaching integration seminars, he remained convinced these attempts were of little value, save in one or two instances. Despite his initial opposition to the idea of a school of psychology, he was one of the few professors

Chapter 1 – A School Is What We Need

who intentionally helped psychology students design projects in his classes that met their special interests and needs.

In the discussion, some faculty pointed out the tie between the Weyerhaeuser money and the idea of a new school. They voiced a suspicion that has continued to haunt the school from that day to this: namely, that Fuller Theological Seminary would never have even considered establishing such a school had it not been buttressed by a million dollar offer from the chairman of its Board of Trustees. These critics expressed the fear that the seminary was being opportunistic rather than logical in accepting such an offer.[20]

Without question, there is some truth to this observation. At this juncture in its history, neither Fuller's faculty nor its trustees were actively seeking to add another school. The seminary was engaged in a perennial financial struggle. A major conflict was brewing over the question of biblical inerrancy. Furthermore, there was a vacuum at the highest administrative level. Harold Ockenga lived in Boston and was an absentee president. Harold Lindsell, the vice-president; and Don Weber, the director of development; both functioned independently with little oversight. They were frequently at odds with one another. The seminary's "plate was full" and the idea of a new school of psychology must have seemed to many at the Santa Barbara meeting as an agenda that had to be dealt with only because Weyerhaeuser was who he was.

Nevertheless, it should be observed that all ideas that eventually become realities are based, in part, on personal interest and historical coincidences. Even Don Weber's original motivation in seeking support from the Weyerhaeusers for strengthening pastoral counseling training at Fuller was grounded in his personal friendship with Lars Granberg and his concern for the mental health of his brother-in-law, former seminary president, Edward John Carnell.

To observe that the original proposal for a school of psychology at Fuller was seriously considered, in part, because of the position C. Davis Weyerhaeuser occupied and his offer of financial support, is to state a historical reality. It does not color or qualify the soundness of the idea nor does it justify mistrust in either the seminary's receipt of the money or those who gave it.[21] Weyerhaeuser's offer to support the establishment of a school of psychology at Fuller was done out of genuine appreciation for his wife's recovery. More importantly, it was an offer that came out of a well-thought-out sense of what the Christian church needed in the last half of the twentieth century.

C. Davis Weyerhaeuser's subsequent involvement in planning for the school testifies to the seriousness with which he took the school of psychology idea. He traveled from Tacoma to Pasadena for meetings on an almost bimonthly basis for the next two years and accompanied Don Weber on calls to the Commonwealth Fund, the Ford Foundation, and the Lilly Endowment in behalf of the project. Some years later, the integrity of his interest was seen in his participation in helping to provide a modern, well-equipped building for the school in the mid-1980s.[22]

A more foundational concern about the idea of a school of psychology focused on John Finch himself. At this point in time, there was no one on the faculty who came from a Wesleyan background. While Finch had served as a Presbyterian church pastor during his graduate school days at Drew University and he attended the First Presbyterian Church in Tacoma, he originally was a Methodist minister, and the ideas he expressed in his lectures appeared to some faculty as tinged with an emphasis on experience more than on the proclamation of eternal truths. They strongly questioned whether his theology would be compatible with the Calvinistic orientation of Fuller Theological Seminary. They read into his interest in establishing a school of Christian psychology an Arminian existentialism. They felt that his basic theological assumptions would not qualify him for faculty status at the seminary. They were concerned that a school would be established which would be based on ideas they concerned erroneous, even heretical. Suspicions about the compatibility of Finch's ideas with Fuller's theological stance continued to be expressed through the years, long after this December 1961 faculty/trustee meeting in which the idea of a school was first considered.

There was one professor, however, who thought the idea was a good one. This was Paul Jewett, professor of systematic theology. Although he agreed with those who expressed concern about Finch's theology, he became excited about the possibility of a new school. He saw the school of psychology as the first step toward a Christian university.[23] He recalled the 1950-51 Fuller Seminary Catalog which had stated, "The purpose of this professional school of higher learning is to offer Christ-centered instruction in any and all subjects pertinent to the gospel ministry, missions (home and foreign), and other related Christian activities."

Jewett presented a diagram to the faculty and trustees. It consisted of concentric circles in which theology was pictured at the center. Other disciplines in varying distances of direct relevance to theology occupied the outer circles. Psychology, according to Jewett, was adjacent to theology and, thus, was the logical, first-step school to be established in this projected move toward a university with many adjunctive programs.

It is not known how many persons knew about Jewett's ideas before the meeting. He had adopted it from the writings of Emil Brunner and continued to use the model regularly in his teaching of systematic theology through the years. What is known is that Jewett's proposal did not result in overwhelming support for the idea. It did result, nevertheless, in enough support to continue the exploration of a new school of psychology.

No firm decision to reject or accept the idea was reached at this fall 1961 meeting of the faculty and trustees in Santa Barbara. The Harrison Committee was asked to continue to explore the project more fully and bring in a report to the March 1962 meeting of the faculty at which time "the faculty will either endorse or reject the proposal." [24]

The Faculty Fact-Finding Committee

Paul Fairweather and John Finch went to work to provide more details for the Harrison "Fact-Finding Committee," officially called the "Committee on Planning Associated Schools." Finch and Fairweather saw that there was a need to convince others that a new school of psychology was a good idea. They feared that the plan might fail in spite of the Weyerhaeuser offer. Their four-page report,[25] prepared for the committee, indicated that they had sought reactions of a number of outstanding professional psychologists and educators, including Paul Meehl, professor at the University of Minnesota, and several psychologists from Pine Rest Christian Hospital in Cutlerville, Michigan.

It was discovered that no graduate program of the type they envisioned existed in the United States. However, they found that O. Hobart Mowrer had a postdoctoral training program at the University of Illinois which was open to ministers. Mowrer was a well-known Presbyterian who had rediscovered the Christian principles of forgiveness and restoration in the midst of a psychotic depression for which he was hospitalized during the very time that he was to take office as the president of the American Psychological Association.

Mowrer became deeply concerned about the ethical roots of mental illness and wrote a volume titled *The Crisis in Psychiatry and Religion*.[26] The thesis of this treatise was that there were two gospels in the Bible. One was the high moral gospel of Jesus' teachings and the other was Pauline gospel of forgiving grace. He contended that most mental illness was due to ethical violations of Jesus' gospel. Because people had super-egos which were too weak, they sinned and became emotionally disturbed. His training program at Illinois emphasized an interrelationship between spirituality and mental health that was similar, in some ways, to the program Finch and Fairweather envisioned.

However, in other ways, Mowrer's program was significantly different. He expressed disapproval of the Fuller project because he felt that it promoted "professionalism." He called fee-for-service psychotherapy "trafficking in guilt." He suggested that Fuller should establish a program which encouraged the church to do its own therapeutic work—apart from professional counselors. Finch and Fairweather acknowledged the truth of what Mowrer espoused, but felt he was too optimistic about the church's ability to handle everyone's problems. They concluded that the University of Illinois program would never meet the mental health needs of the church.

Another Fairweather/Finch interview was conducted with the leaders of the program at Marble Collegiate Church in New York City. Here the members of the American Foundation for Religion and Psychiatry conducted training programs for ministers, but did not train psychologists. Nor did they attempt to explicitly relate theology to their counseling. They emphasized using clinical material as it related to each client's unique personal faith and individual circumstance. They responded favorably to the idea of a school of psychology at Fuller and indicated that they would welcome the opportunity to collaborate.

Another type of program was discovered in Minnesota. Three Lutheran ministers were accepted each year into the doctoral program in psychology at the University of Minnesota under Paul Meehl.

Chapter 1 – A School Is What We Need

Meehl was a notable psychologist who was connected with the development of the Minnesota Multiphasic Personality Inventory and had been very active in the American Psychological Association. In fact, he, like Mowrer, had been president of APA. Meehl was a serious Lutheran layman who was concerned about the spiritual dimensions of health. He had coedited an important book titled *What, Then, Is Man?*[27] He, too, was invested in training Christian counselors but did not have theologians on his staff. He became very excited about Fuller's program and later agreed to serve as the chairman of the National Steering Committee of well-known mental health professionals who agreed to advise the seminary.

Other well-known personages who were interviewed in these trips around the country were Carl Rogers; Stanley Hopper, professor at Drew University School of Theology, Stanley Lindquist, Christian psychologist in Fresno, California; and Walter Houston Clark, professor of psychology at the Hartford Seminary Foundation. All of these expressed strong support for the school of psychology idea.

Several options for training were proposed by the consultants who talked with Finch and Fairweather. These included lay training, collaboration with ministers, short-term counselor training of theologians, and the challenge to individual Christians to integrate their faith and their therapy. Seward Hiltner, professor of pastoral theology at Princeton Theological Seminary, liked the idea of augmenting psychological studies with training in theology. However, he strongly disliked the idea of sequential training in which persons were trained as pastors first and psychologists second. He urged Fuller to make the training simultaneous and to give theology control over the process.

The Fairweather/Finch report concluded that none of these were sufficient to meet the need and that a separate school of Christian psychology was needed.[28] The rationale that was given in the report included the following ideas:
1. The basic problem in mental illness is "spiritological";
2. To communicate with the field of mental health, the church must demonstrate competence in those who represent its point of view;
3. Seminaries are the educational arm of the church and must assume responsibility for training Christian counselors;
4. Faculty should be trained psychologically and theologically;
5. There is a need for an institution to be a center for research as well as a center for training;

6. A school of psychology could contribute to the enhancement of better pastoral counseling;
7. The central objective should be to train persons for the vocation of Christian psychotherapy;
8. Trained Christian psychotherapists can serve Christians who are emotionally disturbed, can function within the church, can interpret the church to other mental health professionals, and can restore the church to its rightful role in the healing ministry.[29]

The Fairweather/Finch report concluded with the recommendations that all students in the new school have seminary training; that the training lead to accreditation and licensing as psychologists; that relationships with nearby universities be sought for enrichment; and that the length of time for achieving the doctorate be about three years beyond the Bachelor of Divinity degree.

Approval in Principle

In the afternoon of March 14, 1962, the faculty voted to accept "in principle" the proposed program for a Ph.D. in the area of Christian psychology.[30] An annual budget of $150,000 was projected. Since the Weyerhaeuser gift totaled $65,000 annually, this left a balance of $85,000 to be raised.

Although it was presumed that the school would be located at Fuller and that prospective faculty would affirm the Fuller Seminary Statement of Faith, a committee was appointed to ascertain whether the school should be established somewhere else such as at the Northwestern Christian College in Eugene, Oregon, or at the Claremont College in California. These options were pushed by Finch, in part as a ploy to spur the seminary to become serious about the school of psychology idea.

Dr. Fairweather became the chair of this committee that was given the task of determining next steps in the plan. Harold Lindsell, vice president of the seminary, was charged with addressing the questions of location and administration. Robert Bower, professor of Christian education, was assigned curriculum concerns, and Dr. Finch was to asked assist in matters of faculty selection.[31]

Although there was still some slight question about whether Fuller was the ideal place, the "handwriting was on the wall." The idea was a Fuller idea. The stimulus had arisen out of lectures given

Chapter 1 – A School Is What We Need

at Fuller. The energy to pursue the idea came from Fuller professors. The decision was made by Fuller trustees and Fuller faculty. The challenge money was a promise from a Fuller trustee. The School of Psychology seemed destined to become a part of Fuller Theological Seminary. Events of the next several months were to make this crystal clear.

Perhaps the time between the March decision and the final seminary commitment to establish the school could be thought of as a period of final reassurance and confirmation that this was the right thing to do. After all, finances for the School of Theology were not too stable at this time, and there was some uneasiness over a nonresident president. The seminary had operated in the red for 11 of its 15 years.

Further, looming on the horizon was a major debate over the authority of the Bible which was to erupt into what has been labeled "Black Saturday" by the historian George Marsden.[32] A struggle for consensus on the inerrancy of the Bible occurred at a faculty/trustee Ten-year Planning Conference at the Huntington Sheraton Hotel in San Marino. Two trustees resigned over what they perceived to be the drift of the seminary away from conservative theology.

However, this Black Saturday, December 1, 1962, could be called "Good Saturday" for the School of Psychology, because it was on this day that a firm decision was reached to go ahead with the establishment of a psychology program at Fuller. On the one hand, the recommendation of the Harrison Committee to proceed received less attention than it deserved in the midst of a sometime vitriolic debate over biblical authority. On the other hand, the report was taken seriously and a thoughtful decision was made. In either case, the die was cast in later 1962 and the narrative of the events that led up to, and followed, this event is the subject of the next chapter.

ENDNOTES

1. By the early 1960s Boston University School of Theology, the Southern Baptist Seminary at Louisville, Kentucky, and Garrett Biblical Seminary in Evanston, Illinois, developed strong doctoral programs in Pastoral Counseling under the direction of Paul Johnson, Wayne Oates, and Carroll Wise, respectively.

   Evangelical seminaries, such as Fuller, had only minimal training in this field. Paul D. Fairweather had only recently been added to the Fuller faculty as professor of pastoral counseling, and Robert Bower, professor of Christian education, was teaching some courses in family counseling. Bower's teaching

was later to become the beginning of master's-level training in marriage and family therapy.
2. Edward J. Carnell to C. Davis Weyerhaeuser, July 7, 1961, at the time Weyerhaeuser became chairman of the Fuller Seminary Board of Trustees.
3. These three lectures by John Finch at Fuller Seminary in 1961 are contained in the Appendix to this volume.
4. The account of this event was shared with me by Don Weber.
5. To date, Fuller Theological Seminary has become widely known for its training in clinical psychology and marriage and family counseling, but it has never achieved distinction in pastoral counseling, in spite of the fact that it has been able to attract such distinguished professors as Samuel Southard and David Augsburger to its faculty.
6. John G. Finch to Paul Fairweather, August 24, 1961.
7. John G. Finch to Don Weber, May 28, 1961.
8. Paul D. 8. Fairweather to John G. Finch, September 13, 1961.
9. There was one crucial exception to this statement. Although the exact form the school took grew out of the Weyerhaeuser/Finch relationship, Harold John Ockenga, Fuller's first president and collaborator with Charles Fuller in establishing the seminary, had considered the possibility that Fuller should establish some graduate training in psychology sometime before 1961. In 1953, at a luncheon with well-known evangelical psychologist, Malcolm Jeeves, Ockenga had expressed the opinion that Fuller might someday add psychology to its curriculum. Jeeves, a neuropsychologist from St. Andrews University, Scotland, and an Intervarsity Christian Fellowship leader, was at Harvard for several terms. He attended Park Street Church where Ockenga was pastor. They often met for lunch and on at least one of these occasions, Ockenga expressed an interest in seeing Fuller offer graduate training in psychology. He had a strong concern for having evangelicals become involved in the dialogue between religion and science, both natural and social. However, his interest was not necessarily "clinical."
10. The writings of theologian Paul Tillich and psychologist Rollo May had become very influential. Exemplary volumes included Tillich's *The Courage to Be* (New Haven: Yale University Press, 1952) and May's *The Art of Counseling* (Nashville: Abingdon Press, 1939).
11. Edward J. Carnell's book on existential theology, *The Burden of Søren Kierkegaard* (Grand Rapids, MI: William B. Eerdmans, 1965).
12. Paul D. Fairweather to John G. Finch, September 13, 1961.
13. For a full account of Annette Weyerhaeuser's experience, read her chapter "Vitality and Power" in H. Newton Malony's edited volume, *A Christian Existential Psychology: The Contributions of John G. Finch* (Pasadena, CA: Integration Press) 89-96. The quote used here can be found on page 93.

Weyerhaeuser's account of these events was personally shared by her with entering students in the School of Psychology at their fall orientation for many years. It is a well-known and appreciated story which she recounts with genuine feeling.
14. Ibid., 93.

Chapter 1 – A School Is What We Need

15. John G Finch to C. Davis Weyerhaeuser, August 24, 1961.
16. Ibid.
17. Ibid.
18. Harold John Ockenga to C. Davis Weyerhaeuser, September 7, 1961. It is interesting that Ockenga did not acknowledge his long-term interest in a psychology program which he had discussed with Malcolm Jeeves eight years before. However, the tone of his letter to Weyerhaeuser does not show that he was surprised by the idea. Certainly, Ockenga's support was needed for the project and there is every indication that he gave wise nourishment during the early months of planning. He mentioned that he was aware that a school of psychology proposal would change the nature of the institution and he did not want the faculty to think they were being bypassed. His caution was more procedural than substantive.
19. Minutes of Faculty/Trustee Planning Retreat, Santa Barbara, California, 2-4 December 1961.
20. Ibid.
21. Those who have worked with C. Davis Weyerhaeuser agree, without exception, with Don Weber's assessment of his integrity. Weber stated, "I have had the pleasure and good fortune to work with Dave Weyerhaeuser within three institutions . . . Fuller, Whitworth College, and Young Life. I have invested a good portion of my career in seeking to build first-rate and responsible Christian institutions. Believe me, Dave Weyerhaeuser is in a class by himself. . . . Dave is a selfless, bright, and gutsy philanthropist. His faithfulness and persistence is exceptional." Letter from Don Weber to H. Newton Malony dated August 17, 1994.
22. This new Psychology Building was built at 180 North Oakland Avenue, Pasadena on the site originally occupied by the Child Development Center. It is a three-story structure with very adequate laboratory, office, and classroom space. It was completed in 1985. Although "official" statements pictured the funds for this project as having been donated anonymously, in reality Davis and Annette Weyerhaeuser donated 3 million and their son, Bill, a graduate of the school, and his wife, Gail, donated 2.5 million dollars to complete the building.
23. December 2-4, 1961, Faculty/Trustee Meeting
24. Letter from Everett Harrison to John G. Finch, February 2, 1962.
25. John G. Finch and Paul D. Fairweather, "Report of Fact-Finding Committee on the Proposed Graduate School of Christian Psychology," Minutes of Faculty Planning Meeting, March 13-15, 1962.
26. O. Hobart Mowrer. *The Crisis in Psychiatry and Religion* (New York: D. Van Nostrand, 1961).
27. Paul Meehl, Richard Klann, Alfred Schmeiding, Kenneth Breimeier, and Sophie Schroeder-Slomann, *What, Then, Is Man? A Symposium of Theology, Psychology, and Psychiatry* (St. Louis, Missouri: Concordia Publishing House, 1958).
28. Finch and Fairweather, Fact-Finding Committee Report.
29. Ibid., 4.

30. Minutes of the Faculty Meeting, March 13-15, 1962.
31. Ibid.
32. George M. Marsden, *Reforming Fundamentalism: Fuller Seminary and the New Evangelicalism* (Grand Rapids, MI: William B. Eerdmans Publishing Company, 1987), pp. 208-215.

CHAPTER 2

How Firm Was the Foundation

"How Firm a Foundation" should be the theme song for Fuller Seminary's School of Psychology. The months leading up to and following "Good Saturday" were riddled with consultations, reflections, committee meetings, plans, and projections that would make the planning for most other projects pale with its brilliance and thoroughness. The foundation that was laid during these months was a "firm" one, indeed.

Concern Over a School of World Mission

The deliberations became so extensive that Charles Fuller, the seminary founder, became perturbed that his hopes for a training school for missionaries might be forgotten. His concern was evidenced by phone calls made by him to his son, Daniel Fuller, dean of the School of Theology, and to Fuller's newly elected president (January 1963), David Allan Hubbard.[1]

One day the phone rang. The dean answered. A voice said, "A school of missions!" Before any response could be made the caller hung up the phone. Shortly thereafter, President Hubbard's phone rang. He, too, picked up the receiver. Again, a voice proclaimed, "A school of missions!" Without further ado, the caller hung up.

Later that morning, Dean Fuller and President Hubbard met in the hall. "Did you get a phone call?" Hubbard asked of Fuller. "Yes, did you?" the dean replied. They both laughed. They had no doubt about the identity of the caller. The voice was well known to them. It was the voice of Charles Fuller, founder of the seminary. He was expressing his anxiety that they would become so involved in planning for the School of Psychology that they would forget his strong desire to establish a school of missions. He saw all the energy that was being put into a "firm foundation" for psychology and was worried that his passion for missions would be neglected.

There is little doubt that the idea of a school of missions had been put on a back-burner during the early part of 1963. The Harrison Committee, which had been commissioned in the spring of 1962 to study the feasibility of a school of psychology, had its duties broadened in the fall.[2] It became one of 11 major committees of the seminary's Ten-Year Planning Program and was renamed the "Committee on Planning Associated Schools."

The report of this committee to the December 1962 meeting had recommended that a committee study further the idea of a school of missions but not move quickly in light of Hartford Seminary's problematic experience with the establishing separate schools within its structure. Further, the report recommended that any thought of establishing a school of Christian education be redirected toward strengthening the Bachelor of Divinity program. Yet, the report stated, "This does not mean that we are questioning the wisdom of the establishing of a school of psychology. We renew our endorsement of it and urge the hearty cooperation of all in effecting its realization."[3]

However, President Hubbard and Dean Fuller got Charles Fuller's message. Shortly after plans for the School of Psychology were put in motion, contact was made with Donald McGavran who was the head of an Institute for Church Growth located in Eugene, Oregon. In the spring of 1965, nine months after the Pasadena Community Counseling Center was opened and just as the first students were being admitted to the School of Psychology, McGavran was persuaded to move his institute to Fuller. Charles Fuller's call was not in vain. A school of missions was up and running.

Thus, within the space of a few years, Fuller Seminary grew from one to three schools. Paul Jewett's idea of a Christian university had begun to take formal shape. Alas, however, this early dream paled in the years to follow. No more schools were added. What was a grand vision became consolidated into a stable troika. Some of the caution expressed in the Harrison Report continued to direct the events that followed.

Nevertheless, in the spring of 1962, Charles Fuller's anxiety was well-placed. His eyes were not deceiving him. Much School of Psychology activity was going on. The foundation of the seminary's School of Psychology was solidly constructed during the months before and after December 1, 1962. If the energy that went into building this foundation can be taken as a clue, then it is understandable why the faculty and trustees took an affirmative decision on Good Saturday. The record is impressive. What was to become a school, replete with training center, faculty, students, and dean, was constructed on strong pillars of thought and reflection.

Building Support

Finch and Fairweather traversed the nation before and after the 1962 "Good Saturday" decision. Prominent persons in religion and mental health were consulted. Davis Weyerhaeuser underwrote every endeavor. Don Weber sought support from the Lilly Foundation. President-Elect Hubbard planned the academic structure to link the three schools together. The American Psychological Association and the American Association of Theological Schools were contacted. Advice was sought. Questions were asked. Critique was encouraged. This frenzy of activity culminated in the first meeting of a National Steering Committee on June 1, 1963, in Chicago at the O'Hare Inn.[4]

The "firm foundation" events that led up to this June meeting are worthy of note. They are testimonies to the depth of conviction and commitment in each of the individuals who gave of their energy and time during this crucial period in the gestation of the School of Psychology. As early as the late fall of 1961, Paul Fairweather had written to the American Psychological Association (APA) asking for curriculum guidelines for training doctoral-level psychologists. There was concern in everybody's mind that those who were trained in the school be acceptable to the profession as legitimate psychologists. They felt that the church could ill-afford to produce counselors who could be discounted by other mental health professionals. Christian psychology should be able to show its effect in the public marketplace. Thus, meeting the standards for secular psychological training was important. The school should do more, not less, that the universities did.

Early in 1962, as he and John Finch prepared their report for the March faculty meeting, Fairweather requested permission from the seminary to publish their ideas in some professional journals. These were sensitive days in that the faculty had not yet given their final approval nor had the idea of a new school been discussed yet with the American Association of Theological Schools (AATS) on

21

which the seminary depended for its basic accreditation. Soon thereafter, President Ockenga spoke with Charles Taylor, director of AATS, and tentative approval was given to publicize the idea of a training program in Christian psychology.[5] These discussions led to the first publication about the proposed school. In the spring 1962 issue of the Christian Medical Journal, an article titled "A Proposed Graduate School of Christian Psychology" appeared. It was coauthored by Finch and Fairweather.[6] Most of the ideas later to be found in the March 14 report to the Fuller faculty and trustees were included in this first attempt to reach the broader professional community. (A copy of this article is contained in the Appendix.)

Other activity was going on simultaneously. In May 1962, a letter from C. Davis Weyerhaeuser to R. Donald Weber indicated that in addition to his commitment to the operating budget of the seminary, he would contribute up to $24,000 toward the expenses of John Finch and Paul Fairweather "incurred in connection with establishing the School of Psychology."[7]

In June of that same year, the seminary's business administrator, Richard Curley, penned a report describing a plan for establishing a school of psychology clinic and classroom/office complex in two campus buildings on Ford Place.[8] The report detailed the refurbishments that would be needed and projected a yearly budget of $189,000. Although it was later decided to physically locate the school elsewhere, the seriousness with which the idea was being treated can already be seen fully six months before a final decision to proceed with the school was reached.

The first of many contacts with esteemed mental health professionals took place during the spring and summer of 1962. Finch reported that when the idea was presented to Rollo May, May stated that if he had his education to do over again he would be attracted to the type of program proposed for the School of Psychology.[9] This was but the first of many encouraging statements by well-known persons.

Seward Hiltner, well-known pastoral theologian at Princeton Seminary, gave his strong support and recommended that Paul Pruyser, professor and director of research at the Menninger Foundation, also be contacted. Pruyser applauded the move to train professional psychologists who would be able to relate theology and psychology in their work. He agreed that accrediting pastoral counselors was not in the best interest of the church or society, but that training psychologists who were Christians was preferable. He volunteered to serve as a consultant to the program and to help rewrite the basic philosophy of the school.[10]

A schedule of visits with charitable foundations was proposed by Don Weber. Fairweather and Finch committed themselves to join him in these efforts to gain further financial support for the school. Matters of curriculum, administration, and the program's relationship to psychiatry were also discussed. Fairweather and President Harold John Ockenga wrote to a number of professionals asking whether they would be willing to add their names to foundation proposals which described the need for a school of psychology. Among those who agreed were:

    Klaire V. Kuiper, M.D., and Gelmer A. Van Noord, M.D., of Pine Rest Christian Hospital in Michigan

    Paul E. Meehl, Ph.D., of the University of Minnesota

    Wilson Van Dusen, Ph.D., of Mendocino State Hospital, California

    Lars I. Granberg, Ph.D., of Hope College, Michigan

    Carroll J. Wright, Ph.D., of the Los Angeles Baptist City Mission Society,

    President Harold N. Englund, D.D., of Western Theological Seminary, Michigan

    Donald F. Tweedie, Ph.D., of Gordon College, Massachusetts, and the Lexington Veterans Administration Hospital, Kentucky

    Reuel L. Howe, M.Div., of the Institute for Advanced Pastoral Studies, Michigan

    Robert B. Munger, M.Div., of University Presbyterian Church, Berkeley, California

    C. Ralston Smith, M.Div., of First Presbyterian Church, Oklahoma City, Oklahoma

    Frank Rosendale, M.D., of the Bremerton, Washington Doctors Clinic

    Robert J. Lamont, M.Div., of Pittsburgh's First Presbyterian Church, Pennsylvania[11]

Needless to say, this was a very noteworthy list. It must have made a positive impression on foundations as well as on the faculty and trustees who made the "go-ahead" decision on that fateful Good Saturday later that fall.

After Good Saturday

"Good Saturday was followed by much activity. Thereafter, planning was based on the foundation of a firm institutional commitment to establish a school of psychology at Fuller Theological Seminary. On January 27, 1963, the first meeting of a full-fledged seminary "Psychology Committee" occurred. No longer was this a fact-finding committee such as had guided the deliberations through the December 1962 decision to undertake the school of psychology project. Nor was it a committee concerned with planning for "Associated Schools." It was now a "Psychology" Committee with power to actually establish the school. Attending the meeting were the new dean of theology, Daniel Fuller; seminary vice-president, Harold Lindsell; and professors Harrison, Bower, and Fairweather, along with Finch, Weyerhaeuser, and Weber. Bower served as secretary to the committee.[12]

For the first time all senior seminary administrators, save two, were present at a meeting explicitly devoted to planning for the School of Psychology. David A. Hubbard, the president-elect, would assume full-time responsibility in the fall of 1963. Although he was absent from this first meeting of the Psychology Committee, he traveled regularly from Santa Barbara to Pasadena during the spring and summer and participated actively thereafter in planning for the school. Richard Curley, seminary business administrator, was also absent, but he had shown his involvement earlier by submitting the aforementioned budget and housing plans. This indicated that the full power of the seminary was now in gear to make the School of Psychology become a reality. The most important decision made at this January meeting was to establish an Advisory Committee of eminent psychologists to interpret the school to the profession, to give prestige to the program, to accommodate the curriculum to APA guidelines, to recommend ways in which the unique contribution of the school could be included in the training, and to facilitate foundation support. Paul Meehl, professor of psychology at the University of Minnesota, was nominated to be chair of this Advisory Committee. In the mid-fall of 1962, he had written Fairweather these words: "You may certainly use my name as one who strongly endorses the projected school of Christian psychology."[13]

Chapter 2 – How Firm Was the Foundation

Two other significant decisions were made at this January meeting of the Psychology Committee. It was agreed to ask for a consultative meeting with Ralph W. Tyler, director of the Center for Advanced Study in the Behavioral Sciences at Stanford. Tyler was a member of the policy-making board of the National Institute of Mental Health who, it was thought, could advise the seminary on the type of training that should be offered and the opportunities for psychologists in national mental health planning. Further, Fairweather and Finch were mandated to "make contacts of an exploratory nature regarding a dean for the School of Psychology."[14]

The Psychology Committee meeting with Tyler did not take place until late May.[15] He asserted that the faculty should be recognized psychologists in order to gain credibility for the training at the school. He cautioned against calling the school a "school of Christian psychology" if the seminary wanted the degree validated by the profession. Tyler was, however, basically supportive of Fuller's plans. He offered suggestions about the type of student that should be admitted and felt that the program should be allowed to develop without much more specific planning. He concluded that the essential qualification for both students and faculty should be a belief in a meaning to life that lay outside natural explanation.

Plans for the National Advisory Committee proceeded rapidly during the spring of 1963. President-Elect Hubbard accompanied Fairweather and Finch to Minneapolis in March for a meeting with Paul Meehl. Also present at this meeting were Donald F. Tweedie, Jr., of the Lexington Veterans Administration Hospital and Gordon College, later to become director of the Pasadena Community Counseling Center, and Lars Granberg, of Hope College who was the former dean of students at Fuller.[16]

At this Minneapolis planning meeting with Meehl, a list of recommended members was agreed upon and a convening of the group was planned for early June at the O'Hare Inn in Chicago. Names suggested for the committee included

Gordon Allport, Ph.D., Psychologist at Harvard
Wayne Holtzman, Ph.D., Psychologist at the University of Texas,
Rollo May, Ph.D., Psychotherapist in New York City
Gelmer Van Noordt, M.D., Psychiatrist at Pine Rest Christian Hospital

Mansell Pattison, M.D., Psychiatrist at the University of Washington
Bernard Ramm, Ph.D., Theologian at the American Baptist Seminary of the West
Evelyn Berger, Ph.D., Psychologist at the East Bay Psychology Center, Oakland
Wayne Oates, Ph.D., Pastoral Counselor, Southern Baptist Theological Seminary
Vernon Grounds, Ph.D., Psychologist/Theologian, Denver Baptist Seminary

The National Steering Committee Meets

Although all the above-named persons accepted the invitation to be on the National Steering Committee, as it came to be called, only five of them were able to be at the first meeting which occurred on June 1, 1963. Drs. Berger, Tweedie, Granberg, Van Noord, and Pattison met with Fuller representatives Hubbard, Weber, Finch, Fairweather, and Weyerhaeuser at the O'Hare Inn near the airport in Chicago. Trustees Larry Kulp, Paul Van Oss, and Stan Olsen were also present.[17] Unfortunately, the chairman, Paul Meehl, found it necessary to resign before that meeting, due partly to what he felt would be heavy demands on his time.[18]

Records of the discussions of this meeting of the National Steering Committee are very complete. They include a summary of the decisions as well as a printed transcript of the discussion. Hubbard chaired the meeting and noted that, while the seminary would make all the decisions, the Steering Committee's suggestions would be responded to very positively in their deliberations. Many topics were discussed and a number of opinions were expressed.

Regarding potential faculty, it was recommend that an adequate knowledge of theology and an evangelical commitment were essential. Further, the committee thought that a concern for relating Christian affirmations to psychological ideas was also necessary. Again, the faculty should reflect a variety of specialties and be at or near diplomate status with the American Board of Professional Psychology.

The "Doctor of Psychology" (Psy.D.), as opposed to the "Doctor of Philosophy" (Ph.D.) degree was discussed. It was felt that the former was a new professional degree that would not be recognized by the National Institute of Mental Health (NIMH). The committee hoped that NIMH would award fellowships to students at the school. Accreditation of the training by the American Psychological Association was also considered important for possible government grants.

There was extensive discussion of whether training at the school should be related to the medical model. The committee recommended that there should be a psychiatrist at the school on either a full-time or consulting basis. It was suggested that the Christian Medical Society be asked to give its blessing to the school.

Regarding resources, the committee recommended that the library needed 12,000-15,000 volumes and 35 journals in order to be minimally adequate. The books on the Harvard List of Books in Psychology were judged to be the minimal collection on which the library holdings should be based. Further, a survey of the library's collection in other related disciplines was planned.

Two other critical issues were discussed: the establishment of a training clinic and the qualifications of a dean. Although the need for practical training had been considered before this meeting, it was here that the necessity of having a training clinic was first seriously considered. This proposal was later to become a priority. In fact, it was to be determined that the clinic was to be opened a year before students were admitted.

Who would be dean was at the forefront of much thinking at this meeting of the Steering Committee. It was thought that a decision on this matter needed to be made soon and that a dean needed to be in place long before students were admitted. In addition to being a practicing Christian, the following qualifications were thought to be important:

- an ability to identify with the perspectives of others
- possession of adequate credentials and reputation
- an ability to relate and build morale
- membership in professional societies and a willingness to represent the school at professional and community meetings
- an outstanding reputation in one psychology area
- experience in graduate education and training
- ability to develop relationships with clinicians
- competence as an ecclesiastical and psychological politician
- possession of fiscal and administrative know-how

These recommendations became the basis of the report of the seminary's Psychology Committee to the Board of Trustees in July, 1963.[19] These ideas became important ingredients in the choice of a dean and the opening of the counseling clinic. The coming of the dean and the opening of the clinic were to happen in reverse order. But before either occurred, several other events happened—some positive, some negative. Describing these will be the subject of the next chapter.

ENDNOTES

1. These events were recounted to me by Daniel Fuller in a personal communication, September 1993.
2. The committee was composed of Everett Harrison, chairman, Paul Jewett, and Paul Fairweather. Being a committee concerned with "Associated Schools" indicates that the idea of Fuller Seminary becoming a Christian university was still very much alive. David Hubbard, when he became president, was also interested in this type of development. This interest, along with Charles Fuller's concern for missions, were probably in many of the faculty's mind in their approval of the bringing of the School of World Missions to the Fuller campus.
3. Report of the Committee on Planning Associated Schools to the Faculty/Board of Trustees Meeting, December 2-3, 1962.
4. Minutes of the meeting of the National Steering Committee, June 1-2, 1963, Chicago.
5. Letter from Harold John Ockenga to C. Davis Weyerhaeuser, February 28, 1962. Ockenga shows his caution here in prematurely announcing that the seminary had approved the establishment of a school of psychology before the faculty had actually voted on it.
6. John G. Finch and Paul Fairweather. "A Proposed Graduate School of Christian Psychology," *Christian Medical Journal* (1962, Spring), pp. 1-2.
7. Letter from C. Davis Weyerhaeuser to R. Donald Weber, May 18, 1962.
8. Memo from Richard D. Curley to John Finch, Paul Fairweather, and C. Davis Weyerhaeuser, June 22, 1962.
9. Report of Faculty Committee on Proposed Fuller School of Psychology, September 25, 1962.
10. Although Pruyser seemed very enthusiastic about the school and willing to help, there is no evidence that he participated at all in further deliberations after this visit with Finch and Fairweather.
11. The seminary archives include letters of agreement from all of these professionals. Among this list, Tweedie later became the first faculty member in the school, directed the establishment of the Pasadena Community Counseling Center, and determined many of the early curriicula and procedural policies of the school. Munger became professor at Fuller some time later. His wife, Edith, was the first woman to graduate from the School of Psychology.

CHAPTER 2 – HOW FIRM WAS THE FOUNDATION

12. Minutes of the Psychology Committee, January 27, 1963.
13. Letter from Paul Meehl to Paul Fairweather, September 10, 1962.
14. Minutes of the Psychology Committee, January 27, 1963.
15. Report of the meeting of the Psychology Committee of Fuller Theological Seminary with Dr. Ralph Tyler, May 29, 1963.
16. Advisory Committee Report No. 1, March 24, 1963. This was the meeting with Paul Meehl in Minneapolis. After this meeting, the name of the committee was changed to "The National Steering Committee."
17. Report of the Meeting of the National Steering Committee for the School of Psychology, Fuller Theological Seminary, June 1, 1963. Also in the archives are three other records of this meeting: A Summary of Action and Discussion of the Steering Committee, Preliminary Report of the Meeting of the Steering Committee of the School of Psychology, and a printout of the audio transcript of the actual discussion.
18. Paul Meehl's resignation from being chairman of the National Steering Committee is somewhat clouded by differing opinions. At the March meeting he had clearly stated that he had no time for secretarial duties and was assured that the seminary would assume these tasks. He seemed enthusiastic and entered fully into the discussions at the March meeting in Minneapolis. However, there was some thought that he may have become incensed over what he perceived to be President Hubbard's demands. He may have felt that he was being dictated to and that his prestige was not being recognized. In any event, he not only resigned from the chairmanship but also from the National Steering Committee and was never involved in the establishment of the School of Psychology thereafter.
19. Report of Progress and Current Status, Proposed School of Psychology, Fuller Theological Seminary, July 15, 1963. This report was submitted to the July 15 trustees' meeting by Paul Fairweather but it was accompanied by another document jointly written with John Finch. This report was titled "A Proposed School of Psychology, Fuller Theological Seminary: Report to the Board of Trustees." The content of the two reports was very similar. However, the latter report suggested that further consultation occur regarding curriculum be undertaken with Carl Rogers and Sydney Jourard and that a meeting of a select subcommittee of the National Steering Committee clarify the philosophy of the school through a discussion of essays prepared by the subcommittee members. This meeting is discussed in the next chapter.

Chapter 3

Two Steps Forward, One Step Back

The momentum that led to the meeting of the National Steering Committee in June 1963 was slowed down a bit by one or two dissenting voices. One of these was Ralph Cooper Hutchinson, the head of an organization called Studies in Higher Education which had been engaged to do a study of the seminary as an adjunct to the Ten-Year Planning Program. He wrote a confidential memo titled "Theo-Psychology at Fuller Theological Seminary" which recommended that the plans for the School of Psychology be delayed. He wrote:

> The concept of a school of theo-psychology is of the utmost significance both to the Christian faith and to the social order. Fuller is blessed that Mr. Weyerhaeuser wishes to place it here rather than in some university. But it is too important to be mangled in the "borning," which appears to be likely if the present implementation program continues. It is here recommended that the implementation be postponed until certain problems are solved.[1]

Integration Versus Overlay Models

Hutchinson gave two reasons for his recommendation that the plans be delayed: The seminary was in a financial crisis and the academic plans for the School of Psychology were "neither logical nor convincing." He felt that the seminary was approaching insolvency and that after start-up foundation grants ran out, there would be a shortfall approaching $100,000 per year.[2]

In regard to the academic plans, Hutchinson concluded that the basic hypothesis on which the idea of a school of psychology was based was that "there is a newly developing and an integrated science, theo-psychology, which involves a distinctly Christian psychological therapy, and that this demands a center of research and teaching in which this science may mature."[3] He felt that the plans

Chapter 3 – Two Steps Forward, One Step Back

as they were developing were a repudiation of this principle of integration.

According to Hutchinson's understanding of the plans, students would take Bachelor of Divinity courses at the seminary but they would take their broad-based psychology courses at a local university. He was correct, as far as he went. Indeed, Professor Paul Fairweather had arranged with UCLA to do much of the teaching of the psychology courses. Hutchinson noted that these university-taught courses would be graduate-level psychology—not theo-psychology—courses. He called this an "overlay" rather than an "integration"[4] model of training. He felt that students could already obtain overlay education by studying psychology in universities after they had finished seminary training. Hutchinson suggested that the school be delayed and replanned. His recommendation was that the curriculum in "theo-psychology" should be an integrated course from the very beginning and should allow for only a small minor of special related courses in either theology or in psychology proper. He concluded, "The only thing wrong with the project as now being implemented is that it won't work!"[5]

Earlier in 1962 John Finch and Paul Fairweather had introduced this term "theo-psychology" in the article they had written in the *Christian Medical Journal*. They had stated, "The unique objective of this school is to provide for the Christian community an adequately integrated theo-psychological conceptual framework within which to conduct Christian psychotherapy."[6]

However, there is no record that Finch or Fairweather agreed with Hutchinson, or felt that the plans should be changed or delayed. In fact, in the late summer of 1963, Finch wrote in a letter to Fairweather that his first impression of Hutchinson was that he was a "windbag."[7] This reaction to Hutchinson's ideas is somewhat puzzling in light of the fact that often Finch himself made similar judgments in the years that followed. His hope was for a model of therapy that explicitly assumed and expressed theological ideas. Nevertheless, at this time he did not foresee any danger, as did Hutchinson, that this would not be accomplished if psychology courses were taught at UCLA—away from the seminary campus without theological input.

Hutchinson's concern about whether all courses in the school's curriculum should be "integrated" as opposed to "overlaid" is an issue that has been debated through the years. From the beginning,

31

even in the Harrison Committee report of December 1962, the plans resembled an "overlay" model.⁸ The model the Harrison Committee proposed included theology courses taken at the seminary and psychology courses taken separately at a neighboring university or at the seminary.

From the very beginning, a series of courses combining psychology and theology were planned.⁹ Called "integration seminars," these courses would be taught jointly by a theologian and a psychologist. However, in the initial plans the prime arena in which integration was to take place was in the supervision of psychotherapy, not in courses which combined the two disciplines. The courses were intended to support integrative clinical work.

It does not appear that Hutchinson's concerns were given serious consideration by any of the planners. In anticipation of this fact, he had labeled his report "confidential" and submitted it solely to Davis Weyerhaeuser. He realized that the idea of a school of psychology had gained a great deal of momentum and enthusiasm. He noted how far the plans had progressed and stated he did not desire to squelch the possibility that the school could accomplish its aim, even with an "overlay" model. He stated in his report, "The miracle is not impossible. It is within the will of God, as is anything. Therefore, "Studies in Higher Education" is not willing to voice, other than to Mr. Weyerhaeuser, our doubts about the possibility of success in this venture. Studies does not wish to discourage a miracle."¹⁰ Hutchinson's report was one "step back" which the "two steps forward" could not stop.

Which Should Come First, Students or a Clinic?

Other expressions of concern about plans for the School of Psychology were expressed by Trustees Stan Olson and Larry Kulp. Olson was the dean of the Baylor University School of Medicine and an administrator of the Texas Medical Center in Houston. Kulp was professor of geophysics and head of the Lamont Laboratory at Columbia University. Both doubted the feasibility of the project.

Before the Chicago meeting of the National Steering Committee in June 1963, Weyerhaeuser, Finch, Hubbard, Harrison, and

Chapter 3 – Two Steps Forward, One Step Back

Fairweather journeyed to Houston for a meeting with Olson and Kulp in the spring of 1963. The unstated, but definite, agenda from Olson and Kulp's standpoint was to talk the planners out of proceeding. From their extensive experience in higher education, they felt that the idea of a "school of Christian psychology" was ill-conceived and that the project would never gain the prestige and respect which was envisioned. At the Houston meeting they listened to the plans and expressed their doubts. On the one hand, their experience in university settings convinced them that doctoral training grew slowly out of strong undergraduate programs whose professors decided to extend their influence upwards. They had never heard of establishing a doctoral program without this type of foundation. On the other hand, they could not conceive of a training program in the helping professions which did not have a clinic-type facility where students could apply their learning. Out of a deep respect for Davis Weyerhaeuser, Kulp, and Olson courteously, but firmly, expressed their misgivings. The Pasadena contingent listened, but respectfully disagreed. Both Olson and Kulp agreed to attend the meeting of the National Steering Committee in June, but continued to have strong doubts. "You don't just announce a doctoral program without long years of scholarly work leading up to it," they contended, "Fuller will be laughed out of town."

The concerns of Olson and Kulp were only assuaged by the Steering Committee's acceptance of their recommendation that the project follow the Mayo Clinic experience of beginning with a medical clinic.[11] They hoped that the School of Psychology planners would see the wisdom of reconsidering the plan after they had some clinical experience. Kulp and Olsen still doubted the basic idea of a school of psychology which would award doctoral degrees and saw this plan of "clinic first, students second" as a delaying tactic.

However, yet another consultation had taken place shortly before the June meeting of the National Steering Committee. This was the consultation with Dr. Ralph Tyler noted earlier. He was excited by the idea of the school of psychology and foresaw no problem with courses taught outside the seminary. He stated that "UCLA should provide training in areas which are not related to the uniqueness of our school."[12] Note Dr. Tyler's use of the word "our" which indicated he had become identified with the project in the course of the interview.

More importantly, it is noteworthy that Dr. Tyler differed from Dr. Hutchinson as to whether "theo-psychology" implied a new type of psychology. In answer to the question whether the name "School of Christian Psychology" would pose a problem, Tyler replied,

> This could create a problem. Try to get a title that does not create confusion. The psychology is not to be Christian—it is the faculty who will be Christian. Emphasis should be on a clinical psychology where Christian commitment motivates the person, rather than the psychology.[13]

In yet another statement on this the issue of the term "Christian psychology," Tyler added,

> My understanding of your use of this term is that you plan to prepare clinical psychologists who will bring their own religious convictions to bear in their professional work. This would mean that the way the psychologist works with people is affected by his religious convictions. . . . There are certain kinds of convictions that guide the Christian who is operating as a clinical psychologist. He [sic] believes in the dignity and worth of the individual human being—thus he will be concerned with the worth of his client. He believes that he can relate the truth of God to immediate experience and everyday life. . . . He would not deny the existence of data, but always in terms of "what does it do to this person as a child of God?"[14]

The National Steering Committee Meets

When the National Steering Committee met in June, Tyler's opinions and recommendations influenced their decisions almost to the exclusion of the concerns raised by Hutchinson. Tyler urged the planners not to define "Christian psychology" more specifically at that point in time but to let the program develop. He recommended seeking a faculty who were well-trained in psychology and had experience in their discipline. He did not suggest that they be required to have theological training but that they have "an adequate theology and an evangelical commitment." Dedication to "certain Christian psychological ideas" was considered most important.

This concern for letting well-trained psychologists develop a Christian psychology rather than requiring that a "theo-psychology" be worked out ahead of time became the principle recommended by the National Steering Committee. As will be seen, this recommendation of Tyler guided the selection of the dean and the early faculty members. It also was an approach contrary to that advised by Olson and Kulp.

As noted earlier, this first general meeting of the National Steering Committee for the School of Psychology took place at the O'Hare Inn near the airport in Chicago, June 1, 1963. The meeting could be called a major "step forward." The meeting set in motion significant actions leading to the opening of a counseling center and, subsequently, the beginning of classes some 12 to 18 months later. Attending this meeting were Drs. Evelyn Berger, E. Mansell Pattison, Lars Granberg, and Gelmer Van Noord, along with Fuller Seminary representatives Hubbard, Finch, Fairweather, and Weber. Weyerhaeuser as well as seminary Trustees Gerrit Groen, Larry Kulp, Stan Olson, and Paul Van Oss also attended. Additionally, Donald Tweedie was present. He was to become the director of the Pasadena Community Counseling Center and the first faculty member of the school.

Some were expecting to see Paul Meehl at this meeting. They did not know that he was having some misgivings about his involvement. Shortly after the meeting, Meehl resigned the appointment and membership on the committee. Most of the participants never knew his reasons for declining further participation.

It was at this meeting that the decision to recommend that the degree should be in "clinical" rather than "counseling" psychology. It was decided that the aim of the school should be to train "therapists" rather than to educate "scholars," as most other doctoral degrees were designed to do. One way to state the goal, according to the minutes of the meeting, would be to eventually provide a psychotherapist to help every pastor in the nation.[15] Also, there was strong consensus that a clinic for practical training should be established alongside the academic curriculum. Both psychiatrists and social workers would be needed to help with supervision and to work with families. The clinic was thought to be the center of the school. There was even talk about making the clinic become one of the Community Mental Health Centers which President John F. Kennedy was proposing. In this regard, a monumental decision about the time for the opening of the clinic was made. In support of trustees Olson and Kulp, the steering committee recommended that a clinic be established at least one full year before students should come and classes would begin.[16]

President Hubbard reported to the Steering Committee that $100,000 had been allocated for purchasing two old buildings for the school and that money had been set aside for starting a library collection of psychology books and periodicals. It was suggested that subscription to 35 periodicals and 12,000-15,000 volumes would be the minimum required library holdings.[17]

Fairweather and Finch proposed an operating budget of $189,000 per year. In addition to $65,000 contributed by the Stewardship Foundation of Davis Weyerhaeuser and an estimated yearly income of $50,000 from clinic fees, an additional $75-100,000 was needed. While some of this would come from tuition, it was thought that there would be a need to subsidize these monies in scholarships, if good students were to be attracted to the program.

There was a difference of opinion about whether funds for the school could be obtained from the National Institute of Mental Health. As it was not clear whether the government would give money to a religious institution, Don Weber reported that four foundations had expressed interest: the Old Dominion Fund, the Grant Foundation, the Lilly Endowment, and the Russell Sage Foundation. However, only the Lilly Endowment came through with $125,000 in funds.

In discussions about the faculty, Fairweather, Bower, and Cole were identified as persons already on the seminary staff who were trained to provide counseling. Robert Bower taught religious education; Don Cole, practical theology; and Paul Fairweather taught pastoral counseling. Later, these men became the nucleus of the first faculty. As we shall see, they were joined by Donald Tweedie, the first director of the clinic; Paul Barkman, the first director of research; and Adrin Sylling, the clinic's social worker.

Of critical importance was the Steering Committee's discussion of the appointment of a dean. They agreed that the selection of the dean was an urgent need and that the dean should be in place a full year before the school opened. They recommended that the dean be "eclectic in spirit," as well as being a well-trained psychologist with administrative experience and a strong commitment to the project. This meant that the dean should not be identified with any one brand of psychology—be it existentialism, psychoanalysis, or behaviorism.[18]

One final issue was considered. It was the issue of how closely should the school be related to the American Psychological

Chapter 3 – Two Steps Forward, One Step Back

Association? The consensus was strongly in favor of working toward APA accreditation. Finch suggested that it would take several years before APA would evaluate the program but that the accreditation would be retroactive.[19] This first meeting of the Steering Committee ended with an enthusiastic vote of unanimous approval that the project should proceed. The committee encouraged President Hubbard to carry an expression of their support back to the faculty and trustees of the seminary.

The motor was running and the machine was beginning to move. The basic structure was beginning to form and some of the major players were positioned. Not least among the signs that things were ready to move were the initials "mf" on the bottom of the Steering Committee minutes which indicated that Marnie Fredrickson was at her place and fulfilling her role as "secretary to the Psychology Project." As her June 1963 letter to John Finch stated:

Dear Dr. Finch,

I have just assumed my new duties as secretary for the School of Psychology. Much as I regretted having to resign from my work with Mr. Weber and the Public Relations Office, I am thoroughly looking forward to this new assignment.

I will be on duty for the School of Psychology for four hours each day or as the work necessitates. Please direct any material or requests that you may have in connection with the School of Psychology to me, here at the seminary. I am setting up files, answering inquiries, and generally coordinating the material on hand.[20]

Margaret Elizabeth Fredrickson, affectionately known as "Marnie," was employed at Fuller Theological Seminary from 1959 until 1978. Initially, she was part-time assistant to the Development Office and eventually became office manager and secretary to Don Weber, the director of development. As noted in her letter, Weber assigned her to the "Psychology Project" in 1963. She became the secretary to all planning meetings after the trustees and faculty had decided to establish the School of Psychology in December 1962. When the Pasadena Community Counseling Center was opened in the fall of 1964, she became secretary to Don Tweedie, the director. Later she became executive secretary to both the founding dean, Lee Edward Travis; and his successor, Neil Clark Warren, until her retirement in 1978. Many people felt that Marnie was the "glue" that held

37

the school together. Privately, some even expressed the opinion that she "ran" the school. All who knew her found her to be consistently affirming, completely supportive, always helpful, and amazingly efficient. She is vividly remembered and deeply loved.[21]

ENDNOTES

1. Ralph Cooper Hutchinson, "Theo-Psychology at Fuller Theological Seminary." A Report to the Ten-Year Planning Committee (April, 1963).
2. Ibid., p.1-2.
3. Ibid., pp.2-4; Ibid., p.4
5. Ibid., p.8
6. John G. Finch and Paul D. Fairweather, "A Proposed Graduate School of Christian Psychology." *Christian Medical Journal*, Spring, 1962, pp. 1-3.
7. Letter from John G. Finch to Paul D. Fairweather, August 22, 1963.
8. Minutes of the Faculty/Trustee Meeting, December 2-3, 1962.
9. Memo from David Allan Hubbard to All College and University Students Interested in Graduate Training in Psychology. (Pasadena, California, Spring 1963), p. 6.
10. Hutchinson Report, p. 6.
11. Report of the Meeting of the Steering Committee for the School of Psychology, Fuller Theological Seminary, June 1, 1963, Chicago, Illinois.
12. Report of the Meeting of the Psychology Committee of Fuller Theological Seminary with Dr. Ralph Tyler, May 29, 1963, p. 6.
13. Ibid., p. 7.
14. Ibid., p. 4.
15. Ibid., p. 5
16. Op. cit., Steering Committee Report, p. 3.
17. Ibid., p. 2.
18. Summary of Action and Discussion of Steering Committee, June 1, 1963.
19. Report of the Meeting of the Steering Committee, p. 11.
20. Margaret E. Frederickson to John G. Finch, June 19, 1963.
21. At the time of the writing of this volume, Marnie Frederickson was living in retirement with her husband Vern in Solvang, California, where she was suffering from Parkinson's disease. (She died on October 27, 1995.)

CHAPTER 4

School Objectives Are Debated —The Clinic Is Opened

Determining the philosophy and objectives of the School of Psychology was a project that had gone on simultaneously with the efforts to open the Pasadena Community Counseling Center in early November 1964. Fairweather had been asked by the seminary Psychology Committee to chair a "Study Committee" which would not only work out the details for the opening of the counseling center, but would determine the objectives, philosophy, and guidelines for the school itself.[1] The membership of this committee was to include persons who might eventually become part of the faculty as well as those who were already there. John Finch, Donald Tweedie, Paul Barkman, Carroll Wright, and Lars Granberg, along with psychiatrist E. Mansell Pattison,[2] became active members of this Study Committee and participated in discussions in the late fall and winter of 1963.[3]

Dialogues About the Goals and Objectives

It was in these dialogues, formed around papers which the committee members wrote to each other, that the basic philosophy of the School of Psychology was fashioned. One of the motives behind these efforts was to meet the continuing concerns of Trustees Olson and Kulp that the seminary might be starting a doctoral program before it had a sound scholarly or theoretical base of ideas upon which to base a curriculum. They continued to note the tradition of university doctorates which developed slowly on a sound scholarly base of prolonged study and publication.

At the second meeting of this committee in October 1963, papers for discussion were presented by Pattison, Wright, and Granberg. Pattison proposed that one of the primary tasks of the school should be an integration of the spiritual/theological understanding of persons into a unity with their biological and psychological dimensions. He said that this would result in an increased apprehension of what the *imago Dei* meant. He added that health and disease were transcendent, ultimate concepts which were not limited to horizontal relationships. In regard to curriculum, Pattison suggested that study at the school should provide the necessary basic theological tools for intelligently pursuing clinical investigation. He perceived the counseling center as providing opportunity for intense interaction among the students and the faculties of both theology and psychology.[4] Everyone affirmed Pattison's ideas.

Carroll Wright proposed that while the church needed to face the problem of mental illness, the School of Psychology should take as its primary task the demonstration of the relation between faith and illness. He stated:

> *If we could demonstrate that all psychogenetically rooted neuroses and psychoses are, in the final analysis, rooted in the demonic-idolatrous image of God, we might convince ourselves of the need for a restudy in depth of "mental illness" and "psychotherapy."*[5]

He noted the available writings of O. Hobart Mowrer, Charlotte Bühler, Carl Jung, Viktor Frankl, Harry Guntrip, Wilfred Daim, and Paul Tournier,[6] all of which he believed provided a beginning foundation for students gaining a deeper theological understanding of psychology. He proposed that the school should conceive of itself as being formed to accomplish the task of spelling out a Christian psychology and for training persons for therapeutic ministry. Wright's ideas were especially appealing to Finch who wanted the school to focus on producing a psychology that was uniquely Christian. Although Wright did not clarify the term "Christian psychology" in his presentation, there is some warrant for thinking that he meant the "father image" approach conceived by Fairweather. In spite of the fact that he had been supportive of Fairweather's ideas, Finch, on the other hand, likely meant his Christian existential psychology, which was somewhat different in emphasis.

The issue of whether the School of Psychology should exist to promote a "Christian psychology" became a matter of contention. Although not a member of the Study Committee, Professor Robert Bower wrote a series of comments on the Study Committee's report. He was particularly disturbed with the continuing references to a "Christian psychology." Bower contended that the term should be downplayed and not used until there was further data gleaned from

Chapter 4 – School Objectives are Debated—The Clinic is Opened

serious research studies. In a set of questions which he wrote after the report of the Study Committee was read at the meeting of the faculty Psychology Committee, Bower stated:

The use of this term (Christian psychology) in much of our publicity, in my opinion, has given men [sic] on the outside (not the least of which are those in NIMH) the feeling that there is such a strong religious interest involved that the school will eventually "collect" data of a psuedoscientific nature in line with previously determined goals and objectives.[7]

Bower was not alone in his concern: Hubbard also affirmed this point of view. He suggested that the seminary should practice "understatement" in it public statements. He pointed out that psychology was "much newer than theology and we do not have the classical creeds of Christendom to guide us."[8]

Finch and Fairweather vigorously defended the opposite opinion. They emphasized the "uniqueness" of Fuller's program. Although they did not mention Hutchinson, they were advocating the kind of "theo-psychology" which he espoused. Practically, Finch and Fairweather called for "boundaries" in the hiring of faculty and in statements about the school's philosophy. They opposed having Freudian, Jungian, or behavioral psychologists on the staff. Fairweather even asserted that "we must come to the place where we "let go" of Freud, etc., and be willing to state the philosophy and presuppositions in which we believe and let ourselves go at this point.[9] Finch added his contention that

the Freudian view of man leaves out God. A Freudian on the faculty would be a great difficulty. We are not off the "main stream" of thought, especially when you consider that it is founded on a Christian view of man as spirit, responsible to God, and free to find God. Freud sees man [sic] as a biological being primarily. This thing plagues all therapy. We have Christian commitment and we must involve this.[10]

President Hubbard replied,

Founders of institutions are obligated to shield the institution from their own prejudices. We must recognize our limitations, and launch this school on a scope of largeness.[11]

He resisted any implication that the seminary had already developed a "Christian psychology" which it was ready to use as a basis of training. Granberg agreed. He cautioned against becoming too specific about relating psychology and theology at a time prior to establishing an adequate base of clinical experience. Granberg suggested that

> the details of the school's philosophy should be regarded as living and growing, hammered out at the forges of intense therapeutic interaction with clients, and frank, relentless dialogue with colleagues, fueled by imaginative research meticulously executed.[12]

It was Granberg's opinion that until that experiential foundation was available, "It seems best to set down a terse summary of the historic creeds of Christendom with special emphasis upon the anthropological propositions." After listing a set of these propositions, Granberg concluded that, while psychotherapy should address itself to all aspects of the human personality, "its paramount concern (should be) healing of the spirit." In a realistic statement of what could be expected, Granberg cautioned against having the School of Psychology identified too strongly with any one psychotherapeutic model:

> It seems to me there is a need to focus on the possible without a feeling of being let down. And the "possible" is bound to be a derivative of available faculty. Good professional training, solid teaching and clinical experience, capacity and desire for growth and largeness of spirit seem to me to be the necessary criteria of staff members. By "largeness of spirit" I mean a discerning openness to all viewpoints and all approaches to therapy regardless of their theoretical soil. . . . Good therapists are usually better than their theories, and their effectiveness is, at least in part, far different reasons than they think, it seems to me.[13]

In general, this debate over the degree to which differences in psychological persuasions would be tolerated is one which continued for some years. Overall, Hubbard's position that the seminary was founding a "school" rather than a "movement," carried the day. Thus, he advocated the inclusion of a variety of viewpoints on the faculty. Finch, on the other hand, was disappointed that the school did not design its curriculum around his Christian existential point of view or employ faculty who agreed with it.

Openness to persons of various approaches can be seen clearly in the appointment of Paul Barkman to the faculty. The Reiss-Davis Clinic for Child Guidance, where he was a Postdoctoral Fellow, was clearly psychoanalytic in persuasion. Rudolph Ekstein, Freud's last student, was a teacher there and Anna, Freud's daughter, was an honorary board member. Barkman was definitely influenced by this point

Chapter 4 – School Objectives are Debated—The Clinic is Opened

of view. At the time of his arrival on campus, he was in classical psychoanalysis and remained so for a year after he was appointed.

Nevertheless, the Finch/Fairweather point of view continued as a strong undercurrent, and is nowhere better expressed than in a letter written later in 1964 by Davis Weyerhaeuser to Peggy Driscoll, trustee of the Weyerhaeuser Foundation to which the seminary had appealed for financial assistance for the new school. Driscoll had questioned the wisdom of starting a graduate program in psychology when there were already-existing programs nearby in major universities. She suggested that the seminary might better work out joint programs wherein students might take their theology at Fuller and their psychology at USC and UCLA.[14] She did not realize she was advocating the "overlay" model which Hutchinson had disparaged so strongly.[15] Weyerhaeuser replied in a manner that showed he favored Hutchinson's "integration" approach:

If I wished to prepare to teach on the subject of capitalism with the purpose of preparing my students to enter successful business careers in a capitalistic society, I would not attend graduate schools in Russia where presuppositions are Communist. . . . The presuppositions of schools of psychology on practically all secular university campuses are behavioristic which in effect asserts that man's [sic] behavior is exclusively the product of inheritance and environment.[16]

At this point in the letter, Weyerhaeuser boldly asserted that the primary theoretical approach of the school was the one that Finch and Fairweather espoused. He continued:

There is a growing disillusionment over the results of the traditional deterministic approach to man [sic] on the part of many top experts in the field. . . . This stands in contrast to the enthusiasm of these same men and others for the existential approach which is proving to be so much more effective. . . . Our school relies heavily on the postulates of existential psychology."[17]

Weyerhaeuser concluded his letter to Driscoll with a statement about the school's relationship to USC and UCLA that has continued to the present despite early plans to have students take some of their psychology classes at these institutions:

If man is basically spiritual, then it is our conviction that schools of psychology, such as those at USC and UCLA with their traditional presuppositions, cannot and do not provide adequate training to meet the

> *emotional needs of man [sic] as he is actually constituted. We, therefore, cannot act on your recommendation. We have gone part-way in the direction you suggest, however, by having already made arrangements with UCLA for 18 hours of graduate courses in such fields as anthropology, social science, etc., which are neutral from a philosophical standpoint.*[18]

Even if Weyerhaeuser was not completely correct in his presumption that certain fields are philosophically neutral, his contention that most psychology courses would be taught at the seminary's School of Psychology has become the norm up to the present time. Whether the teaching of psychology at the seminary has resulted in "theo-psychology" is debatable.

This debate over the uniqueness of the school continued to ferment and became the first issue of discussion at the next meeting of the Study Committee in late December 1963. The thoughts of Pattison, Tweedie, theologian Bernard Ramm, and John M. Vayhinger, chair of the National Steering Committee, guided the discussion. All cautioned against claiming too much for the school. A sample of their statements follows:

> *We need to be careful in not attempting to say that Christian therapists are the best. As a Christian therapist, I can believe that they are; and we may be able to do some research to show that our patients get better faster than those of a person who has the same training and capabilities as I do* (VAYHINGER).

> *Religionists have claimed that religious ideas can make a significant contribution but these claims have not been substantiated by any evidence. It seems to me that our goal might be to look for the common ground of working postulates that will enable us to say, "We propose to see, to demonstrate, if possible, to research into, what contributions the religious frame of reference does give to the psychotherapeutic framework, or to the understanding of man"* (PATTISON).

> *The first position again is that we as Christians believe that—just as we believe in Christian doctors and Christian nurses doing the work of mercy—we believe in mental and emotional therapists. The second position would be that because we are Christians, we have a leverage which these people outside of our circle don't have. It seems to me that we are going to have to be awfully sharp and precise in stating exactly what that leverage is, if we take the second proposition* (RAMM).

CHAPTER 4 – SCHOOL OBJECTIVES ARE DEBATED—THE CLINIC IS OPENED

Dr. Ramm's first statement really implies the second but it may evoke more hostility. . . . I think it is much more politic to start with the first point which I would tend to want to do, except to add a broad statement that we are wanting to find out how best to do it and whether there is support for this. What we maintain may well be the unique contribution of this school, is what is almost universally recognized as being inadequate in contemporary psychotherapy: an adequate, holistic, anthropological approach; goals of therapy, and how to be explicit and self-conscious about the axiological approach you are making, since it can be very easily demonstrated that every therapist introduces significantly, whether explicitly or all implicitly, his own value system into the therapeutic relationship. We can state that we recognize what everybody else does, and so we are proposing to try this particular anthropological point of view, this particular axiological position, and these particular goals of therapy. (TWEEDIE).[19]

Although there was much discussion of differing ideas at this meeting, there was no common meeting of the minds. Fairweather brought the meeting to a close with these words and suggestions:

We must summarize and go on to some further thinking. I feel greatly encouraged and warm of heart in what we have been able to do among ourselves this morning. It is wonderful that we can get together as Christian men [sic] who have this kind of interest, and share in the way we have in openness and honesty. To sum up: Would you men be willing to submit the following statements?

1. The uniqueness of the school in terms of the present need as it relates to the psychotherapeutic effort, and the psychological problems implicit within the psychotherapeutic effort: Dr. John Vayhinger, Dr. Mansell Pattison
2. The uniqueness in terms of the theo-anthropological approach: Dr. Bernard Ramm, Dr. Donald Tweedie
3. The uniqueness in terms of antecedents—philosophically and historically: Dr. John Finch[20]

All agreed to turn in their statements for consideration at the next National Steering Committee meeting which was scheduled for March 20-21, 1964. It is interesting to note that as far as the records at hand, these were the last meetings of the Study Committee. There is no record, either, of the discussion of these assignments at the March meeting of the National Steering Committee. One can only surmise that the good feeling to which Fairweather referred was sufficient, even though it did not result in any definitive statement. There seemed to be a general consensus that Fuller was initiating something unique, but there seemed to be a reluctance to explicitly state this as an affirmation of Finch's Christian existentialism or Fairweather's image therapy.

In fact, Finch's memory is that about ten minutes before the lunch break, Hubbard turned to him and asked if he could summarize his paper in a few minutes. Finch felt insulted by this and answered "No!" He felt that more time should have been given to a discussion of these basic philosophical issues. In general, there seemed to be agreement that the training offered should be solid and scholarly. It should meet all the standards of the American Psychological Association. Also, there seemed to be general agreement that the Christian faith, including its theological and biblical foundation, should provide the basis for understanding human nature, psychopathology, and healing. However, the development of the specifics was left for future development and experience. Granberg's "largeness of spirit" seemed to be the dominant theme among these professionals who agreed to disagree but apparently trusted each other. Some papers were presented at this meeting, but they have not been preserved nor is there any record of dialogue about them. The committee spent most of its time on more practical matters, such as the opening of the clinic in the fall of 1964.[21]

After Lee Travis became dean, the debate over objectives continued, but in a somewhat disguised manner. Neither Travis nor Finch wanted to train pastoral counselors. Both wanted to train psychologists. But Travis wanted to assure that students were well-trained psychologists first and integrators second. Finch wanted to assure they were integrators first, and well-trained psychologists second. These distinctions reflected their different backgrounds. Finch had been primarily trained as a pastoral/philosophical psychologist. Travis had been primarily trained as a hard-nosed, secular psychologist. While both were Christians, their sense of what was needed by those who would integrate faith and practice were decidedly different.

CHAPTER 4 – SCHOOL OBJECTIVES ARE DEBATED—THE CLINIC IS OPENED

The Pasadena Community Counseling Center Opens

In the midst of the dialogue about the goals and objectives of the school, plans for opening a clinic went on apace. The recommendation of the National Steering Committee to establish a clinic one year before students were admitted was affirmed by the faculty and trustees in the summer of 1963. The Psychology Committee took this decision as a mandate and began to make the clinic become a reality. Paul Fairweather and Don Cole were assigned the tasks of selecting a site and working out administrative details. They laid the groundwork that led to the opening of the Pasadena Community Counseling Center in November 1964. By the time of the March meeting of the National Steering Committee, these plans were well on their way. The Pasadena Community Counseling center, or "P-Triple C" (PCCC) as it came to be called, was located at 177 North Madison Avenue in a large, refurbished, two-story, stucco house that was destined to remain the center of school activity until the mid-1980s when it was demolished to make room for a parking lot behind a new psychology building which was being constructed.[22]

Tweedie Becomes Director of the Clinic

Donald F. Tweedie, Jr., became the PCCC "administrative coordinator" in the summer of 1964. There was some discussion over his title. Tweedie was more than "director" of the clinic and less than "dean" of a not-yet-in-existence school. The title "administrative coordinator and chairman of the faculty" was agreed upon as his title until a permanent dean could be chosen. The first task assigned to Tweedie was to renovate the 177 North Madison property. He was asked also to design a beginning curriculum, equip the library with psychology books, establish clinic and staff procedures, and cultivate referral sources. "Administrative coordinator" was the title that seemed to encompass all these duties.[23]

Tweedie came to this position from Gordon College in Hamilton, Massachusetts, where he had been chair of the Department of Psychology for a number of years. He was a well-known Christian psychologist who had written such books as *The Christian and the*

Couch and Logotherapy: An Evaluation of Frankl's Existential Approach to Psychotherapy from a Christian Viewpoint.[24]

While studying with phenomenologist Erwin Strauss at the Veteran's Hospital in Lexington, Kentucky, during a sabbatical leave from Gordon, Tweedie had been consulted about the establishment of the School of Psychology at Fuller and endorsed the project. Subsequently, he played an active role in the National Steering Committee and in the work of a Psychology Study Committee, whose job it was to determine the objectives of the school. Tweedie knew Fuller Theological Seminary well. Earlier in his life, before undertaking graduate study in psychology, he had been a student at Fuller and a classmate of David Hubbard. Although Tweedie had designed plans for a graduate program in Christian psychology at Gordon College, he became excited about being in on the ground floor of the new venture at Fuller. He enthusiastically accepted the invitation to come to Pasadena and to be in charge of the counseling center as well as coordinate plans for the opening of the school. He had hoped that he would be asked to be dean at a later date.

Planning for Opening the Clinic

The final steps leading up to the opening of the clinic and the appointment of Tweedie as administrative coordinator were equal in thoroughness to the deliberations that had culminated in the initial convening of the National Steering Committee over a year earlier. The faculty/staff Psychology Committee had reported to the trustees their progress in July 1963, and had received encouragement to proceed with their plan to begin the school by opening a counseling center the next year.[25] Early in the fall the committee followed through on this mandate and officially set the date of fall 1964 as the time when a counseling center would be opened.[26]

In early spring of 1964 the seminary purchased the Simpkinson property at 177 North Madison Avenue. This was a large two-story house with ample parking and a large front lawn on the corner of Madison Avenue and Walnut Street. When Tweedie arrived in July, his major task was to have this facility refurbished and open for business by early September, a full year before the first students were to arrive. This property was described thusly in a "Summer Progress Report" to the trustees:

Chapter 4 – School Objectives are Debated—The Clinic is Opened

A very excellent piece of property has been procured for the new school at 177 North Madison Avenue, which is one block east of Oakland. It abuts a parking lot owned by the seminary on the corner of Walnut and Madison and also is contiguous with the rear parking lots of two properties used as student dormitories on Oakland. Thus, it will be very convenient in terms of using the seminary library, the chapel, and needed classrooms. The building on the property is a two-story, Mediterranean-style stucco house which is in the process of being renovated for our use. The present layout includes offices for ten faculty-therapists, an office for an executive secretary, a reception room, a waiting room, a kitchenette, and two rooms for which groups therapy shall take place. One of these is conjoined by an observation and recording room. In addition, the area provides three small testing rooms and a student study area.[27]

Tweedie asked for bids on the redecoration. G.W. Manchester, a member of Pasadena's Lake Avenue Congregational Church, was awarded the contract. He agreed to complete the work by the end of September. The first floor included four offices plus a staff room and reception area. The second floor also included a reception area and four other offices. At the cookies-and-punch Open House on opening day in November, all who attended expressed appreciation for a job well done. Marnie Frederickson moved into the office to the left of the reception area and Tweedie settled into the adjacent unit that eventually became the office of the dean. Others chose their places and the Pasadena Community Counseling Center opened its doors for service to the community.

Among the counselors who made up the first staff of the counseling center were three members of the Fuller faculty: Paul Fairweather (professor of pastoral counseling), Donald Cole (dean of students), and Robert Bower (professor of Christian education), as well as five new professionals: Donald Tweedie (administrative coordinator), Paul F. Barkman (psychologist), Harlan Parker (consulting psychiatrist), and Carroll Wright (pastoral and marriage and family counselor. The hope was that these therapists would never counsel full-time. This reduced schedule was to allow them to meet regularly in the staff room to share their experiences and begin developing models and methods for integrating theology and psychology in their clinical work.[28] The counseling center was intended to be the place where the idea of a Christian approach to psychotherapy became a reality. This practical, in-vivo work would become the essence of the "theo-psychology" that would be taught to students in the School of Psychology.

The nonseminary faculty who became part of the clinic came from diverse backgrounds. Tweedie was still back in Massachusetts at the time that Paul Barkman became a Postdoctoral Fellow at the Reiss-Davis Clinic in Los Angeles, while on sabbatical leave from teaching psychology at Taylor University in Indiana. Like Tweedie and Wright, Barkman played an active role in the Psychology Study Committee and the National Steering Committee during the late fall of 1963 and the spring of 1964. As the work progressed toward opening the Pasadena Community Counseling Center, Barkman became director of research for PCCC. He continued in this role when students came in 1965. Also, he coordinated library acquisitions. Barkman remained as a full-time faculty member of the school until the early 1970s.

Carroll Wright was an assistant of Paul Fairweather in their work at the Los Angeles Baptist City Mission and in Fairweather's private practice. They espoused and practiced a form of counseling called "image therapy" that focused on the importance of the father in personality development. This approach combined counseling theory with Christian affirmations and was termed by John Finch as a "valuable contribution to the synthesizing of Christianity and psychology."[29] Wright participated actively in the spring 1964 Study Committee meetings, to be described below. Fairweather recommended that Dr. Wright be a part of the clinic staff. Wright was a counselor in the PCCC and later did some teaching in the school when classes began. He remained with the school until 1968. Harlan Parker, M.D., became the psychiatric consultant to PCCC. He was a Christian who had a private practice in the Los Angeles area and was well-known to many persons at the seminary. Like all other staff members except Tweedie and Barkman, Parker came to PCCC only one day at week at first.

Official Opening of PCCC

In mid-November 1964, the PCCC was officially opened with dedicatory ceremony, refreshments, and a tour of the building. John Finch spoke about the dream of a school of psychology. Paul Fairweather told of plans for classes to begin in 1965 and delivered a

CHAPTER 4 – SCHOOL OBJECTIVES ARE DEBATED—THE CLINIC IS OPENED

speech titled "A Christian Approach to Psychology," which is reprinted in the Appendix to this volume. Tweedie described the services of the center. Hubbard was the master of ceremonies. Of all the major planners, only Davis Weyerhaeuser was unable to come. Shortly after the event, Weyerhaeuser wrote Hubbard:

> Everyone returned to Tacoma enthusiastic about all that they saw and heard in connection with the dedication of our Counseling Center. It was a real blow not to be able to be present, but nothing nicer could have been done for me to than to hear John's entire talk and most of Paul Fairweather's introduction.[30]

Weyerhaeuser continued,

> I took comfort in the fact that I will be down there within a week to see the center for myself, although nothing can ever quite make up for missing the dedication."

His enthusiasm that, at last, all the years of thinking and planning were having tangible results, was widely shared.

Tweedie began to tire of clinic administration very soon. Moreover, he agreed with the need to make the staff at the Pasadena Community Counseling Center multidisciplinary. In the late fall of 1964, he made contact with Adrin Sylling who was the director of adoptions for the Evangelical Welfare Agency in Whittier. Sylling had not heard of the proposed new school before Tweedie called him and asked if he would be willing to consider working at PCCC. Sylling, a licensed clinical social worker and a diplomate with the National Association of Social Workers, was a masterful therapist and a distinguished mental health professional. He agreed to come one day a week to the clinic as part of a plan to make PCCC multidisciplinary. In 1966 he joined the staff full time and became the administrator of the clinic when Tweedie decided to give up the position. During his tenure at the school, Sylling completed requirements for the Ph.D. degree at the University of South Africa (UNISA) and taught clinical interviewing after students arrived. He left to return to full-time private practice in 1980.

Thus, by the time that the first students were admitted into the program in the fall of 1965, the Pasadena Community Counseling Center was a functioning clinic whose fees were contributing significantly to the budget of the fledgling School of Psychology. After Lee Travis became dean, he asked and received permission for the professional staff to bring their private practices into the PCCC.

Subsequently, all faculty were allowed up to a day a week of fee-for-service private practice in their offices.

ENDNOTES

1. Minutes of the Meeting of the Psychology Committee, September 23, 1963.
2. At this time, E. Mansell Pattison, a well-known evangelical professional, was a professor of psychiatry at the University of Washington in Seattle. On some occasions he was considered for a position on the faculty of the School of Psychology but he never came. Nevertheless, he remained interested in the school for many years thereafter and served as a committee member on one or more dissertations as well as gave visiting lectures from time to time. Subsequent to his appointment at the University of Washington, Pattison taught at the University of California, Irvine, and the Medical College of Georgia. Pattison died as the result of an automobile accident in the late 1980s.
3. The deliberations of this group are detailed in the Report of Meetings of the Study Committee, School of Psychology, October 5, November 15, and December 20, 1963. The references to follow are from one or more of these reports.
4. Report, November 15, p. 7
5. Ibid., p. 8.
6. Writings to which Wright referred included:
Charlotte Bühler, *Values in Psychotherapy* (Glencoe, IL: The Free Press, 1962). In addition to her work on values, she was also "one of the founders of humanistic psychology in this country. She was the founder of a movement within an organization, the American Association of Humanistic Psychology, and its own organ, the *Journal of Humanistic Psychology*. She was also a major theoretician; "her altruistic orientation and rigorous research approach combining to produce far-reaching theories of development and human behavior." Gwendolyn Stevens and Sheldon Gardner, *The Women of Psychology: Vol. II, Expansion and Refinement* (Cambridge, MA: Schenkman, 1982), p. 27.
Wilfrid Daim, *Depth Psychology and Salvation*. Translated by Kurt F. Reinhardt. (New York: Frederick Ungar, 1963). Daim was an Austrian psychiatrist who offered a psychoodynamic understanding of redemption and who was very influenced by Otto Rank as well as Sigmund Freud. He was a contributor to the journal *Psychotherapy as a Religious Process*, published by the Institute for Rankian Analysis in Dayton, Ohio. In this book, Daim "examined the need for salvation, the place of the psychoanalytic process as part of the process of salvation, and the place of this only 'partial salvation' within the frame of the total salvation by Christ" (Hendrika Vande Kemp, *Psychology and Theology in Western Thought 1672-1965: A Historical and Annotated Bibliography*, in collaboration with H. Newton Malony (Millwood, NY: Kraus International Publications, 1984) p. 173).
Viktor E. Frankl, *The Doctor and the Soul: An Introduction to Logotherapy* Translated by Richard Winston and Clara Winston. (New York: Knopf, 1955). Frankl, "a Jewish psychiatrist and concentration camp survivor, is

CHAPTER 4 – SCHOOL OBJECTIVES ARE DEBATED—THE CLINIC IS OPENED

well-known in Christian as well as transpersonal circles as the founder of logotherapy, which focuses on the search for meaning in human existence. *Man's Search for Meaning* has been published in 24 languages and named by the Library of Congress as one of the ten most influential books in America." (Hendrika Vande Kemp, "Historical Perspective: Religion and Clinical Psychology in America," In Edward Shafranske, Ed. *Religion and the Clinical Practice of Psychology*, Washington, DC: American Psychological Association, in press, p. 13.) Donald Tweedie studied with Frankl and invited him to lecture at the School of Psychology in 1964-65.

Harry (Henry James Samuel) Guntrip, *Mental Pain and the Cure of Souls*. (London: Independent Press, 1956). This book was also published under the title *Psychotherapy and Religion: The Constructive Use of Inner Conflict* (New York: Harper, 1957). Guntrip was "a major leader in the British Object-Relations School [who] began his career as a Congregationalist minister. The core of this book is an explication of object relations theory, drawing on the works of John Bowlby, W.R.D. Fairbairn, and Phyliss Greenacre as well as his own clinical observations" (Hendrika Vande Kemp, "Great Psychologists as 'Unknown' Psychologists of Religion," (Chapter in book in progress, undated, p. 1). [For Guntrip] Religion is defined as "experiencing a relationship with the ultimate all-embracing reality regarded as personal. Psychotherapy and Christian experience both involve a quest for salvation and the experience of communion." (Vande Kemp, *Psychology and Theology*, pp. 150-151.)

Carl G. Jung, "Answer to Job". *The Problem of Evil: Its Psychological and Religious Origins*. Translated by R.F.C. Hull. (London: Routledge & Kegan Paul, 1954). This is only one of a number of writings of Jung, famous Swiss psychiatrist. In comparison to Freud, Jung's outlook on religion is much more positive and constructive. His famous dictum that treatment of those in mid-to-late life resembled the life-solutions of the great religions illustrates his conviction that religion is a deep-seated, essential part of self-development. In this volume, Jung deals with the righteousness of God in dealing with Job and raises the possibility that Job was more moral than God.

Paul Tournier, *The Meaning of Persons*. Translated by E. Hudson (New York: Harper, 1957). Tournier is the best-known European contributor to Christian personalistic psychology. He emphasizes the "spiritual component of the person which is as real as the mental or physiological" (Vande Kemp, *Psychology and Theology*, p. 214). In 1947 he helped "organize annual international congresses on the Medicine of the Person. Twenty-one books authored by Tournier have been translated into English." (Vande Kemp, "Historical Perspective," p. 12). Tournier lectured at the School of Psychology in its second year.

7. Robert K. Bower, "Questions and Comments on the Psychology Committee Meeting, November 15, 1963.
8. Minutes of the Meeting of the Psychology Study Committee, November 15, 1963. It is difficult to keep the several committees separate, particularly when they meet on the same day as is the case in these November 15 meetings. The three committees were: the National Steering Committee composed largely of non-Fuller Seminary professionals, the purpose of which

was to give counsel and validation to the School of Psychology project; the Psychology Committee composed of Fuller faculty and administrators, the purpose of which was to execute plans for the establishment of the School of Psychology; and the Psychology Study Committee, a subcommittee composed of both seminary and nonseminary persons, the purpose of which was to discuss and suggested objectives and philosophy for the School of Psychology. Both the National Steering Committee and the Psychology Study Committee reported back to the Psychology Committee, which had the responsibility to undertake the actual execution of plans.

9. Ibid., p. 3
10. Ibid., pp. 3-4.
11. Ibid., p. 4.
12. Ibid., p. 4.
13. Ibid., p. 5
14. Letter of Mrs. Walter B. Driscoll to C. Davis Weyerhaeuser, September 22, 1964.
15. Ralph Cooper Hutchinson, "Theo-psychology at Fuller Theological Seminary." A report to the Ten-Year Planning Committee (April 1963).
16. Letter of C. Davis Weyerhaeuser to Mrs. Walter D. Driscoll, October 22, 1964.
17. Ibid.
18. Ibid.
19. Report of Study Committee Meeting, December 20, 1963.
20. Ibid.
21. Report of Progress and Developments, School of Psychology, for Meeting of the National Steering Committee, March 20-21, 1964.
22. In the mid-1980s anonymous donors gave five million dollars for the construction of a new Psychology Building at 180 North Oakland Avenue. This building was dedicated in 1986 and named the John Geoffrey Finch Hall. The building is located where two student dormitories were located originally. In the early 1970s one of the dormitories became the Child Development Center. Several faculty offices had also been located in this building.
23. Minutes of the Meeting of the Psychology Committee, February 22, 1964. At this time, Paul Barkman, psychology professor from Taylor University on sabbatical leave at the Reiss-Davis Clinic in Los Angeles, was nominated to serve on the National Steering Committee. Also, in the same motion that nominated Tweedie to be administrative coordinator, Barkman was appointed part-time research coordinator for PCCC. There was a friendly debate between Tweedie and Barkman as to who was the first person employed by the School of Psychology. It appears that they were both hired at the same time.
24. Donald F. Tweedie, *Logotherapy: An Evaluation of Frankl's Existential Approach to Psychotherapy from a Christian Viewpoint* (Grand Rapids, MI: Baker Book House, 1961)

Donald F. Tweedie, *The Christian and the Couch: An Introduction to Christian Logotherapy*. (Grand Rapids, MI: Baker Book House, 1963).
25. Report of the Meeting of the Steering Committee for the School of Psychology, Fuller Theological Seminary, June 1, 1963: 12-13.
26. Minutes of the Meeting of the Psychology Committee, September 23, 1963.
27. Summer Progress of the Development of the Fuller Seminary School of Psychology and the Pasadena Community Counseling Center, p. 1.
28. Preliminary Report of the Meeting of the National Steering Committee, School of Psychology, Fuller Theological Seminary, p. 3.
29. Letter of John G. Finch to David Allan Hubbard, September 16, 1963.
30. Letter of C. Davis Weyerhaeuser to David Allan Hubbard, November 24, 1964.

CHAPTER 5

A Dean Is Chosen

Behind much of the planning for the opening of the clinic was a haunting preoccupation with the question, Who should be dean of the School of Psychology? As the preparations for the opening of the Pasadena Community Counseling Center progressed, this concern came ever more to the forefront.

The National Steering Committee, at its June 1963 meeting, had stated that choosing a dean was an urgent need in light of their recommendation that a clinic be opened the following year. They felt that the dean should be there during that time to help plan the curriculum, to choose the faculty that would be needed, and to coordinate clinical and classroom training.[1]

The first recorded step in selecting a dean can be seen in a letter to David Hubbard from Davis Weyerhaeuser in August 1963, just a few weeks before Hubbard was to be installed as seminary president. The letter reads:

I am writing to ask you to clarify what steps, if any, I should take in alerting Larry, who is chairman of our Academic Affairs Committee (at least until September 1), as to our desire to have him appraise various candidates for the dean of our new school.[2]

The "Larry" in this instance was Trustee Lawrence Kulp, the physics professor at Columbia University who was greatly concerned that the new school have academic integrity. Weyerhaeuser's question seemed to indicate that the time was approaching when a formal selection process might be needed. That this was the case can a be seen in a subsequent paragraph of Weyerhaeuser's letter to Hubbard:

I happened to be talking with John Finch yesterday and mentioned our conversation about a dean. He feels there are both strong and weak points in connection with the name he prefers, but feels the advantages outweigh the disadvantages. I am asking him to write you about this.[3]

Dean Candidate 1: Paul Fairweather

Subsequently, Finch wrote President Hubbard a strong letter in support of the candidacy of Paul Fairweather, the incumbent professor of pastoral counseling at the seminary.[4] Finch noted that Fairweather had been a part of developing the idea of the School of Psychology from the beginning; had developed a unique integration of psychology and theology based on the role of fathers; had strong academic qualifications; knew the seminary well as one of its professors; was an active practitioner who had attracted several other counselors to work with him; and was not actively seeking the position. Finch regarded this last point as a strong mark in Fairweather's favor.

Fairweather's candidacy did not seem to progress much beyond Finch's letter, however. This was probably due to a growing concern, on Hubbard's part, about Fairweather's many extracurricular interests. He was involved in the Los Angeles Baptist City Mission and had a very full counseling practice in addition to his professorial responsibilities. These interests, plus the disappointment he came to feel about the theology's reaction to his father-image model, eventually led to his having to choose whether to stay at Fuller or not.

In spite of the fact that he showed great enthusiasm for the School of Psychology project and had served as the central resident faculty figure in much of the planning, Fairweather eventually choose not to return to the faculty after a sabbatical leave in 1968. Early awareness about how these many interests might handicap his functioning led Hubbard to be cautious about serious consideration of Fairweather as dean, despite Finch's strong recommendation.

However, Fairweather was an active staff psychologist in the Pasadena Community Counseling Center and School of Psychology faculty member for the first several years of the project. In the initial year that students were at the school, Fairweather's "image therapy" became one of the first presentations in faculty/student dialogues on integrating psychology and theology. His theorizing had a profound influence on a number of early students in the School of Psychology program.

In addition to Fairweather, six other names of possible deans surfaced during this time. One was Vernon Grounds, well-known professor of pastoral counseling and president of the Conservative Baptist Seminary in Denver, Colorado. Another was John M. Vayhinger, professor of pastoral psychology and counseling at Garrett Biblical Institute in Chicago and the chair of the National Steering

Committee. The third was Donald F. Tweedie, Jr., professor of psychology at Gordon College who became the administrator of the Pasadena Community Counseling Center and chair of the faculty until a dean was chosen. The fourth was Gordon Allport, famous professor of psychology at Harvard University. And the fifth was Lars Granberg, who had recently moved from Fuller, where he was dean of students, to Hope College as professor of psychology.

Dean Candidate 2: Vernon Grounds

Several persons expressed appreciation for Vernon Grounds, but felt that the dean should be a psychologist rather than a pastoral theologian. Weyerhaeuser expressed this concern well in his aforementioned letter to Hubbard. He wrote:

> He [Finch] would have serious reservations concerning Vernon Grounds unless it can be established that he is well accepted by the psychological profession. I think I agree with John for the reason that the close connection between the school and the seminary will probably always give rise to the charge that we are promoting theology and not psychology and, unless we have at our head a man who is thoroughly recognized in the field of psychology, we will never be able to successfully refute this charge.[5]

This sentiment was echoed by others who were concerned that the School of Psychology become accredited by the American Psychological Association as quickly as possible. It was felt that a "psychologist" dean was necessary for this accreditation to occur. However, Grounds was held in such high esteem that he later became a featured lecturer in the school's annual integration lecture series.

Dean Candidate 3: John Vayhinger

The third person who was seriously considered during this time was John M. Vayhinger. His candidacy rose and fell several months before Tweedie arrived in Pasadena. Vayhinger was an evangelical Methodist minister/psychologist who received his training at Columbia University and who taught at Asbury Theological Seminary and Anderson School of Theology before assuming his current appointment at Garrett Biblical Institute in Evanston, Illinois. He was asked to join the National Steering Committee in late 1963[6] and subsequently became its cochairman.

Vayhinger was more than a titular cochairman of the committee. He became deeply involved in the deliberations of the Study Committee which became involved in discussing the objectives and philosophy of the school.[7] His thinking so impressed Davis Weyerhaeuser that he wrote a letter in February to former president, Harold John Ockenga, who was still an active trustee, expressing what seemed to be a general consensus that Vayhinger would make a good Dean. Weyerhaeuser's letter stated:

It appears that we may have found our dean of the proposed School of Psychology. Vayhinger is a thoroughgoing evangelical, speaks freely of his conversion experience and, as far as we know, will sign our Fuller creed, which he has in his possession, without any reservations.

Weyerhaeuser added a theological caveat to this last comment: *I believe the only theological question would be a possible Arminian position, but from what I gather this would not be a problem, in view of statements which he has made which demonstrate that he is definitely not a Pelagian in any sense of the word. I am confident that men like Bromiley would be satisfied.*[8]

He closed his letter with a statement indicating he felt assured that Vayhinger was the person. "We are all very encouraged over these recent developments and believe our Lord is directing us step by step."

Unfortunately, yet perhaps providently, in light of later developments, Vayhinger decided to honor his precommitment to leave Garrett and to join the faculty of Iliff School of Theology at the University of Denver and, thus, he was not offered the dean's position at Fuller. He seriously considered the role, but felt that a person who had distinguished qualifications in psychology was needed to bring credibility to the project. Although trained as a psychologist, his teaching, like that of Vernon Grounds, had been mostly in pastoral counseling.

Dean Candidate 4: Gordon Allport

It was Vayhinger who approached Gordon Allport about the deanship. When he returned to Chicago from one of his trips to Pasadena for National Steering Committee meetings, Vayhinger phoned Allport and inquired about his interest in becoming dean. Gordon Allport, a distinguished professor at Harvard, wrote one of the seminal books on the psychology of religion shortly after the end of the second World War. His book, *The Individual and His Religion: A Psychological Interpretation*[9] was one of earliest volumes that signaled an end to a long drought in American psychology during which the psychology of religion was considered a "taboo" topic.[10] His research program in Intrinsic/Extrinsic Orientations to Religion was beginning at this time.[11] It was destined to play a dominant role in research for the next four decades.

Vayhinger knew of Allport's reputation and thought he would bring to the school the eminence the project needed in its inception. Allport had heard about Fuller's School of Psychology project and was pleased to be asked to consider becoming the dean. He replied, "I am very honored but I am too old. I think the school needs a younger person. However, if I were to start a school of Christian psychology I would pattern it after the one at Fuller."[12]

Dean Candidate 5: Donald Tweedie

Tweedie's candidacy was another matter, however. He did have the psychological qualifications. He was a Christian psychologist who had distinguished himself as an academician and a scholar. He was the chair of the Department of Psychology in an accredited Christian college and was well-versed in psychological phenomenology and existential theory. In addition, Tweedie knew Fuller well and identified with the seminary's evangelical roots. He had theorized, both in speech and in writing, about the essence of Christian counseling. He had seriously thought about establishing a graduate school of Christian psychology at Gordon College, where he was teaching. His acceptance of the position as administrative coordinator of the Pasadena Community Counseling Center was based on his expectation that he would be seriously considered for the position of dean.

However, the position was never offered to Tweedie, although he functioned as acting dean in some crucial ways during the planning for the clinic opening and in the following months before, and after, Lee Travis assumed the position. In his role as "chairman of the faculty," most of the early curriculum and procedural guidelines for the School of Psychology were developed by Tweedie. Even after Travis arrived, Tweedie continued to advise him on decisions and actually drew up many of the details for opening classes in the fall of 1965.

Chapter 5 – A Dean Is Chosen

Of course, the direction that events took might have been different had Tweedie, or any one of the other candidates, become dean. It is not clear why Tweedie's candidacy failed, but there is some indication that his and Hubbard's styles were not compatible enough to have predicted a positive relationship had he become dean. They had been seminary students together and knew each other well. Tweedie had a large family and felt that he needed to have additional monies beyond those that the seminary was able to offer for their support. Hubbard remained somewhat uncomfortable with Tweedie's style of setting limits on his time and investment.

Dean Candidate 6: Lars Granberg

However, Hubbard was comfortable with Lars Granberg. The minutes of the June 1, 1964, meeting of the Psychology Committee, at which the president submitted a set of procedures and guidelines for the opening of the Pasadena Community Counseling Center, included the following statement:

a. *I feel that if we do not proceed with deliberate haste to select a dean, we will not be able to maintain our time schedule. Furthermore, we will lose the impetus which the launching of the clinic will give us in terms of public relations and community interest. Also, to postpone the beginning of the school will mean that more and more we are involved in a clinical operation, rather than an educational one.*

b. *Dr. Granberg seems to me the best person on the scene. His theology is above reproach, his academic competence is generally recognized within the seminary family. His skill as a team leader is legendary. He will give us the leadership around which we can rally and move forward.*

c. *I recommend his appointment to be made as of September 1, 1965.*[13]

Little is known about what happened to Hubbard's recommendation of Granberg. It was not necessary for the Psychology Committee to approve this recommendation because the appointment of deans was a presidential prerogative. Probably, the chief reason that Granberg was not seriously considered was the appearance of Lee Travis on the scene in the summer of 1964. In an October 1964 letter to Granberg announcing the appointment of Travis, Hubbard offered Granberg the position of director of academic affairs in the School of Psychology and indicated that he would be among those considered for dean when Travis retired, an eventuality that Hubbard suggested would not be long coming in light of Travis' advanced age.[14]

Dean Candidate 7: Lee Edward Travis

Travis brought a proven background in the training of doctoral students that no one of the other candidates possessed. Trustees Olson and Kulp had explicitly stated to Hubbard that only an experienced scholar who had directed the study of advanced students would pass muster with the board. As it turned out, Travis more than met their qualifications.

Lee Edward Travis was a clinical psychologist in private practice in Beverly Hills who had only recently retired after 20 years of teaching at the University of Southern California (USC). Prior to coming to USC in 1958, Travis had been professor of psychology, director of the Speech and Hearing Clinic, and chair of the Psychology Department at the University of Iowa where he had earned his doctorate in 1924.[15] Travis had chaired over 200 doctoral dissertations during a distinguished career and was among the 20 most quoted psychologists in American psychology in the 1940s and '50s. He had pioneered the use of electroencephalography in the United States and had authored or edited four volumes including the definitive *Handbook of Speech Pathology*.[16] In addition he had written over 90 professional articles. Further, he was a licensed psychologist in the state of California and a diplomate in clinical psychology of the American Board of Professional Psychology (ABPP). He had all the credentials for being a distinguished first dean of the School of Psychology at Fuller Seminary. In addition, he was a Christian.

The events which led up to choosing the man who was to become the first dean of the School of Psychology have become almost legendary. What happened in the summer and fall of 1964 preliminary to the appointment of Lee Edward Travis overshadowed each of the other candidacies in a manner that has assumed monumental proportions. It is to that story that we now turn.

During the late spring of 1964, the mood among the four central figures in the School of Psychology project (Weyerhaeuser, Hubbard, Fairweather, and Finch) could best be described as one of

Chapter 5 – A Dean Is Chosen

moderate-to-high anxiety. The opening of the clinic was fast approaching and still there was no viable candidate for the deanship on the horizon. John Finch expressed it best when he stated, "We were feeling desperate."

Lee Travis' name had been suggested to Fuller almost one year before he was seriously considered for the deanship. A lost note on Marnie Frederickson's desk explains the delay. Hal Hirsch, a member of Bel Air Presbyterian Church in West Los Angeles and a Fuller theology student, gave Travis' name to Marnie Fredrickson, the secretary who had been assigned to the psychology school project in the late spring of 1963. However, she misplaced it and put it out of her mind in the midst of the press of other matters which were occupying her energy. Hirsch had thought that the seminary might like to know about his therapist [Travis], who was directing the Counseling Center at his church, Bel Air Presbyterian.

In the spring of 1964, almost a year after he first gave Travis' name to Fredrickson, Hirsch found that Travis had not been contacted. Once more, he suggested Travis' name to Marnie. She apologized for misplacing it and passed Travis' name on to President Hubbard. Hubbard contacted Louis Evans, Jr., the pastor of the Bel Air church, and found that Travis was a highly respected ruling elder and he was, indeed, the director of the church's Counseling Center. Evans reported that Travis had agreed some two years earlier to give one day a week of counseling to those who came to the church for help. He had volunteered his services following a chance encounter at a church supper where Travis and his wife, Lysa, coincidentally sat near Evans and his wife, Colleen. Travis had insisted that they sit near the exit door in order to leave early in case the meeting became boring. Dr. and Mrs. Evans came late and sat nearby. The two couples began talking, and when Dr. Travis asked how he could help, the pastor said he had been praying for someone to come along who could offer some counseling help at the church as he was feeling overwhelmed by the number of people who were seeking his help.

Why Travis, a clinical psychologist in private practice in Beverly Hills, should have had any interest in volunteering his services to the church is a question that had its roots in a religious experience occurring only a short time earlier. Out of courtesy to Lysa, Travis had agreed one afternoon to drive by the church that was being built off Mulholland Drive on the crest of the hill above their house in

Psychology and the Cross

Encino, California. He had called the new building a "monument to superstition," but agreed reluctantly to go to a worship service with her the following Sunday.

At the time that he attended this service, Travis would not have called himself religious. He had grown up in Iowa as a member of the reorganized Church of the Latter Day Saints, but had not been in church since adolescence. He was a hard-nosed scientist who espoused materialism and scientific rigor. At the University of Iowa, and later at the University of Southern California, he had distinguished himself as an early researcher in the physiological investigation of brain waves and the treatment of speech disorders. His students knew him as an empiricist who had little patience with sentimentality or non-experimental investigation. Like many psychologists of that era, Travis espoused a positivistic understanding of truth based on the methods of the physical sciences. One of his students reportedly said that Travis was a full-blown atheist who prided himself on his anti-religious statements.

During these years, Travis, like many American psychologists, considered religion to be a "taboo topic." Religion was superstition. Yet something life-transforming happened to Lee Travis the second time he attended Bel Air Presbyterian Church. The first time he was there had been uneventful and he went again more out of deference to his wife than out of interest in what was going on. On that second fateful Sunday morning that he attended in the spring of 1960, the church was so crowded that the Travises had to sit in the open-air, overflow area where the service was broadcast to them.

At some point in this service a set of strange emotions overtook Lee Travis. He became flushed and euphoric. Tears began to pour down his cheeks. A sense of transcendence overwhelmed him. He was profoundly moved. Although later he could not account for the experience in terms of exactly what Dr. Evans was saying, he credited the event to a religious awakening that changed his life. On hearing of the experience, some of Travis' friends recommended he consult with a neurologist. They felt he had probably experienced a cerebral stroke. Travis knew better, however. At the time Fuller first contacted him, Travis' account of this event was as follows:

"I was a new Christian, only about three years old. For 40 years I had been an agnostic, with my belief system rooted firmly in scientific determinism and in the concept of man being a closed system

Chapter 5 – A Dean Is Chosen

sufficient unto himself. There was no God and no need of one. Neo-Darwinism explained the origin and meaning of life. Then the Lord searched me and knew me that warm spring morning in 1961. He carried me away in his love, telling me that he was acquainted with all my ways and that I could never flee from his presence. In overwhelming joy and gratitude, I committed my life totally to him."[17]

It was shortly after this experience that Travis volunteered to start the counseling center at Bel Air church. In a letter of recommendation which Louis Evans later wrote to Hubbard on Travis' behalf, he stated that Travis had become a faithful member of the church and a regular student of the Bible. Evans stated in his letter:

Four or five years ago, I first met Dr. Travis flushed with an interest in the church and the particular relationship between the church's ministry to people in emotional need. . . . His commitment to Jesus Christ seemed firm and clear and in the months which have followed, he has grown mightily in his understanding of the Scriptures and in his belief in what Christ alone can do in the human heart. He sees human therapy as simply the "narthex" to divine therapy. Because all therapy is limited to the therapist, he feels God alone can do the ultimate task of renewal.[18]

Over the years that followed, Travis became a deeply appreciated part of the congregation and an elder.

This was the Lee Edward Travis who agreed to meet for lunch in early May of 1964 with Finch and Fairweather. Finch described the meeting as occurring in a dark restaurant where one could barely see across the table but where seeing was not nearly as important as sensing. "I knew immediately that this was the man who should be our dean," Finch reported. "This is the man we want," he said to Marnie when they returned from lunch.

This sense of being in the presence of a significant person was echoed many times by others who met Travis in the years to follow. In the course of the conversation, Finch told Travis about his "dream" of a school where Christian psychologists could be trained. He boldly told Travis that "the Lord is leading me to put my finger on you for the job." Travis made an interesting reply to Finch's assertion. He said, "I don't know anything about theology." Finch replied, "That is good; I'm glad you don't. You will write your own theology." Little did Finch known how true Travis' admission was. He was a genuine, gentle Christian who turned out to be the ideal dean for the new school. But Travis was never known for his theological sophistication.

He said on many occasions to his colleagues in theology, "Teach me; I'm an eager student."

Travis' reflections on the restaurant meeting clearly indicate he was feeling inspired. He wrote:

As John [Finch] talked I would drift in and out of a transcendent state. I was led not by them, not by any human being really into paths beyond the stars, into time eternal, into a charge that I must accept—the founding deanship of a new school of Christian psychology. I was carried along still one more time in the loving arms of the Lord, in a state of complete surrender out of which I would be free and capable in serving him. Time over lunch melted into forever. Practice, patients, and Beverly Hills passed out of mind. I walked out into the warm spring sun of the early afternoon a new being full of joyous sounds ringing in my ears. I had heard the sweet siren song of service that I had been born for this day, for this destiny. The farm [his family home in Iowa], Graceland Academy, and Iowa University, research, teaching, writing, practicing, and the Bel Air experience all made sense now. They were all of a piece, one piece, to serve my Creator and know his presence forever, never again to be lonely. The place and the time of service were at Fuller.[19]

In a letter to Travis the week following this first lunch, Finch wrote that he had a similar feeling:

I have a certain glow which originated in Beverly Hills in our meeting together and which I am nurturing and maintaining. In nonpoetic language, it was a delight to make your acquaintance.[20]

Finch sent Travis some articles and stated in his letter,

I trust these articles will do two things. One, help to clarify the magnitude of the problems with which we are confronted and two, how very much further we need to go and how greatly we need your assistance.[21]

One handwritten letter, dated in early June 1964 to President Hubbard clearly shows Travis' characteristic humility coupled with his growing interest and sense of destiny. It reads,

Forgive the informality of pen and ink but I want to thank you for your letter that promised to keep me appraised of the development of the School of Psychology at Fuller. . . . I feel strongly that the program you have in mind is the greatest advance in clinical psychology that has occurred in my lifetime. To me it is a thrilling and inspiring concept and I would feel honored and blessed to have anything to do with its development. Appreciating your interest in me and I am always your attentive listener. Most prayerfully, Lee E. Travis.[22]

Chapter 5 – A Dean Is Chosen

Travis was as convinced as Finch and others that he was the man for the job, even at this early date in the exploration. Shortly after this luncheon, the decision to offer Lee Travis the deanship became the object of earnest consideration. It continued over the next six months. During the intervening weeks, Travis was a frequent visitor to the seminary. He listened and he advised. President Hubbard sought the counsel of others, both within and without the seminary. In a letter to Davis Weyerhaeuser in mid-summer, Hubbard asked for "a written summary of your impressions which can be part of our dossier on him [Travis]."

One letter to Hubbard from Nicholas Bercel, M.D., expressed well the attitude of the professional community toward Lee Edward Travis. Bercel wrote, "This is the first time in the 20 years I have known Dr. Travis that I am asked to write a reference letter about him—which is probably due to the fact that he is generally too well known." Bercel went on to detail Travis' many accomplishments:

Dr. Travis is the greatest expert on speech pathology in the world today. He was for many years head of the Department of Psychology at the University of Southern California, a pioneer in child psychiatry, psychophysiology, and a top authority on psychotherapy in general. I cannot think of anyone more suited to head such a program as you are contemplating." [23]

A summer progress report dated August 26, 1964, did not mention Travis by name but indicated that

We are presently in conversation with a mature psychologist who has a professional pedigree which is practically peerless. His recommendations, both personally and professionally, are exceedingly high, and he has expressed the willingness to accept the responsibilities of the deanship of the School of Psychology in its initial years. [24]

The report ended with a statement of exultation about the project. It stated:

The details of development of the School of Psychology are phasing in well. In every major area we are convinced that this is a "house which the Lord is building" and we are rejoicing in the challenge of the task. It is the conviction of those of us involved, and many of those with whom we talk concerning the School of Psychology, that Fuller Theological Seminary is making a significant contribution to the advancement of the Kingdom of Christ in this new project.[25]

A strategic letter from Davis Weyerhaeuser to John S. Lynn of the Lilly Endowment toward the end of September reflected the direction in which thinking about the dean was going. A request for seed funding had been made to Lilly. In addition to stating that a budget was being sent in a few days, the letter read:

> *I was down at Fuller for a meeting of the School of Psychology Committee last week and was very pleased with the developments. We met with Dr. Lee Travis, whom we are considering as our dean, and I was again tremendously impressed with him, both as a Christian and as a man of distinction in the area of psychology. He displayed excellent leadership capabilities and I feel that he, therefore, can get our school off to a good start.*[26]

The Lilly Endowment did some investigating on its own and concluded that Lee Travis was, indeed, a psychologist of distinction in whom they could put their trust. The possibility of his appointment as dean was the determining point in their decision to award Fuller a $125,000 grant. The letter informing President Hubbard of the award stated, "Since, in our judgment, it is very important that Dr. Lee Travis be appointed as the dean of this new school, we are designating that $40,000 of this amount is for his salary for two years."[27]

Travis jokingly stated again and again, "I never agreed to come." But on many occasions, Travis did come to Fuller until, after an interview with the Executive Committee in September of 1964, he was officially appointed to the position of dean by the seminary Board of Trustees in November. Although his full-time appointment did not begin until summer, he came one or two days a week beginning in January 1965.

This recommendation of the Lilly Endowment was followed with enthusiasm. In fact, there was already strong consensus that Travis was the person for the job. The public announcement in early December 1964 stated both that Travis had been appointed dean and that the Lilly Endowment had pledged $125,000. Which came first, the appointment of Travis as dean or the award, is unknown.

In January 1965 Lee Edward Travis became the first dean of the Graduate School of Psychology at Fuller Theological Seminary. He remained as dean until 1975 at which time he was succeeded in that role by Neil Clark Warren, one of the first faculty members Travis appointed after he assumed his post. A poem Travis wrote soon after his religious experience reveals that he felt God had determined that

Chapter 5 – A Dean Is Chosen

he would fill a special role. His willingness to go where God led is evident. Fuller was the answer to that call to service.

> *Save me for you, spare me for your purposes*
> *May I live more, ninety and nine years more*
> *Only for you may I live ninety and nine years more.*
> *You need not spare me just for me*
> *You need not spare me from pain and suffering*
> *Or from sorrow and hurt and the discouragement of failure*
> *But please spare me for ninety and nine years more*
> *To witness to the men of my lengthened life*
> *As only an extraordinarily lengthened life can witness*
> *In a world of incredulity and utter scorn*
> *In a world of sure prediction and no surprises*
> *In a world of meaningless clock-like momentum*
> *Grinding inexorably the finest atoms into nothingness*
> *Let me witness to thy purposes*
> *Striding ever far behind in your everlasting footsteps*
> *Yet striding in every strengthened faith and clearer hopes*
> *Declaring unflinchingly the truth of your presence.*
> *A truth so clear for all to see who will pause to see*
> *Needing strongly the sheer living physical witness to this truth*
> *Living more, living ninety and nine years more*
> *I will be this vital witness of this truth*
> *I will be the limitlessly open truth abounding for all to see*
> *My older companions of contemporary doubt and customary futility*
> *Playing a faceless role for their own selfish making*

> *For them, give me life to serve you, just to*
>   *serve up*
> *Not at all in any way just to serve me*
> *Always in all ways just to serve you*
>   *To serve you*
> *Have I asked too much, am I too presumptuous*
>   *to ask at all?*
> *Already you have walked with me and have talked with me*
> *Ought I to be sufficiently grateful to accept my short life?*
> *Just for me I would not ask for anything more*
>   *than my short life*
> *But for you I would ask even for an extension*
>   *of my short life*
> *To live ninety and nine years more in the*
>   *witnessing of your will be done*
> *Upon this earth, this contemporary world of*
>   *unconcern for you*
> *I would ask your favor and your forgiveness*
> *Bless me, oh Lord, for your sake*
> *Bless me, oh Lord.*[28]

During his tenure, Travis led the school in building a strong faculty, in achieving accreditation by the American Psychological Association, in the beginning of what later became a comprehensive Psychological Center, in the establishment of an annual integration lectureship named for John Finch, and in the graduation of 69 doctoral candidates.

As noted earlier, Travis was never known for his theological acumen. In fact, one person reportedly said that his theological examination by the faculty prior to his appointment as dean was "a disaster." In spite of what his pastor had written, Travis was, and remained, a theologically naive, yet trust-filled Christian. Many would label him a "mystic" who believed strongly in the presence and power of God but whose religious knowledge never approached his psychological sophistication. Yet, through it all, Travis was an eager learner, a masterful visionary, a constant supporter of innovation, an eminent example, and a lovable friend. As one faculty recruit said, "I had heard little of Fuller Seminary before I arrived, but I knew within 15 minutes that Lee Travis was a person with whom I could work and on whom I could depend." His successor as dean, Neil C. Warren, expressed a sentiment of many who knew him when he said, "He was, without doubt, the best human being I have ever known."

One of Travis' former students at the University of Southern California summed up well the feeling of many who came to know and trust him in his days at Fuller Seminary. In the book *Psychologist Pro Tem* honoring Travis at his eightieth birthday in 1976, Russell Haney wrote:

Here was the Lee Travis of Saturday morning, of coffee and donuts, of the open door. The professor, who, with the eager and loving support of his wife, Lysa, welcomed students to his home. Perhaps the memories of many are best focused on the challenges, gentle searching and insistent, almost urgent supportiveness offered by the chief. Many were told "You can do it—go to it—and come back when you think it's done." Many were astounded at being told "OK—go think about it—try it—be careful—but it's worthwhile—it's worth trying—come back and tell us." It was difficult to believe that our ideas would find so much recognition—or be so valued. One after the other, we found ourselves in orals for our preliminary examinations—or in our final doctoral orals. And one after the other, we realized again that he was there to help us succeed—to help us be the best that we could be.[29]

Those of us who had the good fortune to know and work with him would echo these words of Dr. Haney:

To the leadership of Lee Edward Travis goes much of the credit for what the School of Psychology is and has become. A Service of Inauguration for Lee Edward Travis as dean of the School of Psychology at Fuller Theological Seminary was held in Payton Hall on the seminary campus on Monday, December 6, 1965. Travis' speech, "Man: In Search of Him," is reprinted in the Appendix to this volume. The address is "vintage Travis." It set the tone for the next decade in which Travis would lead the School of Psychology in a search for the nature of human beings in their organic, mental, and spiritual dimensions.

ENDNOTES

1. Report of the meeting of the Steering Committee for the School of Psychology, Fuller Theological Seminary, June 1, 1963, Chicago, Illinois.
2. Letter from C. Davis Weyerhaeuser to David Allan Hubbard, August 27, 1963.
3. Ibid., p.1
4. Letter from John G. Finch to David Allan Hubbard, September 16, 1963.
5. Letter from C. Davis Weyerhaeuser to David Allan Hubbard, August 27, 1963.
6. Minutes of the Meeting of the Seminary Psychology Committee, November 15, 1963.
7. Vayhinger accepted the invitation to attend the next meeting of the Study Committee, a subcommittee of the Seminary Psychology Committee assigned the task of deciding on the philosophy and objectives of the new school. This Study Committee met on December 20, 1963, and Vayhinger was present. The minutes of the committee meeting revealed him to be an active participant, a style he maintained from that time on.
8. Letter from C. Davis Weyerhaeuser to Harold John Ockenga, February 11, 1964.
9. Gordon W. Allport, *The Individual and His Religion: A Psychological Interpretation* (New York: Macmillan, 1950).
10. See William Douglas' chapter "Religion" in Norman Fareberow's *Taboo Topics*. (New York: Atherton, 1963, pp. 80-95)
11. Although the seminal article in *Extrinsic-Intrinsic Religious Orientation* (EIRO) research was not published until 1967, the theory had been anticipated in Allport's concern for mature and immature religion in the 1950 volume. The first publication in EIRO studies was Gordon W. Allport and J.M. Ross, "Personal Religious Orientation and Prejudice," *Journal of Personality and Social Psychology*, 5 (1967): pp. 432-443.
12. Personal communication in interview with John M. Vayhinger, October 16, 1994.
13. David Allan Hubbard, "Proposed Operating Procedures for the Fuller Theological Seminary School of Psychology," Archives of Fuller Theological Seminary, mimeo.
14. Letter from David Allan Hubbard to Lars Granberg, December 16, 1964.
15. A complete resume of Lee E. Travis' background can be found in Paul C. Clement and Donald F. Tweedie's edited volume *Psychologist Pro-Tem: In Honor of the 80th Birthday of Lee Edward Travis* (Los Angeles, CA: University of Southern California Press, 1976).
16. Lee Edward Travis, *Handbook of Speech Pathology and Audiology* (New York: Appleton-Century-Crofts, 1971). This was a revision of his earlier edited book *Handbook of Speech Pathology* (New York: Appleton-Century-Crofts, 1957).
17. Lee Edward Travis, *Ensnared in Love* (Pasadena, CA: Integration Press, 1986), pp. 40-41.

Chapter 5 – A Dean Is Chosen

18. Letter from Louis H. Evans, Jr., to David Allan Hubbard, July 22, 1964.
19. Travis, *Ensnared in Love*, p. 40.
20. Letter from John G. Finch to Lee Edward Travis, May 14, 1964.
21. Ibid.
22. Letter from Lee Edward Travis to David Allan Hubbard, June 4, 1964.
23. Letter from Nicholas A. Bercel to David Allan Hubbard, August 17, 1964.
24. Summer Progress of the Development of the Fuller Seminary School of Psychology and the Pasadena Community Counseling Center, 1963: p. 2.
25. Ibid., 2
26. Letter from C. Davis Weyerhaeuser to Charles G. Williams, September 10, 1964.
27. Letter from Charles G. Williams to David Allan Hubbard, October 20, 1964. Williams was the director for religion of the Lilly Endowment, Inc. Contact with the Lilly Endowment had begun at least a year earlier through Don Weber, Fuller's director of development. Weber and Hubbard had a consultation in Indianapolis on November 1, 1963, with John Lynn and Harold Duling, Lilly staff. In addition to their concern over the quality of the dean, which led them to direct that part of their monies be used for Travis' salary, they were also interested in the quality of students that would be attracted to Fuller's program. Thus, they directed that a major part of the money left in their $125,000 grant be used for student scholarships.
28. Travis, *Ensnared in Love*, pp. 18-19.
29. H. Russell Haney, 29. H. Russell Haney, "USC: The Years of the Clinician." In Tweedie and Clement's *Psychologist Pro Tem*, pp. 29-43.

CHAPTER 6

Students Come—Classes Begin

The public announcement that Travis had been appointed dean also stated that the School of Psychology would open in the fall of 1965.[1] The name "Fuller Graduate School of Psychology," by which the program was to be subsequently known, first appeared in this announcement. The program was described as one in which graduates would receive the Ph.D. in Clinical Psychology after six years of studying both psychology and theology in a curriculum which included practical clinical training. That the school was "in business" can be seen in the invitation for interested persons to write the registrar [Marnie Frederickson] at the 177 North Madison Avenue address rather than the seminary registrar office, which was located on Oakland Avenue. For almost a decade thereafter the School of Psychology produced its own catalog separate from that of the seminary. The North Madison building was the headquarters for the School of Psychology until the mid-1980s, at which time it was torn down to make way for the new building at 180 North Oakland.

The early spring 1965 announcement of the opening of the school stated that details of the curriculum, which would be "geared to meet the requirements of professional accrediting agencies," would be announced in the next few weeks.[2] Behind this seemingly innocuous statement lay an ongoing debate. From a very early point in the planning, it had been determined that the school would produce "psychologists" who could meet the requirements for licensure in the states in which they chose to practice because they had been trained in a graduate program which was approved by the American Psychological Association (APA).

The reader may remember that Ralph Hutchinson had questioned whether plans which included courses in secular psychology, such as might be taught at UCLA, would be appropriate for a curriculum in "theo-psychology," which he perceived to be the purpose of the Fuller program.[3] He called teaching psychology and theology in separate courses an "overlay" rather than an "integration" model. By the time of this first official announcement that the School of Psychology would open in September 1965, Hutchinson's warning had been disregarded.

As early as December 1962, the report of the Committee on Associated Schools to Fuller's Ten-Year Planning Conference had included a list of projected courses for the school which could easily have been copied from any extant program in clinical psychology in any major university.[4] Except for the fact that all courses were to be taught at the seminary and no courses were to be taken at UCLA, the "overlay" model had become the format that was to be followed. The prime concern was to pass the scrutiny of the APA and to guarantee to the professional community that students had studied "real" psychology.

Without question, the appointment of Lee Travis as dean indicated that obtaining credibility within the psychological community had high priority. Providing the world with psychotherapists who would have the respect of society, as well as the trust of the church, was the aim. Travis' letter of appointment had specifically stated that he would be the "academic director of the entire program."[5] In that position he was expected to design a training program in psychology that resembled those of the Universities of Southern California and of Iowa, institutions of which he had been a part for much of his past.

One might think of this period in the history of the School of Psychology as a "honeymoon" time in which all the primary figures were getting along well together. One of Travis' first letters was written to John Finch, inviting him to journey down from Tacoma one Wednesday a month "to help with appointment of faculty, creation of curriculum, and selection of students."[6] Travis was trusting that he and Finch saw the task through similar eyes.

Although John Finch appeared to agree with the concern to provide a training program which would receive accreditation by the American Psychological Association, he later took the position that this was a very constraining approach. Earlier, it was noted that he had called Hutchinson a "windbag" for suggesting that teaching psychology separately from theology was ill-advised. However, he soon came to agree that teaching psychology as it was taught in secular universities was, indeed, a weakness of the program. From Finch's perspective, traditional courses, such as statistics, personality, and physiological psychology, were not as important or as essential as courses in Christian existentialism. Truly, Finch's vision was for the training of Christian psychologists rather than psychologists who were Christians. Although Fairweather in earlier discussions had joined Finch in contending that the school should be focused on Christian psychology, he did not contest the move toward a curriculum or faculty that reflected broader perspectives.

The concern which Finch had expressed in discussions with Hubbard about whether psychoanalysts and behaviorists should be employed as faculty became increasingly strong over the years as he realized that existential psychology was going to be presented as only one elective option among many other courses. During these early months of curriculum planning, however, things seem to go along harmoniously. Finch seemed well pleased with the way plans were developing.

Actually, PCCC administrator Tweedie designed much of the early curriculum. Having been chairman of Gordon College's Psychology Department for over a decade before coming to Fuller, he knew what a well-rounded psychology curriculum should include. Furthermore, he had talked with Travis and agreed with him on the kinds of courses that should be offered. On December 9, the day after the letter of appointment had been sent to Travis, Tweedie sent Hubbard a note suggesting how the opening of the school in the fall of 1965 might be announced. Although his note did not list the courses, it stated that "the curriculum in academic psychology and the practicum in clinical experience will be well above the minimal recommendations for the doctoral program of the American Psychological Association."[7]

The Hubbard Memo

Soon after the above-mentioned announcement in the spring of 1965, a four-page memo from President Hubbard was sent to "All College and University Students interested in Graduate Training in Psychology."[8] A picture of Travis, Hubbard, and Tweedie graced the top of this publication. The memo announced that after three years of study by a National Steering Committee and a Faculty Advisory Committee, the Fuller Seminary Board of Trustees was launching a new School of Psychology. The establishment of a 15-year trust by

Chapter 6 – Students Come – Classes Begin

one of the seminary trustees, C. Davis Weyerhaeuser, and a generous three-year grant from the Lilly Endowment were credited with making the project possible.

The memo reviewed the three years of study and preparation which led to the launching of the new School of Psychology and invited interested students to apply immediately. It stated that "this will be a theologically oriented program, based on a Christian view of man." In a highlighted section, the memo noted that "the needs of contemporary society are creating new and challenging roles for psychotherapists" and that "Fuller believes it is both the opportunity and the responsibility of the church to be involved in this training." The memo contained the detailed list of course titles that had been promised in the earlier announcement. It prescribed what students would be taking across a six-year span. The mastery of four languages and statistics was required. These were to be the "tools" for mastering psychology and theology.

During the first three or "pre-clinical" years, students were to take eight hours of biblical and theological courses and eight hours of psychological courses each quarter. Summers were to be spent in learning Greek and Hebrew.

During the last three or "clinical" years, students were to spend their summers studying French and German. This was to prepare them for taking two-hour psychology seminars in these languages during their fourth and fifth years. Further, they were to take four-hour courses each quarter in applied psychology. In each of the last nine quarters, they were to take two-hour psychology-theology seminars which integrated their study in these two disciplines. In addition to these studies, students were to be involved in clinical clerkships, externships, and internships each of these last three years. The dissertations and qualifying exams were to be completed during the last year of study.

The memo stated that tuition would be $1,200. Room rent would range between $4.65 and $7.20 weekly, and meals could be purchased during the week for $12.25. Two postdoctoral fellowships of $6,000 each were announced. An application form was also attached. Pictures of visiting and full-time faculty were also included. Travis, Tweedie, Fairweather, and Cole were listed as full-time faculty. Under Barkman's picture it was noted that he would be full-time by the time school opened in the fall. The memo also listed several visiting faculty. Among these was Harlan Parker, a psychiatrist and Adrin Sylling, a social worker. Sylling was destined to assume Tweedie's role as full-time director of the Pasadena Community Counseling Center. At this time, however, he was still the director of the Evangelical Welfare Agency in Whittier, and was only part-time. Donald Wayne Hall, was described as an "experimental" psychologist from the University of Colorado. Clayton Durward Roa, was listed as a postdoctoral fellow.

The memo also gave the membership of the National Steering Committee. By this time, the chairman, John Vayhinger, had moved from Chicago to Denver where he was teaching at the Iliff School of Theology. Interestingly enough, John Finch, at whose suggestion the School of Psychology had been initiated, was not mentioned in the memo, except in a section listing "special lectures." Here he was named, along with Viktor Frankl, Ph.D., of Vienna, Austria, and Paul Tournier of Switzerland. Donald Tweedie had studied with Frankl and written a book on his thinking titled *Logotherapy: An Evaluation of Frankl's Existential Approach to Psychotherapy from a Christian Viewpoint.*[9] Tournier was an internationally known Christian psychiatrist with whom Tweedie was also personally acquainted.[10] Frankl and Tournier, along with Finch, gave invited lectures during the 1964-65 year when only the Pasadena Community Counseling Center was operating. Special lectures were delivered by O. Hobart Mowrer of the University of Illinois and Perry London of the University of Southern California during the following year, 1965-66, which was the first year students were in residence.[11]

Thus, Finch began a pattern he was to continue for many years. He came to the school and spoke in classes as well a on special occasions every year until the early 1990s. In the 1970s Finch began teaching a one-week intensive course that included academic credit. At this time, many students responded positively to his model of "Christian existentialism" and journeyed to Tacoma for three weeks of "intensive therapy"[12] under his guidance. Some years later, a book detailing Finch's model was published. This volume, *A Christian Existential Psychology: The Contributions of John G. Finch*[13] included testimonies from Annette Weyerhaeuser and a number of other persons who had benefited from his approach. Yet, in spite of Finch's influence in this way and his contribution to the planning of the school, he was never a part of the full-time faculty. For many years he was listed as a part-time, or visiting professor in the yearly seminary catalogs.

The First Class

Nineteen students matriculated in late September 1965 and began their study as the first class in the new School of Psychology. There were 18 men and one woman. Ten of this number were to finish their studies and graduate with doctorates in clinical psychology. Their names and the year in which they graduated are as follows:

Ronald W. Ohlson, 1970; now a psychologist in Anchorage, Alaska

David W. Donaldson, 1970; now a psychologist in Denver, Colorado

James R. Bell, 1970; now a psychologist in Olney, Montana

James R. Oraker, 1970; now a psychologist in Colorado Springs, Colorado

Samuel N. Lo, 1971; now a psychologist in Pomona, California

Clifford L. Penner, 1971; now a psychologist in Pasadena, California, and a trustee of the seminary

John S. Fry, 1971; now a psychologist in Newport Beach, California

David W. Condiff, 1972; now a psychologist in Glendora, California

Allan P. Hess, 1972; now a psychologist in Venice, California

James V. Van Camp, 1972; a psychologist whose address is unknown

Several in this first class eventually graduated with terminal master's degrees. These were: Joseph Solman, Remigo Bon Gabriel, Nikola Andonov, Richard Burr, and David Corbin. One student, Delano Goehner, was well on his way to completing his studies when he took ill with serious stomach complications and died in early 1970. There is no record of what happened to the other students in this group.

Almost every student who applied in the spring and summer of 1965 was admitted. Lee Travis decided to include everyone who expressed an interest. Marnie Frederickson also made some decisions. Al Hess, who was a student in theology, talked with Marnie and was advised to think over whether he wanted to give himself wholeheartedly to many years of psychological study. A few days later he returned and told her he was willing to do so. "You're in!" she responded. John Fry, too, was already a student at the seminary. He was one of a number of Young Life leaders who had come to Fuller for theological study but who transferred into the School of Psychology. James Oraker also had been a staff member of Young Life. After graduation, he returned to Young Life employ.

Thirteen of those in this first class had previously completed Bachelor of Divinity degrees. Others came directly from undergraduate training. Cliff Penner, for example, had moved to Seattle after graduating from college in order for his wife, Joyce, to complete nursing school. They attended University Presbyterian Church where Robert Munger was the minister. One Sunday in the spring of 1965, David Hubbard preached at the church and told about the new School of Psychology which would be opening that fall. After the service, Cliff spoke with Hubbard and became interested in attending the school. Hubbard suggested that Cliff speak with John Finch, who was located in nearby Tacoma. After the interview, Finch reported his approval to Travis and Cliff was admitted.[14]

A number of the students in the first class were married. Soon after students arrived, Lee Travis and his wife, Lysa, began a weekly meeting for wives which continued for a number of years. Many women felt that their ability to stand the stress of graduate school was greatly enhanced by these weekly meetings. The Travises nurtured these wives and talked to them "as if they were their own children." They gave the women a sense of community and a feeling that they belonged to a project that was significant and worthwhile. Often, the Travises would have the whole student body over to their home in Encino for food and fellowship. The Travis home, on Red Rose Drive in Encino, was an opulent residence complete with a swimming pool and a warmly decorated living room. These students, and many after them, felt embraced and accepted in a manner that they remember with great appreciation.

However, a number of the students in the first class were unmarried. They lived together in "Dorm 190," one of a series of older homes on Oakland Avenue. They became known as a somewhat ribald group who were distrusted by neighbors on each side, who were more pious theology students. The male psychology stu-

Chapter 6 – Students Come – Classes Begin

dents in "Dorm 190" had a habit of celebrating each others' birthdays with parties which evoked the disdain of the other students. Although rather mild according to secular standards, these birthday parties included spiked punch, the singing of Kingston Trio songs, and a cold shower for the "birthday boy." On one occasion in mid-May of the first year, a knock came at the door. In walked two burly police officers who reported that they had received a complaint about the noise the party was making. Naturally, the psychology students presumed that their more spiritual colleagues in the nearby dorms had lodged the protest.

John Fry was at the party. The next day, Dolores Loeding, then secretary to the dean of the School of Theology, approached Fry as he walked to class. With a sly grin on her face, she stated, "I heard about your party last night, John Fry!" "Where?" queried John. "At the faculty Scholarship Committee meeting," Loeding answered. This worried Fry because he was seeking some scholarship monies at that time. He wondered whether they would consider him a good risk or not, in spite of the fact that the party had been rather mild in comparison to parties that took place in off-campus settings.

Some months later, Lee Travis caught up with Fry and, putting his arm around him in a fatherly manner, said, "John, I feel really badly to have to ask you about this, but Dr. Hubbard wanted me to find out what really happened at your party last May."[15] Although his concern was real, Fry got his scholarship. The party did not affect the amount! The group in "Dorm 190" was not as ill-behaved or irreligious as others perceived them to be. One of their memories was the pious sign on Sam Lo's fish bowl: It quoted St. Paul's statement, "Love never fails."

Every student took six weeks of Greek during the summer before classes began in the fall of 1965. In the second summer they took Hebrew. The study was so concentrated and the pressures so great that students became very anxious and tense. During the Hebrew class, some of the students called Don Tweedie to know if they should seek to hospitalize a theology student who was acting bizarrely in reaction to the stress. He was walking around belligerently confronting others and trying to start a fight with anybody who would challenge him. By this time, students in the first class felt they had become proficient enough in psychopathology to be able to identify a person in need! Tweedie calmed them down and told them to keep observing the other students' behavior. The whole incident subsided.

The First Graduate

The first graduate of the School of Psychology was not among those students who entered in the fall of 1965. William "Bill" Evans entered a quarter later, in the Winter Quarter of 1966. He defended his dissertation in late spring of 1969 and received his doctorate at the June graduation, a year ahead of nine first-class students. Evans called himself a "class of one." He describes his entrance into the School of Psychology as a unique combination of circumstances. Evans had trained for the ministry and had completed seminary training at the Presbyterian Seminary at San Anselmo, California. Then, he had gone to Scotland where he worked on a doctorate in New Testament for a year prior to attending the Ecumenical Institute in Switzerland for a time. Undecided about his life work, Evans went into business but soon decided to return to ministry and became the minister to youth at First Presbyterian Church in Alberquerque, New Mexico. While there he took psychology courses at the University of New Mexico and became interested in further study. During one of his trips back to Los Angeles, he met Lee Travis. His brother, Louis Evans, Jr., was the pastor at Bel Air Presbyterian Church where Travis had his life-transforming religious experience. It was only natural that Travis would have a special feeling toward Bill Evans. Travis encouraged him to apply to the School of Psychology and offered him the position of research assistant. "We'll pay your tuition, " Travis promised.[16]

In early January of 1966, Evans called Travis and accepted his offer. With all of his past study, Evans was afforded advanced standing. Travis allowed him to study on his own without attending class and "test out" on courses when he felt he was ready. He even promised Evans that he would not have to take comprehensive exams. When the other students heard of this arrangement, they protested and Travis reneged on his promise. Evans had to take the examinations. This was very troubling to Evans, who had planned on not having to take the exams and thought Travis had gone back on his word. But he acquiesced and began to prepare. During the two

Chapter 6 – Students Come – Classes Begin

months that he was preparing for the comprehensive exams, Evans was on internship at Camarillo State Hospital. He would wake up at 5:00 a.m. and prepare study cards for the day. At spare moments, he would take out his cards and go over them. He passed five of the six exams the first time he took them.

As Evans states it, "Travis needed to graduate someone and I needed a Ph.D. in Psychology. Our needs worked well together. I was a maverick, but I was not a loose cannon. I determined to do a good dissertation and make him proud of me." Evans worked with behaviorist Milt Wolpin of UCLA on a project that became his dissertation—The "Deconditioning of Snake Phobia."[17] Several of the other students helped him complete the project. Supposedly, one snake escaped and took up residence in the heating ducts of the Psychology Building on Madison Avenue. Since one of the ducts was situated near the feet of Marnie Frederickson, she reportedly remained in mortal fear that this snake would come out and bite her.

The project was completed and Bill Evans defended his dissertation in the late spring of 1969. Travis made him rewrite it six times before he approved it. By the time of the oral defense, Evans was so anxious that he accused Travis of creating stutterers rather than healing them! The defense was held in the seminary dining room. Bleachers were erected to accommodate the crowd. There was a printed program. Most members of the seminary community, as well as many guests, were present. The Dissertation Committee, which was chaired by Travis, included Donald Lindsley and Milt Wolpin from UCLA, Paul Clement and Neil Warren from the School of Psychology faculty, and Calvin Schoonhoven from Fuller's theology faculty. Questions were asked by each committee member as well as by those in the audience. Travis answered one question Evans couldn't answer, after which Evans retorted, "Why didn't I say that?"

Evans won the distinction of being the first graduate because David Donaldson had trouble with his project. He had to start over and did not finish before Evans had completed his work. After graduation, Evans worked for the County of Los Angeles, taught at California State University, Northridge, and presently is a consulting psychologist in private practice in the Los Angeles area.

The Second Class

By the fall of 1966 the student body had grown to 45; two women and 43 men. Of those in the second class, 16 eventually graduated. They were as follows

    David C. Bock, 1972; now a psychologist in Pasadena, California

    Theodore "Ted" M. Johnson, 1972; now a psychologist in Manheim, Pennsylvania

    Haddon "Don" E. Klingberg, 1971; now dean of the chapel at North Park College, Chicago, Illinois

    Joseph "Joe" R. Venema, 1971; now a psychologist in Pasadena, California

    David F. deVidal, 1970; now a psychologist in Lake Oswego, Oregon

    Kenneth P. Lott, 1970; now a psychologist in Encino, California

    J. Lewis "Lew" Mylar, 1970; now a psychologist in Colorado Springs, Colorado

    Donald D. Roberts, 1970; now a psychologist in Spokane, Washington

    Jack E. Oakwright (formerly Wright), 1970; now a psychologist in Sandpoint, Idaho

    Paul W. Kelly, 1972; now a psychologist in San Diego, California

    Gary W. Reece, 1978; now a psychologist in Glendora, California

    Scott T. More 1973; now a psychologist in Costa Mesa, California

    Thomas J. Malcolm, 1972; now a psychologist at Azuza Pacific University, Glendora, California

    Kenneth H. Loudon, 1974; now a psychologist in Aldergrove, British Columbia, Canada

    William "Bill" T. Weyerhaeuser, 1975; now a psychologist in Tacoma, Washington

    Frank Edward Nocita, 1972; deceased[18]

Travis reflected on these years in the mid-1980s. He wrote:

The school has matured. The first year 25 people applied and we took them all. The next year we were more selective in admitting about 35 students out of twice that number of applicants.[19]

Travis was correct. By the time he retired in 1975, the School of

Chapter 6 – Students Come – Classes Begin

Psychology had graduated a total of 69 Ph.D. recipients and had awarded 11 terminal master's degrees. One anomaly was entering student Leon Yao who earned "As" in all his course work but failed his internship. When offered a doctorate in experimental, rather than clinical, psychology, he declined and left the program.

No one of the three women who were members of the first two classes ever earned degrees. However, Travis had the honor at the last graduation ceremony in which he was dean to confer on Edith Munger the first doctorate awarded to a woman. Munger was a professional trained in social work who entered the school when she was in her mid-50s. At that time, she was the oldest student to have entered the program. There was some doubt that she would ever finish, and Professor Malony told her she was "too old to undertake graduate education." She proved him wrong by finishing her degree in record time. She completed a major study under the direction of Neil Warren on students who did or did not complete their seminary education.[20] Subsequently, Munger helped establish the counseling center at the First Presbyterian Church of Hollywood and was in private practice both in Pasadena and in Menlo Park, California, during the time when her husband, Robert Munger, was an associate at the Presbyterian church there. A scholarship fund in her honor, for second-career women has been established.

The Graduate School of Psychology continues to admit entering students some 30 years after that first class began their studies. Hundreds of students have come and gone. What began as a class of 19 in the fall of 1965 has become a student body of 254 women and 155 men in 1995 studying in two divisions: Marriage and Family Therapy and Clinical Psychology.

ENDNOTES

1. News Bureau, Fuller Theological Seminary, "Fuller Announces New Psychology Dean and Foundation Grant," December 2, 1964.
2. Memo from David Allan Hubbard re: The New School of Psychology of Fuller Theological Seminary and its Ph.D. Program in Clinical Psychology, Spring 1965.
3. Ralph Cooper Hutchinson, "Theo-Psychology at Fuller Theological Seminary: A Report to the Ten-Year Planning Committee (April, 1963).
4. Fuller Seminary Foundation—School of Psychology, December 1962: p. 2.
5. David Allan Hubbard to Lee Edward Travis, December 8, 1964.
6. Lee Edward Travis to John G. Finch, December 17, 1964.

7. Donald F. Tweedie to David Allan Hubbard, December 9, 1964.
8. Memo from David Allan Hubbard, Spring 1965.
9. Donald F. Tweedie, *Logotherapy: An Evaluation of Frankl's Existential Approach to Psychotherapy from a Christian Viewpoint.* (Grand Rapids, MI: Baker Book House, 1961).
10. Paul Tournier was a Swiss psychiatrist who became internationally known for his book *The Meaning of Persons* (London: SCM, 1957) and other writings. "In 1947 Tournier joined with Alphonse Maeder . . . and Jean de Rougement, both members of the Oxford Group, to organize annual International Conferences on the Medicine of the Person. . . . Twenty-one books authored by Tournier have been translated into English." Hendrika Vande Kemp "Historical Perspective: Religion and Clinical Psychology in America," in E. Shafranske (Ed.) *Religion and the Clinical Practice of Psychology* (Washington DC: American Psychological Association, in press).
11. O. Hobart Mowrer was professor of psychology at the University of Illinois who had become well-known for his controversial thesis in *The Crisis in Psychiatry and Religion* (Princeton, NJ: Princeton University Press, 1961. The late Perry London was professor of psychology at the University of Southern California who became well-known for his contention that psychotherapists were secular priests in the volume *The Modes and Morals of Psychotherapy* (New York: Holt, Rinehart, Winston, 1964).
12. "Intensive therapy" was John Finch's unique psychotherapeutic adaptation of Arthur Janov's *The Primal Scream* (New York, Dell, 1970). In this experience, clients journeyed to Tacoma for a three-week period of daily therapeutic sessions with a break on weekends. During this time, they were boarded in one of several homes/cabins owned by Finch. They were instructed to have little or no contact with the outside world and to spend the time introspecting and keeping a journal of their experience. Each day they spent one hour with Finch who led them in an exploration of their relationships with parents and other life-figures on whom they might have become dependent. The goal of the therapy was to lead them from dependency to independence and, finally, to interdependency. Integral to the experience was a reconnecting of the person to God—the spirit of the person with the Spirit of God. Finch encouraged clients to read the Gospels of Mark and John and realign themselves to Christ. He contended that the root problems of life were grounded in persons trying to build their lives on other foundations than was possible when persons rediscovered their true selves as meant for relationship with God. Finch used a quote from the Baghvad Gita, the Hindu scriptures, which stated, "Do your duty to God without thought for the fruit of the action." Called "Nishkamakarma," this quote became the theme of the goals of therapy. It presumed that emotional disturbance resulted when persons did not do their duty to God by grounding their life in relationship to Christ.
13. H. Newton Malony, *A Christian Existential Psychology: The Contributions of John G. Finch.* (Pasadena, CA: Integration Press, 1980).
14. Recounted by Clifford L. Penner in interview with H. Newton Malony, Fall 1994.

Chapter 6 – Students Come – Classes Begin

15. Recounted by John Fry in interview with H. Newton Malony, July 1994.
16. Recounted by William O. Evans in interview with H. Newton Malony, September 1994.
17. The title of William Evans dissertation was "The Effectiveness of Visual Imagery on Phobic Behavior when Accompanied by Electric Shock." Evans' dissertation made no attempt to integrate theology and psychology. It reflected the effort during this time to produce dissertations that would evoke the respect of the nonreligious psychological community as well as the approval of the American Psychological Association. As will be seen in the chapter on APA accreditation, this approach was not recommended by Irving Alexander, one of the consultants to the school. He suggested that if the school produced dissertations similar to those that could be written at schools like USC or UCLA, it could not claim any distinctiveness and, therefore, might forfeit its reason for being. This has continued to be an issue for debate at the school.
18. Prior to his death Frank Nocita had a successful private practice in Toluca Lake, California. He was devoted to the School of Psychology and made significant financial contributions on a regular basis. He committed suicide after a lingering depressive illness in late 1980. A memorial fund for helping persons handle stress in professional practice has been established in his honor.
19. Lee Edward Travis, *Ensnared in Love*.
20. The title of Edith Munger's dissertation was "Personality, Motivation and Experience—Their Effect on Persistence in a Theological Seminary."

The "Four Horsemen," clockwise from top left: Paul Fairweather, John G. Finch, C. Davis Weyerhauser, David Allan Hubbard

Members of the first faculty (from top, left to right): Paul Barkman, Robert Bower, Paul Clement, Donald Cole, Paul Fairweather, H. Newton Malony, James Oakland, Adrin Sylling, Lee Edward Travis, Donald Tweedie, Neil Warren

Deans shown clockwise from top left: Lee Edward Travis (1965-1975), Neil S. Warren (1975-1982), Archibald D. Hart (1983-1995), James D. Guy (1995-present).

Administrative assistants (from left): Marnie Frederickson (1965-1978), Dorie Lott (1978-1982), Bert Jacklitch (1982-present).

First class

Second class

Above: Paul Clement in Child Development Center

Left: 177 No. Madison building—headquarters of School of Psychology before 180 No. Oakland building

Top: Lee Edward Travis with student Steve Meyer in Psychophysiological Lab (garage of 172 No. Madison)
Below: Donald Tweedie lecturing in seminar room at 177 No. Madison. Student at left is James Oraker.

Lee Edward Travis in his office at 177 No. Madison

Chapter Seven

Travis Builds a Faculty

When Travis became dean, Tweedie, Barkman, Fairweather, Cole, and Bower composed the faculty. He inherited them. They were all there when he came. They were the "founding" faculty. Except for Don Tweedie and Robert Bower, they would all be gone by the early 1970s. In the interval, Travis brought together a faculty of his own choosing. When he retired as dean in 1974, the faculty included a group of psychologists who were to determine the direction of the School of Psychology for the following 15 years and beyond. This group included Paul W. Clement, Neil C. Warren, H. Newton Malony, James A. Oakland, and Archibald D. Hart.[1]

During the first year of classes, it became clear that curtailing his involvement in private practice was going to be difficult for Paul Fairweather. Although he was very invested in the starting of the School of Psychology, his role had become less central as the Counseling Center opened and classes began. Along with Carroll Wright and others, he provided services to the public through a counseling center in Glendale. Eventually, Fairweather decided that he could not reduce this involvement nor could he bring his practice into the Counseling Center, as all faculty were encouraged to do on the one day a week they were given for private clinical work. The plan was for faculty to use their counseling for modeling and student training. Fairweather's decision to leave the faculty, however, was primarily due to the negative reaction of the theology faculty to his "image therapy." In his teaching, Fairweather had urged students to confront their parents and work through their dependence on them. Fairweather contended that parents, particularly the father, were the prime determinants of one's mental "images." This included one's concepts of God.

Fairweather taught one of the early integration seminars with George Ladd, one of Fuller's well-known New Testament professors. He used his "image" theory as a basis for discussion. One of Fairweather's hopes had been that there would be integrative discussions among the faculties when the School of Psychology was opened. He saw his theory, about the importance of fathers in determining personality and faith, as the first in what would become regular dialogues about clinical issues from a Christian point of view.[2] Unfortunately, he had not anticipated Ladd's strong negative reaction to his ideas. Ladd complained to Hubbard about what he perceived to be highly questionable, even heretical, aspects of Fairweather's thinking. The issue became so controversial that Hubbard asked ethics professor James Morgan to try to settle it. A full faculty meeting was called to discuss the matter. Fairweather's sense that he was going to be severely criticized caused him to decide not to attend the meeting. He sent his colleague Carroll Wright to represent his point of view. He was deeply hurt and discouraged and he resigned soon thereafter.[3]

The second faculty member to leave was Donald Cole, a charismatic Baptist pastor who had taught with Fairweather at the Baptist Seminary in Covina. He had received a doctorate in psychology from the University of London and he transferred from the theology to the psychology faculty when the school was opened. Cole was an immensely entertaining lecturer who was in great demand, and he was deeply appreciated when he was on campus. But often he would be away delivering an invited address at a college campus or on a military base. Apocryphal stories depict Cole as calling the school 30 minutes before class time asking Marnie to tell the students he could not be there because he was speaking to U.S. troops in Korea. Like Fairweather, Cole found it very difficult to reduce his commitments away from the School of Psychology.

By the spring of 1969, both Fairweather and Cole were gone. The next to leave was Paul Barkman. He had served the school well in procuring the foundational volumes on psychology for the library and in deciding which journals were necessary for a a graduate program in psychology. He also taught courses in personality theory and determined the criteria for postdoctoral fellowships. However, it became apparent to Barkman that the heavy involvement in research necessary to mentor doctoral students was not as satisfying to him as clinical work. He resigned from the faculty in June 1970 and established his private practice in the high desert community of Twentynine Palms, California. Several postdoctoral students have been part of his practice. Most recently, Barkman has founded a high-tech, sophisticated service called Counselaid which provides personality, career, and organizational evaluations and consultations.[4]

Tweedie remained with the school until 1976 when he left to go into full-time private practice. He had a large family and making ends meet was a constant concern for Tweedie. He did much counseling outside the school. At one point in the late 1960s, he had satellite counseling centers in three places and considered leaving his teaching. At this time, no private fee-for-service was allowed in the offices at the School of Psychology. Sometime before he left, an agreement was reached with the seminary for allowing the use of faculty offices one day a week. This agreement still holds today. However, because of Tweedie's needs, he was allowed two days of private practice. He taught his classes but attended no committee meeting. Nevertheless, even these arrangements became difficult for Tweedie because of family demands.

Robert Bower's involvement in the school was never more than part-time. His primary duties were as professor of religious education in the School of Theology. He counseled part-time in the Pasadena Community Counseling Center and attended some faculty meetings. During the 1970s he developed a pastoral counseling program in which some of the psychology professors taught on occasion. Bower's main accomplishment, however, was the establishment of a master's program in marriage and family ministries (MFM) in the School of Theology. By 1973 a feeling of competition had developed between Bower's program and the School of Psychology. He began to teach courses in psychological testing and in counseling methods which the faculty of the School of Psychology felt were their province. They saw Bower as encroaching on their territory and as allowing students to use tools and methods for which they were undertrained. Although Bower died in 1978, this tension continued to exist for the next decade, well into the 1980s. The marriage and family program was very successful financially and the School of Theology was very reluctant to give it up, although the psychology faculty continued to protest. In 1989 the MFM program was transferred to the School of Psychology where it remains a strong program to the present time. Questions about the overlap between the Clinical Psychology and Marriage and Family programs are still being debated.

Among his other talents, Travis had an unusual ability to be firm and gracious at the same time. He was supportive of the departures of both Fairweather and Cole. He perceived them to be pastoral

Chapter 7 – Travis Builds A Faculty

counselors rather than psychologists, more public figures than graduate school professors. They left with good feelings toward Travis and the seminary. Their leaving gave Travis his first opportunity to select a faculty of his own choosing. The dilemma, as Travis saw it, was this:

> I inherited Don Tweedie and his PCCC staff as faculty members. These people were a great starting team. There was one critical problem; only Don and I had earned the Ph.D. degree from an institution approved by the American Psychological Association as qualified to give training at the doctoral level in clinical psychology. For the school to be approved by APA, we would need to have more faculty members graduating from approved programs.[5]

In the first move to build a faculty with proper credentials, Paul W. Clement and Neil C. Warren were selected by Travis to join the faculty of the School of Psychology in the fall of 1967. Travis called them "my boys." He saw them as the down payment on a dynamic graduate faculty he hoped to establish at the School of Psychology. Clement came from the Harbor/UCLA Medical Center where he was a staff psychologist and Warren came from the University of Chicago where he had just completed his doctoral training.

Paul Wayne Clement

Neither Warren nor Clement were new to Southern California. Both had attended Pepperdine University as undergraduates and Clement had received his master's degree there. Furthermore, both knew about Fuller's new School of Psychology. Clement had toured the Fuller campus with friends in the fall of 1965 as the school's first students were arriving. In fact, Clement had even thought he might like to teach there, but had not seriously considered applying because he thought that all of the school's professors were required to have had seminary training.

The source of Clement's misinformation was Robert Bower, who was the teacher of a Sunday school class at Sunnyside Baptist Church which Clement was attending while a student at Pepperdine University in the early 1960s. Bower told Clement about Fuller Seminary's plans to establish a school of psychology, stating that he thought all the school's professors would have to have seminary training in addition to their psychological training.

Interestingly enough, in the early 1960s, Clement was planning to attend seminary, learn Japanese, and become a missionary psychologist. Bower had encouraged Clement to keep in touch as his education progressed. The only circumstance that caused him not to enter seminary after completing his doctoral training at the University of Utah was the birth of a child. He felt he needed to find a job to support his young family rather than go on to seminary as he had planned. Thus, Clement accepted a position as the first full-time staff psychologist assigned to Harbor Hospital by the UCLA School of Medicine. While in this position, he was contacted by Travis and invited to become a faculty member of the School of Psychology at Fuller. In January of 1967, when Clement was in his second year at UCLA, Travis sent a letter inviting the hospital to send a representative to a meeting to discuss clinical training for students at the School of Psychology.[6] Clement was the only psychologist who had ever heard of Fuller, so he agreed to go to the meeting.

Due to the scheduling problems of the other psychologists, after the meeting Clement and Travis went to lunch by themselves. At lunch, Clement expressed regret that the hospital was not ready to accept trainees, but he shared thoughts about the training of psychologists in general. That evening, he told his wife about the meeting with Travis. He said that he was surprised to see such a distinguished psychologist at Fuller and told her "I think I like him."[7] It turned out that Travis had a similar feeling; he liked Clement enough to consider employing him.

Several weeks passed. Clement put the meeting with Travis out of his mind. One morning soon thereafter, the secretary at the hospital notified Clement that Travis was on the line. When Clement answered the phone, Travis stated, "I'm not going to beat around the bush. I want to offer you a job." Clement was surprised. He still thought that a Fuller appointment required theological training. Yet, he agreed to talk. Subsequently, he learned that he did not need to have studied at a seminary but agreed to take the theological examination required of all new seminary faculty. At his theological examination, Clement expressed a position about the integration of psychology and theology for which he would subsequently become well-known. Called "orthogonal integration," Clement's belief was that being a Christian believer and being mentally healthy were unrelated. Like independent dimensions, such as height and color preference, mental health and spiritual maturity are unconnected, or "orthogonal," to each other. He stated that he had changed his earlier belief that, even if one was not successful or rich, one would be mentally healthy if one was a Christian.

Clement's position pleased several of the theological faculty. Both George Ladd and Edward Carnell had been struggling with emotional disturbance. They were puzzled as to why their Christian faith had not helped them overcome their depressions. They were comforted by Clement's remarks. Further, Geoffrey Bromiley, Fuller's eminent historical theologian, had long contended that the social/behavioral sciences could not be integrated with Christian theology. Like Karl Barth, Bromiley was convinced that these human sciences could tell us little about the essential nature of the human being. When Clement left the room after his examination, Bromiley exclaimed, "I could teach with that man."[8]

Clement accepted Fuller's offer and became an assistant professor and director of clinical training at the School of Psychology in the fall of 1967. When he told his colleagues at UCLA about his decision to leave, they thought he was crazy. Clement replied, "I'm betting my professional life on my decision."[9] Clement taught child clinical psychology at the school for many years. He led the school through its first and second American Psychological Association accreditation site visits. Somewhat later, Clement established the Psychological Center at the school. This was the first free-standing training center for clinical psychologists in the nation. Travis' reflection on Clement was this: "In a deep sense, Paul just came; no dickering, no bickering, no agonizing, no study of his aptitude for Christian psychology. He came because he had to come, just because he could not possibly do anything else."[10] Clement would agree.

Clement eventually had the opportunity to teach an integration seminar with Bromiley. What Clement had to say infuriated and appalled Bromiley. From Clement's point of view, Bromiley was talking a language that was unknown and foreign to him. When Clement commented on the problem with the seminar in a joint faculty meeting, Bromiley decided not to say what he thought. The problem was swept under the rug, so to speak. From Bromiley's perspective, this experience confirmed his opinion that only those psychologists with advanced theological training should become involved in such dialogues.[11]

Neil Clark Warren

Neil C. Warren also joined the School of Psychology faculty in the fall of 1967. After undergraduate education at Pepperdine, Warren completed Master of Divinity studies at Princeton Theological Seminary. Although reared as a member of the Church of Christ, Warren had become a Presbyterian by the time of his graduation from seminary. In the spring of 1967, he finished work on his doctorate in clinical psychology at the University of Chicago. His was the ideal combination of training for the School of Psychology.

Warren wrote 32 letters to persons and programs around the country hoping to find a position that would combine his theological and psychological training. Several people wrote to him about Fuller Seminary's new School of Psychology. They suggested he might want to investigate it. In turn, a relative of Warren's casually mentioned his name to someone at the school, thinking that the administration might be interested in a person with his training. Warren wrote to Travis about the program and Travis responded. When he learned the program was not yet accredited by the American Psychological Association, Warren's interest waned. Travis, however, perceived that Warren had the type of preparation that would make him an ideal professor at Fuller, so he pursued Warren and invited him to come to the seminary for a visit.

Another obstacle to his interest arose when Warren saw Fuller's Statement of Faith, which all faculty members were supposed to sign. Once again, he questioned whether the School of Psychology would be the place for him. Warren felt that the statement contained sections that were too conservative for him. He told Travis about his misgivings and Travis replied, "Well, we'll work it out so that you won't have to sign!" On second thought, Travis changed this promise by stating, "Well, tell us the sections you will sign and we'll let it go at that."[12] By this time, Travis was very eager to see Warren join the faculty. He may have promised more than he could deliver. Warren agreed to a visit to the school. He came, not so much on the basis of Travis' promises about the Statement of Faith, but because of what his friend Larry Parker promised. Parker was a professor of psychology at the University of Redlands who had studied under Lee Travis at the University of Southern California.[13] He encouraged Neil Warren to come for a visit to Fuller because, "once you meet Lee Travis, you will know in an instant that you could work with him."

Parker's assertion proved to be true. There was no doubt in Warren's mind after encountering Travis that Fuller was the place he wanted to be. As Travis wrote, "He and I joined in the service of the Lord; he young and vital, later to become my successor as the dean of the school."[14] Warren passed his theological examination with little difficulty and assumed the position of assistant professor and director of research in the School of Psychology in the fall of 1967. He taught statistics and research design for a number of years. Because of his background in client-centered therapeutic processes, he also taught courses in basic counseling skills. Following Travis, Neil C. Warren became the school's second dean in the winter of 1975.

Henry Newton Malony

The third "Travis boy" joined the faculty of the School of Psychology two years later, in the fall of 1969. When H. Newton Malony received a colorful brochure describing the School of Psychology, he was professor of psychology at Tennessee Wesleyan College in Athens, Tennessee. The brochure intrigued him because it described a form of training which paralleled his own preparation. Like many of the early students in the School of Psychology, Malony had returned for doctoral training in clinical psychology after completing a seminary education. Malony had earned his theology degree at Yale and had served as a United Methodist pastor for several years.

Malony had long hoped that he would some day have the opportunity to combine his theological and psychological training. Although he was a full professor at Tennessee Wesleyan and he was enjoying undergraduate teaching, the brochure inviting students to apply to Fuller's School of Psychology caught Malony's fancy. He wrote to Travis, "Thank you for sending me the description of your program at Fuller. I will encourage our students to apply. Should you ever have any need for more faculty, I might be interested." Travis received Malony's letter in late January 1969. Due to the press of other issues, Travis did not respond to Malony's letter until mid-March. By that time, Malony was interviewing for positions at Duke and Boston Universities. He only considered Fuller's interest seriously after neither of these positions were offered to him. As he later stated:

> *I agreed to come for an interview at Fuller because I had never been further west than Denver. I misperceived Fuller as a fundamentalist bastion and did not think I would be happy there. However, I was not around Lee Travis for more than 15 minutes before I knew I would be happy there. He was truly an empowering, supportive man.*[15]

Malony's theological examination took place in late spring. The pattern at that time was for the entire theology faculty to be present and for Daniel Fuller, the dean of the School of Theology, to start the examination with the question "How do you like our Statement of Faith?" Malony answered that he affirmed it, that it basically encompassed the tenets of the historic Christian faith. Fuller followed with his second question, "Are there parts of it that you like better than others?" In reflecting on the experience later, Malony said,

> *I didn't know what to say. I perceived this as a no-win situation; if I failed to express support for any part of the statement, I might be disqualified. On the other hand, there were parts of it about which I had some misgivings; I would lack personal integrity if I said I agreed with these parts when I didn't.*

After a minute of thought, Malony stated to the faculty:

> *Before I answer, I want to say that you are interviewing me for a position in psychology, not theology. I am not a theologian; I am a psychologist. However, I am a religious person. What I believe is important to me. I am not about to tell you I believe something when I don't—just to get a job here. So, here goes: I hope that last statement about the last judgment isn't true. I hope that God will eventually win in the life of every person; I hope there is no eternal hell. But I know that the Bible contradicts my opinion and implies otherwise. Nevertheless, I hope it is not so.*

Malony passed the examination and joined the faculty in the fall of 1969. He did not know that his opinion that God would finally win over the heart of every person was shared by Karl Barth. Malony, like Barth, was known as a "closet Universalist" from that day on. His colleague, Neil Warren, said the theological examination was masterful; the best he had ever heard. However, it must be acknowledged that the school was still young and only a very few theological examinations had occurred! Malony taught courses in organizational consultation and directed the Church Consultation Service for a number of years. He later became the director of programs in the integration of psychology and theology. One of his early books portrayed him and his colleagues as "psychologist Christians," rather than "Christian psychologists."[16]

James A. Oakland

James A. Oakland joined the School of Psychology faculty in 1970. He came to Fuller from the University of Washington Medical School in Seattle where he was a psychologist who dealt with problems experienced by children with spinal bifida. One of his research publications concerning the application of behavior modification by parents in dealing with these children came to the attention of Paul Clement, who gave the article to Travis. Travis contacted Oakland and inquired about his interest in coming to Fuller. Travis stated, "By now I was thinking in terms of the popular phrase, 'the four horsemen,' in acquiring the next new member of the faculty."[17] Oakland turned out to be that fourth horseman.

Travis' inquiry spurred Oakland to reflect on his life goals. His self-examination reached a crisis shortly thereafter when Oakland was attending a meeting of the American Psychological Association. He couldn't sleep and decided to get up to write in his journal. He became aware that, although he was a confirmed Northwesterner, having grown up in Montana, he was not all that much interested in medical school education or in pediatric psychology. He decided to investigate the Fuller School of Psychology more closely.[18] The fact that the School of Psychology was located in a seminary was a positive factor for Oakland; its location in the Los Angeles area was not. He had grown up in the Assemblies of God denomination and was a serious Christian. He had been interested in relating his psychology to his faith and had been active in the American Scientific Affiliation.[19] In fact, he was a consulting editor to the association's journal. However, the religious affiliation of the school was secondary to the fact that it was a training program in professional psychology rather than in medicine. Oakland decided he wanted to be part of that kind of education and agreed to come to Fuller. Travis wrote about Oakland's decision:

> To me, from the first view of him coming off the plane, I thought of an apostle, possibly John. Surely here was a modern one. This feeling persisted as we related to each other for some hours during his visit. He

went back home to think over joining us. I knew he was right and prayed that he would leave his lucrative and challenging work in Seattle to labor at Fuller. A few weak fears arose in me that he would not come. I prepared myself for failure. The phone rang. He was at the other end. My heart was beating rapidly and hard. I was prepared to give a final pitch. Then he said, "We have thought over your offer very carefully and we're coming." I wanted to ask him to repeat that but finally answered, "Thanks, thank you so very much." With the gift of uncanny sensitivity to the feelings of others, Jim serves us all as the therapist to the therapists.[20]

Jim Oakland and his family moved to Pasadena in 1970. As he said, "I knew very little about theology and passed the theological examination as a serious, but unsophisticated, believer." Later, he became more interested in theology, took courses at the seminary, and taught integration seminars with Jack Rogers and Glenn Barker. Oakland only taught full-time at the school for five years. During this time he specialized in personality theory and adult psychotherapy focusing his research on clinical interaction. He was committed to investigating the dynamics of therapeutic interventions. He entered psychoanalytic training and taught courses in this field for several years, even after he reduced his teaching to part-time. In 1980 Oakland resigned from teaching at the school entirely. In 1985 Oakland returned to Seattle and entered private practice there. However, during his tenure at the school, he influenced a number of students to become serious psychotherapists. Several of them followed Oakland into psychoanalytic training.[21]

Archibald Daniel Hart

A new Ph.D. in Psychology from South Africa came to the school as a postdoctoral fellow in 1971. This was Archibald D. Hart, who later joined the Fuller faculty and who was to become the third dean of the school in 1982. How Hart first heard about the school is integrally related to the beginnings of African Enterprise in Pietermaritzburg, his home town. In 1962 a group of Fuller Seminary students conducted an evangelistic mission in Peitermaritzburg at the invitation of a local pastor, Calvin Cook. Hart, a resident of this city, helped plan this mission and assisted in setting up a board of persons which was to form the basis of African Enterprise.[22] When this group

Chapter 7 – Travis Builds A Faculty

returned to Fuller, one of them wrote Hart about the new School of Psychology which was being established. Richard Peace, who was later to join the theology faculty, thought that Hart, who was taking courses in psychology at the University of Natal, might be interested in these developments. At the time, Hart, who was a civil engineer by training, was the assistant city engineer of Pietermaritzburg. Hart's boss wanted to prepare him to eventually become the chief engineer. He thought that Hart's training would help him in human relations, making him become a better leader and a more effective engineer. So he had sent Hart for some psychological training at the university.

Hart didn't think much more about Fuller until two years later when he met a missionary couple who had attended a conference at the Narramore Foundation in Southern California where two psychologists from Fuller had spoken. Donald Cole and Don Tweedie were introduced as professors in Fuller's new School of Psychology. Arch Hart listened to their presentations on the tapes the missionaries gave to him. These tapes were Arch Hart's first introduction to the field of Christian psychology. He had not realized before that there were psychologists who were seriously trying to integrate their faith and their practice. By this time Hart had finished his master's degree in psychology and was offering consultations in the evening from an office in his home, counseling primarily with ministers and other religious persons. He began to wonder whether he should come to Fuller to finish his doctoral studies. This was 1965 and the school's first students were arriving. He wrote to Don Tweedie about this idea. Tweedie advised him to remain at the University of Natal and to come to Fuller later as a postdoctoral fellow after he had completed his degree at his own institution.

Hart followed this advice, writing to Tweedie shortly after receiving his doctorate. He wrote that he wanted to come to Fuller for further study. He had begun to reconsider his engineering career and was wondering whether he should become a psychologist full-time. He had been offered a psychologist position with the Research Institute in South Africa and was perceived as a valuable asset for the type of physiological research they were doing. Travis, rather than Tweedie, answered Hart's inquiry and invited him to come to Fuller as a postdoctoral fellow. Hart was surprised to receive a letter from Travis, whose name he knew well. In his work he had begun to read the literature on brain waves and psychopathology in which Travis' name appeared repeatedly. Hart thought that the "Travis" who was at Fuller was probably the son of the scholar about whom he had read. To his surprise, when he arrived he realized that Travis was the notable researcher himself. Travis and Hart immediately struck up a close friendship and working relationship. The early psychophysiological and EEG laboratory was set up during Hart's postdoctoral tenure.

Hart stayed nine months at Fuller. Shortly before he was to return to South Africa, Paul Clement took Hart to lunch and asked him if he would be interested in joining the faculty. Hart was very pleased to be asked and was interested. Like Clement, Warren, Malony, and Oakland, Hart had a sense that being at Fuller was where God wanted him to be. He returned to South Africa, but in 1973 Arch Hart, with his wife and three daughters, returned to Fuller to join the faculty of the school.

His return was due, in no small measure, to the efforts of Richard "Mac" McCrady, the first postdoctoral fellow at the School of Psychology. "Mac," whose Ph.D. was in physiological psychology, came for retraining in 1970. He wanted to become a clinician. Mac and his wife Jean befriended the Harts and greatly admired the wealth of Arch's talents. When the Harts returned to South Africa, Mac encouraged Travis to get them back if at all possible. Travis respected Mac's advice and soon began the process of seeing if Arch was interested. The rest of the faculty fully agreed with this endeavor.

When Hart returned to Fuller, the seminary was experiencing difficult days financially. Hart was only paid $7000 the first year. Because Hart was not a citizen, it took three to four years for the Harts to obtain permanent legal status. Before the faculty position could be officially offered to him, the job had to be widely advertised in order to guarantee that no American citizen was being deprived of a job. Eventually, such well-known persons as President Ronald Reagan and Billy Graham were asked to intervene in the process. Finally, Hart and his family became citizens, and he has remained with the school ever since.

Hart never had a formal theological examination. At one point, Provost Barker said to him, "Arch, we've never had a theological exam for you, have we?" When Hart replied, "No," Barker called Paul Jewett over and they asked Hart a few questions. This was Arch Hart's theological examination! When the second dean, Neil C. Warren, went

CHAPTER 7 – TRAVIS BUILDS A FACULTY

on sabbatical in 1981, Arch Hart became acting dean. When Dean Warren resigned, Hart became the school's third dean in 1982. Travis wrote of Hart:

> *His coming was really irrational. The circumstances surrounding it defy any kind of rational analysis. Trained in engineering as well as psychology, he can sense the spirit in the machine. He can shift from building a computer to healing a soul in anguish. Above all, his daily modeling of a Christian psychologist inspires the entire seminary. Surely the Lord sent him to us.*[23]

These five persons became the faculty Travis recruited. Along with Donald Tweedie and Adrin Sylling, they made up the team during the Travis years. They have been joined by many other notable colleagues since this time.[24] But in every case, their joining the faculty occurred after Travis was no longer dean. It is not that these five were the best, or the last; they were simply the first.

During these early years of the school, the faculty functioned under a set of procedures recommended by President Hubbard in the summer of 1964, a few months before the opening of the Pasadena Community Counseling Center. They read as follows:

> *It is understood that the faculty members' work load will consist of staff meetings, chapel services, therapeutic counseling, and teaching responsibilities. In addition it is assumed that a faculty member will take all necessary steps to keep abreast academically and professionally in his chosen specialty. A commitment to professional competence requires that each faculty member proceed as rapidly as is practical toward state certification and diplomate status within ABPP. For this commitment, a professor will receive the amount of salary normally paid to a man of his rank within the seminary, plus $5,000 increment as partial compensation for what he would receive in outside practice, and for the rigid time commitment which membership in this faculty involves.*[25]

These procedures were in place when the school began. Due to the efforts of Don Tweedie, the $5,000 increment in lieu of private practice was changed. However, concern among the School of Theology faculty about psychology faculty's income has remained a source of tension. As time went on, only Travis, Clement, and Malony achieved the Diplomate Clinical Psychology status with the American Board of Professional Psychology (ABPP), although all these professors became licensed by the state of California.[26]

ENDNOTES

1. These were the five professors employed by Lee Edward Travis during his tenure as founding dean of the School of Psychology. He wrote about the circumstances surrounding each of their appointments in *Ensnared in Love* (Pasadena, CA: Integration Press, 1986), pp. 53-55.
2. Paul Fairweather, in interview with H. Newton Malony, fall 1993.
3. Ibid.
4. The address for Counselaid and Paul F. Barkman is 6476 Adobe Road, Twenty-nine Palms, California 92277, phone 619-367-6198.
5. Travis, *Ensnared in Love*, op. cit., p.50.
6. Paul W. Clement in interview with H. Newton Malony, fall 1994.
7. Ibid.
8. David A. Hubbard in interview with H. Newton Malony, fall 1993.
9. Clement, op. cit.
10. Travis, op. cit., p. 53.
11. Geoffrey Bromiley in interview with H. Newton Malony, winter 1994.
12. Neil C. Warren in interview with H. Newton Malony, spring 1993.
13. William R. Parker became well-known for his seminal research on prayer reported in a book with E. St. Johns, *Prayer Can Change Your Life: Experiments and Techniques of Prayer* (Carmel, NY: Guideposts Associates, 1957).
14. Travis, op.cit., p. 54.
15. The several quotations are from my own memories of what I said on these occasions.
16. H. Newton Malony, *The Psychologist Christian: The Religious Experience of Eighteen Psychologists* (Lanham, MD: University Press of America, 1976).
17. Travis, op. cit., p. 54.
18. James A. Oakland in interview with H. Newton Malony, fall 1994.
19. The American Scientific Affiliation is an association of Christian scientists, both social/behavioral and physical. Its publication *The Journal of the American Scientific Affiliation* (JASA) has now become *Perspectives on Science and Religion*.
20. Travis, op. cit., p. 55.
21. Donald Bosch and Anne Glasser were two of these students who were influenced by James Oakland. Both went into psychoanalytic training.
22. Archibald D. Hart, in interview with H. Newton Malony, fall 1994.
23. Travis, op. cit., p. 55.
24. Faculty of the School of Psychology up to February of 1995 are as follows in alphabetical order. It should be noted that as of 1989, the Marriage and Family Program, originally in the School of Theology, became the Marriage and Family Division of the School of Psychology. In the list that follows, the designation "MF" will refer to faculty in that division while the designation "PS" will refer to faculty in the Clinical Psychology Division.

Chapter 7 – Travis Builds A Faculty

Wayne T. Aoki 8/95—present PS
Jack O. Balswick 9/82—present MF
Judy K. Balswick 9/82—present MF
Paul F. Barkman 7/64—6/71 PS
Colleen Zabriskie Benson 9/80—12/83 PS
Jeffrey P. Bjorck 11/90—present PS
Robert K. Bower 9/58—2/78 PS (by death) Pastoral Theology
Warren S. Brown, Jr. 12/81—present PS
Paul Cameron 8/76—8/79 PS
Paul C. Clement 9/67—9/88 PS
Donald Cole 9/61—6/69 PS (originally Theology)
John H. Court 3/89—12/94 PS
Nellie Delmar-McClure 9/83—6/84 PS
Paul D. Fairweather 9/60—6/66 PS (originally Pastoral Care and Counseling)
John Fantuzzo 9/80—6/83 PS
David W. Foy 4/87—8/92 PS
James L. Furrow 9/95—present MF
James D. Guy 7/95—present PS and MF
Winston E. Gooden 9/84—present PS
Richard L. Gorsuch 9/79—present PS
Dennis B. Guernsey 8/78—8/92 PS
Archibald D. Hart 7/73—present PS
Phyllis P. Hart 9/76—8/82 PS
Richard A. Hunt 10/85—present PS and MF
Vivian S. Lamphear 11/86—9/88 PS
Cameron Lee 12/81—present MF
Lee Lipsker 8/86—6/95 PS
Susan L. Lichtman—11/90—1/93 PS
Lawrence V. Majovski 7/79—8/80 PS
H. Newton Malony 9/69—present PS
Linda Mans-Wagener 9/82—7/85; 9/95—present PS
Leonardo M. Marmol 7/93—present PS
Clinton McLemore 9/75—6/86 PS
Thomas L. Needham 9/89—present MF
James A. Oakland 8/70—12/78 PS
Sheryl S. Osato 12/88—4/90 PS
Philip S. Pannell 9/92—present
George Rekers 9/75—6/77 PS
Charles R. Ridley 7/83—9/90 PS
Glovioell W. Rowland 9/80—8/83 PS

103

Lewis B. Smedes 7/90—9/94 PS, MF
Alvin J. Straatmeyer 9/80—8/86 PS
David A. Stoop 9/95—present PS and MF
Janice M. Strength 4/92—present MF
Adrin C. Sylling 10/66—8/80 PS
Siang Yang Tan 9/85—present PS
Jorge J. Taylor 9/93—present MF
Lee E. Travis 12/64—10/87 PS
Nancy S. Thurston 9/90—present PS
Donald F. Tweedie 7/64—8/76 PS
Hendrika Vande Kemp 9/76—present PS
Charles Wallace 9/71—6/92 PS
William F. Wallace 8/76—8/83 PS
Myrna Walters 9/86—3/88 PS
Neil C. Warren 9/67—6/82 PS
Janet A. Yang 1/93—present PS
Visiting Professor: John G. Finch 9/64—6/91

25. David Allan Hubbard, "Proposed Operating Procedure for the Fuller Theological Seminary School of Psychology," June 1, 1964, mimeo.
26. Subsequent faculty, Alvin J. Straatmeyer, Richard A. Hunt, and Lawrence V. Majovski also received the Diplomate in Clinical Psychology by the American Board of Professional Psychology.

CHAPTER 8

Attaining APA Accreditation

Attaining credibility with the American Psychological Association was a goal of the School of Psychology from the time of the initial planning. In November 1961, only months after the idea of a school was proposed, Paul Fairweather had written the APA for information about the criteria for approved graduate training in psychology. Soon after the first students arrived in the fall of 1965, Lee Travis wrote Arthur Brayfield, the executive director of the APA, for an update on these standards.[1] His letter stated that "one of our chief concerns is to obtain the blessings of the APA."[2] Within a week, Sherman Ross, the executive secretary of APA's Education and Training Board, answered Travis' letter and sent him information on the accreditation process. Over the next several years, efforts were made to meet these standards. On at least three occasions, outside consultants visited Fuller and advised the faculty on the progress that was being made. These consultations eventuated in the school making its first application for accreditation in late 1973.

Consultation with Eliot Rodnick

The first consultant to the school on APA accreditation was Eliot H. Rodnick, professor of psychology at UCLA. He spent a half-day with the faculty in May 1967. His major concern was the size of the faculty, which he felt was far too small to be acceptable. The second consultant visit was made in May 1968, after Travis had added Paul Clement and Neil Warren to the faculty. As early as the late fall of 1966, Travis had conferred with the APA as to who might be the best consultant to advise the school on what should be done to prepare for APA accreditation. The APA recommended Irving Alexander, a visiting professor in the Department of Social Relations at Harvard, who was, at that time, the chair of APA's Accreditation Committee.

Consultation with Irving Alexander

When Alexander accepted Fuller's invitation, he was still at Harvard, but by the time of his consultation visit in May 1968, he had become the chair of the Department of Psychology at Duke University. Alexander had been a member of the National Institute of Mental Health Training Grant Section and had visited every training program in clinical psychology that existed in the United States at that time. Although his first letter indicated he could come in March 1967, his move to Duke delayed his visit until over a year later. This gave additional time for the school to strengthen its program.

At the conclusion of a day-and-a-half of interviews, Alexander met with the School of Psychology faculty to share his impressions. Present at this May 23, 1968, meeting were Professors Barkman, Bower, Clement, Cole, Finch, Travis, Sylling, and Warren. Tweedie was out of town. Alexander's comments were negative and discouraging.[3] Alexander concluded that the curriculum at that time was only equal to a "reasonable undergraduate program in a good, small college." Overall, he did not feel that the courses were up to graduate school standards. He recommended that the faculty be doubled in size, without adding to the student body, and that only students with undergraduate majors in psychology be admitted in the future.

The most novel comment that Alexander made was his observation that there was a misplaced emphasis in the program on the problems of psychopathology. He did not believe that clinical psychology could be taught through a focus on the amelioration of emotional problems. Since the stated purpose of the school was to provide psychologists for the church, Alexander felt that normal personality theory should be the prime focus of the curriculum. It was his opinion that most church persons were not mentally ill. They were "complex," however, and psychologists could offer a great service to them in helping church persons deal with individual differences and the complexities in normal personalities. To emphasize psychopathology would be putting the cart before the horse.

At the time of consultation with Alexander, the school had only been in existence for three years, four, if the establishment of the Pasadena Community Counseling Center is included. Alexander felt that too much was being attempted too soon. He noted that the goals of the school had not been stated clearly enough and that the school was not uniformly accepted by the other seminary faculties. He sensed that the School of Psychology was a threat to certain members of theology faculty. Since the school's goals required collaboration and full support from the other faculties, he felt this distrust could be disastrous is it was not abated.

In another vein, Alexander sounded a theme which has continued to fuel debate. He expressed the opinion that the School of Psychology was too concerned with acceptance by external groups, such as the American Psychological Association. He recommended that the school turn its attention to what it truly wanted to do, and to do it well. He said that if Fuller did what it set out to do really well, APA approval would likely come with little effort. He proclaimed: "I want to disabuse you all of the notion that somehow the criterion of success is acceptance by something out there. The criterion of success will be acceptance in here."[4]

This opinion had been debated repeatedly through the years. However, such a dialogue has never delayed the school's efforts to achieve APA accreditation even though, on almost every occasion, claiming uniqueness while meeting APA standards has not been easy or convincing. By no means has the APA been as eager as Alexander predicted they would be to honor uniqueness. Moreover, meeting APA standards has been moderately constraining at times, and efforts to meet these requirements has consumed much energy. Although history has proved Alexander wrong in a general sense, his caution that Fuller, because of its nature, might deny its essential purpose in order to meet some outside institution's standards, remains a haunting possibility.

Of equal importance to APA accreditation was Alexander's bold statement that he was not sure that the faculty had decided what its prime purpose was. He said:

On the one hand I find the presentation of a model which says we really wish to train clinical psychologists who will have some relation, hopefully, with the church or church-related activity. That's one kind of thing. I also detect the feeling from some remarks I've heard that we're interested in training clinical psychologists, period. I also have the feeling from some of the things I've read that we wish to train psychologists in the sense that they need not be clinical psychologists in the limited sense of the word, but that they may actually be researchers, or they could be teachers, or whatever they want.[5]

Alexander suggested that unless there was a consensus among the faculty as to the prime purpose of the training the school provided, the effort would be "doomed to failure." He further predicted that unless the school directed its energy to providing a type of training that could be obtained nowhere else, it would not succeed. He felt that there should be a reexamination of the goals of the school which would take advantage of the unique attributes of the institution and its faculties. Thus, as Alexander perceived the situation, the purposes for which the school existed might turn out to be much more limited, but much more achievable. His words stated it well: "There is something in my mind that says I would rather find distinction about something, than mediocrity about a lot of things."[6]

Alexander's comments had a strong impact on the faculty. They did not perceive themselves to be as fragmented in their thinking as he did. Travis said it well:

This has been in the back, I think, of most of our minds—just what he said: We can't be a big "University of Michigan" department. Irving tells me that they have over 100 members. They can deal with any phase of psychology—in the laboratory, in the clinic, etc. I think we must do what we intend to do and hope it's unique and worthwhile and defend it and support it, and let accreditation and approval happen if they will. So I think we come back again and again to our intentions at Fuller. We must increasingly sharpen our intention and declare it and pursue it.[7]

One significant interaction occurred in response to Alexander's observation that "I think you are going to have to work out very explicitly what your relation is to the church and the credo which this institution professes. I don't think you can bypass that issue."[8] Travis reacted by saying that all the faculty had in mind church-related services. Turning to John Finch, however, Travis corrected himself and said that Finch had in mind "Christian psychotherapy." Finch, then, offered to speak for himself. He expressed his conviction that training psychologists about a "Christian view of the nature of man" was more important than providing services to the church. Finch said to Alexander:

I think you have done us a great service in pointing out that we must adhere to our uniqueness, and I will define this uniqueness, as I see it. Our uniqueness, as Christians, is a Christian view of man [sic]. . . . Psychology, by virtue of its limited view of man, has really no answer to the problems of man.[9]

In answer to Alexander's question about whether this meant to bring persons back to God or the church, Finch continued:

Chapter 8 – Attaining APA Accreditation

To bring him back to be himself in truth, an authentic person. As far as functioning in the church is concerned, I wouldn't want to function in a church. I'm in private practice. . . . If it's church-related in the sense that they want to send referrals, then that is okay.[10]

This statement by Finch revealed two things. First, it was obvious that there was no consensus as to the way "Fuller trained" psychologists were to relate to the church. Travis' vision was to train psychologists who would join with the church in education and counseling. Finch's vision was to train psychologists who would receive referrals from the church but always be separate from it. Alexander was right in noting that agreement had not yet been reached on the purpose of the school. Probably this difference of opinion over church relationships influenced reaction to the other observation Alexander made about the overemphasis on psychopathology and a lack of emphasis on normal personality development.

The second revelation that came out of this interaction between Finch and Alexander was the observation that Alexander disagreed with Finch's emphasis on the uniqueness of "a Christian view of man." After hearing Finch assert that the spiritual nature of the human being was missing from modern psychology which he, Finch, felt lacked the *weltanschauüng* of philosophy and theology, Alexander suggested that Finch's ideas were not peculiar to Christianity. "I don't like the fact that you usurp this for Christianity," Alexander commented, "I don't think there would be any difference in the stated purpose that any orthodox analyst would have and the purpose you stated right here."[11] Finch vigorously defended his contention that his ideas were distinctively Christian. He replied, "When I say it's Christian, it has very specific, explicit relation to Jesus Christ. I make absolutely no apology for this. I am a Christian without question or doubt."[12] Finch stated that he, because of his Indian background, knew firsthand that the Christian view of the human being was distinctly different from that of the other major religious traditions. He was also convinced that no major theory of psychology included the essence of his Christian point of view.

Alexander was not persuaded. He countered with the following: *Well, I don't get any feeling at all about what the translation of that point of view means in what you do. See, because even when I talk to John [Finch], in the final analysis he tells me that it's all in his head, but when he's out there treating a patient . . . he wants to build in this person some notion of wholeness. Now, okay, I say that's fine. But I don't know what's Christian about it.*[13]

Finch contended that Alexander was wrong. He insisted that his ideas about human nature were the novel, unique, and Christian concepts around which the school was established. He went so far as to state, "We got the million dollars for the lectures I gave," referring to his presentations in the spring of 1961. Finch was correct in saying that his lectures presented a viewpoint that health and psychopathology were essentially dependent on whether persons acknowledged their true natures and responded in decisive faith to the call to be who God created them to be—autonomous spirits whose true natures resided in their relationship with God, the Holy Spirit.

This interaction between Finch and Alexander portended a dialogue which was to continue for many years. Finch continued to insist that the school was founded to advance his Christian view of man [sic]. He became concerned when the curriculum did not focus upon this emphasis. He was disdainful of sociobehavioral methodology and general psychology, both of which became essential components of the "scientist/professional"[14] model on which the training program of the school was constructed. Further, Finch was often critical of ideas which did not explicitly affirm his point of view. Through the years, he insisted that the donors (the Weyerhaeusers) were disappointed in the school because it had not turned out to be the type of training program they envisioned. At times he expressed the opinion that APA accreditation was not a worthy goal if it interfered with or militated against his vision that the school teach a curriculum narrowly focused on his Christian existential viewpoint.[15]

On the other hand, Travis and the faculty heard Alexander well. They continued to seek APA accreditation and to fashion their training around basic psychological knowledge at the same time that they offered many opportunities for students to integrate their Christian faith with their psychological acumen. Nevertheless, they did not limit the models whereby this could be done to the one recommended by Finch. Neil Warren expressed this consensus well at the May 23 meeting with Alexander:

You (Alexander) started out by saying that you thought we'd have no chance at all if we were operating on a model of trying to teach students to be psychologists of various kinds. . . . I got a little worried because that's been the model I've been operating on. And I gather, as a faculty, we've been more on the model that is trying to train people to be clinical psychologists who perhaps will go into teaching, or into clinical practice, or will do research, or a combination of any of those, with a primary interest in integrating, in whatever place they find themselves, theology and psychology.[16]

Alexander, however, sounded a warning of an issue that has plagued the school up to the present, namely, how broad can the training of the school become and still be unique. He answered Warren by asking:

Be realistic. . . . To turn around and say to anybody you know, you can't find anything in our program that you won't find any place else—I think that's nonsensical. And if you said to me, "But I'm going to give them research experience that is going to relate clearly to the problems of psychology and theology or to the spiritual relationships of man," or something like that, or to the investigation of dogma, or the building of faith, I would say, "Ah, here's something that makes sense." But if you tell me that he's going to work on eyelid conditioning because he knows something about research, save your time and money.[17]

Consultation with Ronald B. Kurz

The third APA consultant to the School of Psychology was Ronald B. Kurz, the associate educational affairs officer of the association. He visited Fuller in February, 1971. By the time of Kurz's visit, Tweedie had prepared a statement on "research" at the school which emphasized a focus on religious-related studies. Tweedie stated:

As research patterns develop and goals clarify, the faculty has special interest in the evaluation of positive personal resources in persons identified by a personal commitment to the Christian faith. In a large measure the empirical investigation of Christian anthropology is the "raison d'etre" of the School of Psychology.[18]

This clarification met some of the concerns which Alexander expressed.

Another development at the school by the time of Kurz's visit was the leadership provided by Paul Clement in his role as director of clinical training. In this role, Clement became the driving force that led to the school's finally making an application for accreditation two years later. In the fall of 1970, the faculty authorized Clement to make a request for an official preaccreditation, consultative, site visit from APA Department of Educational Affairs, the body with responsibility for accrediting graduate training. Kurz was this person.

Kurz's impressions were more positive and encouraging than Alexander's had been three years earlier. By 1971, the school had 11 graduates, a student body of 70, a full-time faculty of seven, a part-time faculty of four, and 50 adjunct supervisors. Kurz's report described the program thusly:

The primary goal of the program in clinical psychology is to train clinicians who are equipped to act as a bridge between the clergy and the mental health professions, clinicians who will speak the language of the clergy and the religiously oriented person. The program attempts to integrate psychology and theology in theory, research, and practice. Furthermore, it espouses the scientist-professional model and attempts to produce clinicians who are broadly trained in basic psychology as well as professional practice and who will be able to contribute to the data and theory of psychology as well as to professional practice. A unique research concern of the school is the psychological study of religious experience.[19]

In a memo to Lee Travis soon after Kurz's visit, Paul Clement stated,

[In] the year and a half that he has worked for APA central office, he [Kurz] has never visited a clinical psychology training program which excited him as much as ours did. He felt that our goals of training a special kind of mental health professional who will act as a bridge between the mental health establishment and the churches is very distinctive. Furthermore, he believed that there is a clear relationship between our curriculum and our stated goals.

However, Kurz's enthusiasm did not affect his realistic appraisal of the school's readiness for accreditation. He suggested that the school would not be approved until it increased its faculty to a minimum of 10 and an ideal size of 15. Further, he expressed concern over the diversity and breadth of the staff. He noted that most courses in general psychology were taught by clinicians whose primary training had not been in these areas. Research did not seem to have as central a place among the faculty as Kurz said was optimal. He noted that some faculty were supervising research but doing little or none themselves.

CHAPTER 8 – ATTAINING APA ACCREDITATION

Kurz complimented the student body. He felt they were representative of psychology graduate students across the nation in ability, motivation, and skill. However, he decried the financial stress they were put under by the lack of fellowship monies available to them and such facts as their having to pay tuition while on internships. He felt that the administration did not fully comprehend the financial resources needed to conduct graduate education in psychology.

Kurz affirmed the strength of clinical experience which students obtained by a minimum of two half-time internships but felt that they should be allowed clinical contact earlier than their third year, which was the norm in 1971. He was impressed with the training afforded through the Pasadena Community Counseling Center and noted the uniqueness of the Church Consultation Service which was being developed as a facility for relating psychological training to religious institutions.

Overall, Kurz did not feel that the School of Psychology was ready to apply for accreditation. He did not think the program would be approved until facilities and funding were improved, faculty size was increased, and the financial stress on students was reduced. Further, he said the necessity of students having to go to other institutions for library resources and computer facilities should to be remedied.

The First Application for APA Accreditation

There was much discussion of the Kurz report among the faculty and other psychologists in Southern California. In spite of the concerns expressed by Kurz, the faculty authorized Clement to request an application for accreditation toward the end of 1971. Clement hoped that he would be able to submit the application in time for the Committee on Accreditation to approve a site visit by June 1972.

Although the ability of the school to complete the application as quickly as Clement had hoped delayed possible approval for six months, the faculty's decision to proceed in spite of Kurz's discouragement was based in part on the accreditation of the Western Association of Schools and Colleges (WASC) which had been awarded the seminary in May 1969, just a week or so before William Evans was awarded the first Ph.D. degree in Clinical Psychology. This WASC accreditation, which was strongly supportive of the School of

113

Psychology, had occurred only because Lee Travis has insisted on it. Fuller Theological Seminary had long been accredited by the American Association of Theological Schools (ATS) but had never before sought accreditation by WASC. Earlier in his tenure, Travis had said to Hubbard, "I do not want to be a part of anything that is not accredited." Both Hubbard and Travis agreed that approval of a graduate psychology program by ATS would not suffice for credibility among professional psychologists. Further, they decided that APA would never approve a program that did not have prior approval by a regional accrediting body.

When contacted, WASC responded that they only accredited institutions, not separate schools within a program. Thus, Fuller Theological Seminary applied for, and received, full accreditation from WASC in 1969. And the doctoral degree offered by the School of Psychology was included, with strong affirmation in the report. By the time WASC approval was awarded, the whole seminary was hopeful and involved. A gala celebration of this news was held at the La Strada restaurant in Glendale.

In addition to the encouragement received from WASC approval, several other events convinced the faculty to seek APA accreditation when they did. A conference on training in clinical psychology held at Vail, Colorado, in 1971 had encouraged an expanded definition of the kinds of programs which would be approved to include training which emphasized clinical practice. Theretofore, university academic departments had controlled the definitions of training and had overemphasized experimental and laboratory studies. This encouragement provoked the establishment of the Council for Directors of Clinical Training, of which Paul Clement became a charter member. His experience on the council, coupled with site visits he had been asked to make to other training programs seeking APA accreditation, convinced Clement that the Fuller School of Psychology was doing as well as any and was better than some.

The First APA Site Visit

With these facts in mind, the school officially applied for an APA accreditation site visit. A committee of Irvin Sarason, Kenneth Purcell, and Arthur Wiens made an official site visit to the school on December 4 and 5, 1972. These psychologists were well-known and respected

Chapter 8 – Attaining APA Accreditation

professionals. Sarason, the chairman, was from the University of Washington; Purcell was from the University of Denver; and, Wiens was from the University of Oregon Medical School. Their report contended that the situation at the school was essentially unchanged since the consultative visit of Ronald Kurz, in spite of the fact that by the time of this visit, 30 persons had received their doctorates and a new Psychology Building had been designed and planned.

The school received the report of this APA accreditation site visit on January 30, 1973 from Raymond Vorus, administrative associate in the Educational Affairs Office. The report was negative. For several reasons, the site visiting team did not recommend accreditation. Philosophically, the report[21] questioned whether APA wanted to accredit programs in clinical psychology which did not take place in a broader context in which other specialities were being trained. This related to the fact that substantive courses in psychology were being taught by clinicians who had not specialized in those areas, a situation that had been previously noted. They felt that the program lacked depth and that the faculty was still too small.

Judging psychology to be a behavioral science, the report concluded that the Fuller program did not match the intentions of the Boulder "scientist/practitioner" model. They observed that much of the research had been conducted or chaired by Clement and that the strength of the program was heavily dependent on Clement and Travis. They questioned how stable the program was in light of the fact that Travis was 78 years old and destined to be replaced within a year and that Clement could decide to leave.

The question of academic freedom was also raised in light of the requirement that faculty sign the seminary Statement of Faith each year. The report stated:

Yet another basic question concerns the required Statement of Faith. This is a matter of the nature of academic freedom. In the site visiting team's view, the required Statement of Faith at the least represents a limitation on the diversity to which the students can be exposed and at the most represents a totally unworkable burden with regard to academic freedom and the nature of liberal education.[22]

The report, however, indicated that the visitors were impressed with the students and graduates. They concluded that the interns were rated as good or better than those from other programs except in the area of research. The graduates were occupying positions similar to those from other institutions. In fact, the five who were teaching in colleges was a higher percentage than many other clinical psychology training programs. One graduate was directing a children's home and another was in charge of the Alaska Department of Health and Welfare. They noted, also, that there was a higher percentage of graduates relating their services to the needs of churches than would be found among other institutions. They considered this to be a strength. The report noted the unique attempt of the program to relate psychology and theology. It mentioned the disagreement among students as to the value of having to take Greek and Hebrew and questioned whether professors in psychology or theology had enough leisure to interact in depth with each other in the integration seminars.[23]

The School of Psychology's Response to the Report

In accordance with the APA Committee on Accreditation policies, the school was invited to respond to the site visit report. This response[24] was sent to APA in early May 1973, after extensive discussions among the faculty, students, and select psychologists from the community. The response took strong exception to the report. It stated:

Those who have read the report have pointed out that the report is filled with inconsistencies and is discrepant with a number of sources of input to the site visit team. There are discrepancies with previous accreditation reports written on the Fuller program. There are discrepancies with feedback received from the practicum and internship trainers. There are discrepancies with feedback received from present students, graduates of the program, and employers of the graduates. There are discrepancies with much factual data to which the team was exposed and/or had access. And there are discrepancies with standard procedures for writing accreditation reports.[25]

Regarding the issue of academic freedom, the school's response quoted previous WASC accreditation reports in stating that Fuller was a seminary which held forthrightly to a conservative and evangelical interpretation of Christianity but that "the only possible issue would be whether such a stance interferes with the free exercise of the intellect in education." The previous reports suggested that they saw no evidence of such an interference and, in contrast, "the opposite seemed to be true; religion seems here to strengthen the motivation to education."

The school's response also challenged the inference that students were not exposed to diversity by noting the opportunity for student contact with many other professionals in the Los Angeles area. Further, while the need for more faculty was acknowledged, the response countered the criticism that substantive courses were taught by clinicians by quoting Nevitt Sanford's contention in a previous WASC report to the effect that fragmentation was avoided by this practice. He even recommended that the school should "resist any pressure from APA to move in the direction of bringing in any more specialists." Further, it was noted in the response that the WASC report had evaluated the psychology classes as taught by "well-informed people using good text materials."

The response confronted directly inferences in the site visitors' report that the program was overly dependent on Clement, that the seminary was financially unstable, that a modern foreign language was required, that facilities were inadequate for student research, and that the leadership of the school was uncertain due to Travis' impending retirement. It further countered the implication that it was too early to judge the professional performance of graduates. The fact that one graduate was president of his state's—and another the president of his county's—psychological association was noted but not taken into account in the site visitors' report. Finally, the response contended that aspersions cast on the quality of the school's dissertations were based on only casual perusal of the manuscripts.

All in all, the response of the faculty contended that the site visitor's report was biased in favor of a university-based model. It asserted that Fuller training was producing superior clinical psychologists from a different approach which the site visitors failed to grasp and which they discounted. The validity of the report was, therefore, seriously questioned.

The APA Committee on Accreditation considered the site visitors' report and the school's response at its meeting in late May 1973. It decided that the discrepancies were so great that it could not decide whether to accredit Fuller's program or not. It therefore proposed that another site visit be made in the fall. They recommended that the visit focus on "the diversity and depth of the program, the breadth of knowledge and research competency of the faculty and students, and the relationship between the required Statement of Faith and academic freedom."[26] Paul Clement was able to negotiate the nature of the visit, however, into a general site visit rather than one which had only a limited focus of attention. He insisted that the tenor of the old site visitors' report was negative and that a complete two-day visit, replete with in-depth interviews, was necessary to give the best opportunity for the school to make its case. Clement also asked that one member of the committee be from a nonuniversity-based program which primarily trained professionals to deliver psychological services to the public.

The Second APA Site Visit

The APA agreed to all of Clement's requests and a second site visit occurred on December 4 and 5, 1973, fully one year after the initial accreditation visit. The visitors were Irwin Altman, chair of the Department of Psychology at the University of Utah; Marilee Fredericks, director of the Des Moines Child Guidance Center; and William L. Simmons, director of clinical training at the State University of New York at Albany. In addition to the impressions it gathered from two days of interviews, the committee was given a new self-study which the school completed for this purpose. The committee's report was basically positive and the school's faculty sent a letter to APA in early 1974 indicating it felt it had been evaluated fairly. The faculty was pleased that the report declared, "It appears that Fuller is quite successful in providing very good professional training."[27]

This second site visitors' report to the APA Accreditation Committee was more positive than the first. It stated that psychology and theology were taught separately from one another and that psychology was taught within a scientific, empirical framework. The school's clearly stated objectives provided opportunities for students who might be "misplaced" in other settings. The report noted that the integration seminars, taught jointly by a theologian and a psychologist, allowed students to ask "interesting and significant research questions that might be received with suspiciousness or ridicule in more traditional psychology departments."[28]

The report further stated that the school was well established. Although it needed better financial support for students, more faculty, better library holdings, and support for faculty development, the school had a productive faculty, a liberal sabbatical policy, adequate dissertations, and a highly motivated student body. No evidence was found that the Statement of Faith compromised academic freedom. The report did recommend more faculty, better research facilities, higher priority on the recruitment of women and minorities, and the selection of a new dean who would be of the same caliber as Lee Travis. It concluded with the affirming statement that Fuller "does have unique characteristics, a seminary base and a small exclusively clinical faculty, but there is no doubt that it is a psychology program, training psychologists."[29]

Full APA Accreditation Awarded in 1974

In January 1974, Fuller Theological Seminary's Graduate School of Psychology was awarded full accreditation by the American Psychological Association. The California state psychologist announced the approval and noted that Fuller was the first professional school in the country to be approved.[30] The announcement also noted that the school's director of clinical training, Paul W. Clement, was the president-elect of the California State Psychological Association.

Soon after being notified of APA's approval, a grand celebration was held at the school. Many at the school pointed with pride the following fall to the inclusion of the school's name among the 49 approved programs in the country who were listed in *The American Psychologist*.[31] Since this first approval the school has been reevaluated several times. Each time serious questions have been asked about the relationship of the program to a theological seminary. Adequate academic freedom and diversity have had to be demonstrated every time.

ENDNOTES

1. Files in the institutional archives of Fuller Theological Seminary are replete with APA statements, *American Psychologist* articles, and other materials pertaining to accreditation which were assembled over the next decade and utilized in the school's efforts to attain APA accreditation.
2. Letter from Lee E. Travis to Arthur Brayfield, December 21, 1965.
3. Transcript of the May 23, 1968, feedback session of Irving Alexander with the faculty of Fuller Seminary's School of Psychology.
4. Ibid., p. 22.
5. Ibid., p. 2.
6. Ibid., p. 5.
7. Ibid., pp. 6-7.
8. Ibid., p. 24.
9. Ibid., p. 25.
10. Ibid., p. 25.
11. Ibid., p. 28.
12. Ibid., p. 29.
13. Ibid., p. 30.
14. The "scientist/professional" model was based on the decisions of the Boulder, Colorado, conference on clinical training in psychology which took place in August 1949.
15. A fuller description of Finch's ideas can be found in the volume edited by H. Newton Malony, *A Christian Existential Psychology: The Contributions of John G. Finch* (Lanham, MD: University Press of America, 1980).
16. Transcript of May 23, 1968, op. cit., p. 40.
17. Ibid., p. 43.
18. D.F. Tweedie, Jr., Memo on Research at the School of Psychology, 1967.
19. Ronald B. Kurz, Fuller Theological Seminary: Doctoral Training Program in Clinical Psychology, visited February 17, 1971.
20. Paul W. Clement, APA consultation visit from Dr. Ronald B. Kurz on February 17, 1971, School of Psychology, Fuller Theological Seminary, mimeo.
21. I.G. Sarason, K. Purcell, K., & A. Wiens, A. *APA Accreditation Site Visit Report* (Washington D.C.: American Psychological Association, 1973).
22. Ibid., p. 7.
23. The integration seminars were mistakenly labeled "interaction" seminars on page 4 of the report.
24. Letter to Raymond A. Vorus, Educational Affairs Office of APA, from Paul C. Clement and Lee E. Travis, dated May 10, 1973.
25. Ibid., p. 1.
26. Letter from Ronald B. Kurz to David A. Hubbard, dated June 11, 1973.
27. Altman, I, Fredericks, M. and Simmons, W. *Site Visit Report: Fuller Theological Seminary, Doctoral Program in Clinical Psychology.* (Washington, D.C.: American Psychological Association, 1974, p.1).

Chapter 8 – Attaining APA Accreditation

28. Ibid., p. 2.
29. Ibid., p. 6.
30. The announcement of the school's approval was included in a column titled "In Brief" on p. 6 of the *California State Psychologist*, February 1974. The Institute of Advanced Psychological Studies at Adelphi University has challenged Fuller's contention that it was the first professional school to be approved. However, although the institute was, in fact, approved earlier than Fuller, it is related to a university, and is not a professional school in the strict sense of the word.
31. "APA-Approved Doctoral Programs in Clinical, Counseling, and School Psychology: 1974." *American Psychologist*, November 1974, p. 844.

CHAPTER 9

Integration

From the very beginning, the integration of psychology and theology, of faith with practice, and of belief and life had been a prime goal of the School of Psychology. The very title of this volume, "Psychology and the Cross," attests to this ideal and derives from a statement of John G. Finch, whose dream led to the Graduate School of Psychology at Fuller. Finch expressed the goal of the school to be one of "planting the cross in the heart of psychology." These words are engraved for all to see on a plaque in the courtyard of the Psychology Building on the seminary campus at 180 North Oakland. They are mounted beneath a splendid bronze Greek *psi* out of which emerges a Christian cross. The very first published statement about the school stated the seminary was proposed to establish a "graduate school of Christian psychology."[1]

Called "Christian psychology" by Finch and Fairweather and "theo-psychology" by Hutchinson, the effort to relate psychology with the cross came to be known as "integration." Vande Kemp noted that the goal of integrating psychology and theology had a rich history and was, in fact, a reintegration effort that began after the late nineteenth-century attempt to emancipate psychology from philosophy and theology.[2] However, the term itself has a more recent history. She wrote:

> *The peculiar but common term "integration" to describe interdisciplinary efforts by theologians and psychologists was first used in reference to psychology and the religious realm in 1953 by Fritz Künkel, founder of "we-psychology." . . . Künkel established the [Christian] Counseling Center in First Congregational Church at Los Angeles in the 1940s, and in 1952 founded the Foundation for the Advancement of Religious Psychology. Künkel described his work after 1943 as the "integration of Christianity and psychology.". . . The editors of* Pastoral Psychology *adopted this description in a 1953 biographical sketch of Künkel (The Man of the Month, 1953) and extended it in 1955 to Gordon Allport, who was depicted as "an outstanding leader in the movement on integration of psychology and religion" (The Man of the Month, 1955, p. 59). In 1954 Künkel contributed the opening article on "The integration of*

Chapter 9 – Integration

Religion and Psychology" to the Journal of Psychotherapy *as a religious process. . . . Rickel [the editor] in turn employed the term in this journal to describe Paul Tournier. . . . With the publication of Biddle's* Integration of Religion and Psychiatry *in 1955, "integration" was firmly ensconced as the title for a movement that dominated the 1960s and 1970s, paving the way for the later emphasis on psychotherapy and spirituality.*[3]

The accomplishment of this ideal was the *raison d'etre* on which the school was established. Both Clement and Malony developed tripartite models of the task. Clement called it integration in "theory, research, and practice,"[4] and Malony termed it "integration at the level of principles, of profession, and of person, the 3Ps"[5] A combination of these two approaches might be diagrammed as follows:

```
    PRINCIPLES       PROFESSION         PERSON
         ↖ ↗           ↖ ↗           ↖ ↗
    THEORY           RESEARCH          PRACTICE
```

This diagram suggests that there might be issues of "theory," of "research," and of "practice" at each of the three domains of integration. Practice would be the way a psychologist thinks and talks about principles. Practice would also be the way the psychologist thinks and acts in professional counseling. Practice would further involve the way psychologists understand and identify themselves. And, of course, at each of these levels, there would be theoretical perceptions and research backgrounds. As integration has been conceived at the School of Psychology, it, no less than the training that was provided in the separate disciplines of theology and psychology, has been brought under the rubric of the "scientist-professional" model.[6] This approach understood the function of the psychologist always to be the thoughtful application of serious reflection. This would be true whether psychologists were functioning in the domains of principles, or profession, or of personal self-understanding.

The initial plans for integration included four facets:
(1) integration in clinical practice at the Pasadena Community Counseling Center
(2) intrapersonal integration in which students sought to combine theology and psychology within their own personal experience

(3) integration among schools through dialogue and debate among faculty

(4) integration through courses jointly taught by professors from theology and psychology.

Integration in Clinical Practice

In regard to the integration in the professional practice of psychology, one of the prime reasons for opening a clinic one year before students arrived was to provide a setting where those who would become professors could develop models and processes of integrating the Christian faith with their counseling. Plans included ample time for the staff to meet together to engage in dialogue about how such integration was being done. It was hoped that by the time students arrived, a body of knowledge would be developed which would become the core of integration. This hope undergirded Trustees Kulp and Olsen in their contention that doctoral programs should be based on bodies of knowledge that had been developed. They resisted any thought that this integrative knowledge would be left to the students to develop or that it would be part of the ongoing process after the school opened its doors.

That these first years of treatment and discussion were valuable for the practice of integration there can be no doubt. As the initial memo from President Hubbard announcing the opening of the School of Psychology stated:

The faculty-staff will be actively engaged in the therapeutic work. Students will be trained intensely and under close supervision in individual, group, milieu, and family therapy, with careful attention given to the spiritual dimensions of personality.[7]

The encouragement of Granberg in Study Committee discussions to let the theory develop out of practice rather than predetermine it beforehand, was followed. As John Finch expressed it:

The hope was that as the psychologists who were working with the patients at the clinic gained their information, they would try out a Christian psychology on them, and then bring the experiencing of that into their training.[8]

This kind of integrative supervision has occurred from the opening of the Pasadena Community Counseling Center until the

Chapter 9 – Integration

present. However, there have been two expressed disappointments in the way this professional practice integration has evolved. The first has been the observation made by student trainees that their supervision was weighted more heavily toward current psychological theory than to integrative possibilities. They have felt that integration was only occasionally mentioned. The second disappointment has been that expressed by John Finch. He consistently noted that emphasis had not been placed in training and supervision on the Christian existentialism which he espoused under the term "Christian psychology."

As the early years came and went, Finch became increasingly frustrated with what he perceived to be a lack of attention to integration. He would remind the faculty that they were not being true to the intent of those who gave the money to start the school. He was always eager to tell the faculty about reports he had heard from students who complained to him they were not getting the training in integration for which they came to Fuller. While the faculty chafed under Finch's persistent criticism and felt his observations were exaggerated and unfair, they have had to admit that clinical integration has been much more difficult than they imagined.

The negative criticism by John Finch has been an almost constant concern of the faculty, however. Finch was a regular visitor to the school. At least three times each year he would be on campus for several days during which he would meet with students and faculty. He, along with Annette Weyerhaeuser, would always share with new students the story of the founding of the school during orientation week. Then, at the time of the Integration Symposium in January, Finch would also be present. Finally, in the Spring Quarter, he would teach a one-week intensive course in Christian Existentialism. By the late 1960s, the times that Finch was to be on campus were looked upon with some apprehension by the faculty. He perceived the school's curriculum to be going in a direction that he did not like and he never hesitated to express his opinions. Regularly, he would cast aspersions on the seminary's evangelical position by speaking of the institution as "Fuller Theological Cemetery." The School of Psychology faculty became very defensive around him and, while courteous to him in a formal way, decided to ignore Finch in their planning.

An illustration of this faculty stance happened at the summer conference Finch held each year. Newton Malony was the visiting speaker in 1973. In a small group meeting at the conference, Malony was asked by someone, "What is the attitude of the psychology faculty toward John Finch?" Malony answered openly and honestly, "He is tolerated." Admittedly, answering in this fashion indicated naive social judgment on Malony's part. He should have known that what he said would be reported quickly to John Finch, and it was. The question itself should have made it very clear to Malony that Finch was sensing the faculty's attitude toward him.

Some months passed. The jaded feelings toward Finch persisted among the faculty, as did Finch's negative evaluations, whenever he came to Pasadena. Knowing that this kind of mutual animosity was not good, Dean Travis, with whom John got along fairly well, called an all-day retreat to try to work out a more positive relationship between the School of Psychology faculty and Finch. The faculty and Finch met together at the Passionist Fathers' Retreat Center in Sierra Madre. Almost immediately after the meeting began, Finch volunteered, "I understand from what Newt said last summer at the conference that you just tolerate me. Is that right?" While this was the truth, it did little to help solve the problem. Faculty tried to share with John how uncomfortable they felt around him. He, in turn, became defensive and insisted he was simply telling the truth as he and others saw it. Travis stammered and gave an ambiguous answer to John's accusations. The day ended in an impasse.

Relationships between Finch and the School of Psychology remained cool and ambivalent for many years. Everyone knew that the Weyerhaeuser family was very close to Finch. There was always the feeling that Finch had to be handled cautiously because the Weyerhaeuers might be offended. There was even the feeling that were it not for their support, the faculty would be much more confrontive with Finch. Most faculty felt his attitude was pompous, unfair, and incorrect. They saw themselves as serious Christians who were doing a good job of integrative training. They felt he was blind to what was really going on in the area of integration at the school.[9]

Yet it should be stated that during all of these stressful times, Finch remained an unselfish supporter. He donated his house in Tacoma to the school when he moved across Puget Sound to Gig Harbor. He channeled monies given to him by anonymous donors to the school and regularly made sure that the dean had upwards of $50,000 each year in a discretionary fund. Finch even secured support from a friend so that students could come to Tacoma for three weeks of intensive therapy at no cost to themselves save for groceries and plane fare. He made cars available to students so that they could come from their cabins to see him once each day during their time in therapy. Many students profited deeply from this experience, which was based on his model of Christian psychology.

Professors Malony, Phyllis Hart, Judy Balswick, and Clint McLemore, as well as theology professor Lewis Smedes, went through this intensive therapy experience and found it very helpful. Several testimonies to the value of this therapy can be found in the book *Christian Existential Psychology: The Contributions of John G. Finch*.[10] There is little doubt that personal integration was enhanced for many persons through this process. Many who experienced intensive therapy reported Finch to be a decidedly different person as a psychotherapist than he was as a visiting professor at the School of Psychology. In his psychotherapeutic role he was experienced to be a warm, supportive, and helpful person.

One facet of clinical integration that functioned well for almost a decade was the Church Consultation Center. Established in the spring of 1970 and directed by Malony, the CCC provided students training opportunities to offer service to churches. Several students did their internships in this center and all students in courses on organizational consultation learned to give speeches, conduct leadership training, help establish church counseling centers, advise on problems and conflicts, lead retreats, and consult with pastors on counseling issues and the dynamics of pastoral ministry. Three examples of this kind of practical integration were the establishment of a ministers' group which met weekly for sharing and counsel, the provision of assistance to the First Presbyterian Church of Hollywood in offering a counseling service, and the evaluation of ministerial candidates for several denominations.

Intrapersonal Integration

In addition to the opportunity to explore their own personal integration of psychology and theology through intensive therapy, students were assigned to encounter groups for their first two years of the program beginning in 1970. These groups were described in the seminary catalog in the following manner:

> **Psy 580 Intra-Personal Integration (0)**
> *All students participate in encounter groups with other members of their class throughout their first two years in the school. The goals of this experience are to help each student become more aware of his impact on others and to work toward becoming a more integrated person. Students are encouraged to examine the relationship between their faith and their decision to enter clinical psychology.*[11]

These groups were led by faculty members. They met weekly and often included marathon weekends or overnight sessions. These groups were discontinued in the late 1970s, when it became apparent to the faculty that there were unavoidable conflicts of interest involved—even when faculty determined they would have nothing to do with decisions involving their group members. This awareness was prompted by changes in the APA code of ethics. However, students who participated in these groups routinely looked back on them with warm feelings and felt they added greatly to their efforts at personal integration.

One other aspect of personal integration has been the encouragement to students to become involved in their own psychotherapy. The administration has subsidized the fees that have been charged, although the faculty did not require that students engage in their own therapy. Many, if not most, students have taken advantage of this help and have felt their own therapy added greatly to their efforts to become integrated persons. Entering into intensive therapy with John Finch was also one of the ways that some students undertook this type of integration.

Interfaculty Integrative Dialogue

The next way in which integration was intended to occur was in a series of integrative dialogues and debates among the faculties of theology and psychology. As noted earlier, Paul Fairweather was keenly interested in seeing this type of integration established, but became hurt and disillusioned after his encounter with George Ladd. After this debacle, no systematic interfaculty dialogue was started during the first several years of the school. However, in

1971, Travis sent a memo to President Hubbard suggesting an elaborate plan for starting the dialogue again. After noting the successful development of the school in the first six years, Travis stated:

Now may we turn our energies and creativity to what might be termed the second phase of our development, namely, to the task of realizing our uniqueness and destiny conceived by the founders of the school. This conception placed singular emphasis upon the integration of theology and psychology in the training of clinical psychologists. It was not enough to offer the finest training in orthodox clinical psychology (the scientist-professional model). Fuller had to acquaint and imbue the student with the truths of theology and make every effort to relate these to psychology in various forms of psychotherapy. To launch a more concerted effort at integration may I make the following proposal.[12]

Travis' proposal was to divide the entire faculty of the seminary (approximately 30 total) into five groups of six each. Each group would meet monthly for integrative dialogue. Travis urged the president to initiate such a plan and see that it was successful. Why Travis' plan never materialized is unknown.

Regular interfaculty dialogue about integrative issues has not been a reality during any period of the School of Psychology's life, save as a part of the annual lecture series, to be discussed below. While there have been periodic times of discussion among groups of faculty, this pattern of dialogue has never become an officially supported or promoted endeavor. Fairweather's original dream remains just that, a dream.

Integration Seminars

Originally it was planned that students would take courses in theology (including ethics, church history, biblical studies, etc.) and in psychology (including all facets of the discipline) after which they would take courses which brought the disciplines of psychology and theology together. It was thought that these integration seminars should be undertaken only after students had prepared themselves at the doctoral level in both disciplines. This preparation was intended to include the ability to work with both foreign and biblical languages as well as the research methodologies of psychology.[13] Thus, students were to enroll in these integration seminars toward the end of their training.

Initially, Paul Fairweather was assigned the role of planning for and teaching these integration seminars. The first such seminar was taught during the fall term of 1966 by Fairweather, Hubbard, and Carroll Wright on "The Problem of Suffering."[14] The following term, Fairweather and Wright taught a seminar on "Dualism in Flesh and Spirit" with New Testament professor George Ladd.[15] In the spring of this first year of integration seminars, Tweedie joined with New Testament professor Everett Harrison in teaching on the topic "Human Spirit and Holy Spirit."

The next two years of integration seminar topics and teachers were as follows. They reflected a variety of important themes and included the involvement of a number of faculty members from both psychology and theology.

Fall 1967: Neil Warren (in his first term as psychology professor) and Calvin Schoonhoven, theology professor of hermeneutics, taught a seminar on the topic "Schleiermacher"

Winter 1968: Travis and James Daane, theologian, taught a seminar on the topic "Sin and Forgiveness"

Spring 1968: Paul Clement (at the end of his first year as psychology professor) taught with historical theologian Geoffrey Bromiley on the topic "Theological Anthropology." This was the ill-fated seminar in which Bromiley had such negative feelings about Clement's convictions

Fall 1968; Paul Barkman, from the psychology faculty, taught with systematic theologian Paul Jewett on the topic "The Accurate Assessment of Religious Belief"

Winter 1969 Tweedie and William LaSor, Old Testament biblical scholar, taught a seminar on the topic "The Psychological Meaning of Old Testament Terms"

Spring 1969: Donald Cole and religious educator Robert Bower (who was also a psychologist and who counseled part-time in the Pasadena Community Counseling Center) taught a seminar on the topic "The Psychological and Spiritual Factors in Marriage."

This original pattern changed over the years. First, a decision was made in the early 1970s to do away with all the language requirements, unless a student elected to study for the M.Div. degree. After considering a survey which concluded that the rank of graduate programs in clinical psychology was inversely related to the number of required languages, the faculty decided that requiring four languages (Greek, Hebrew, German, Spanish or French) was unnecessary. Further it was determined that Statistics, not foreign languages, was the tool on which psychologists depended. The psychology faculty urged the theology faculty to think of the psychology students as Master of Arts students rather than Master of Divinity students. "English language" biblical studies became the norm and replaced language-required courses for psychology students soon thereafter.

The second way in which the integration seminar curriculum has changed pertains to the time at which the seminars are taken. Students began to complain that they had to wait until the last years of their training for these courses. Integration was a central reason that they came to Fuller and they wanted to become involved sooner than the fourth year. So, in the early 1970s, students were allowed to take their integration seminars whenever they desired. They were required to take four such seminars during their training. Students were even allowed to design an integration seminar based on their own unique interests if they could find a theologian and a psychologist who would agree to work with them. The only requirement was that they take the course titled "Introduction to Integration Seminars" taught once a year during that time, by professors Jack Rogers, from theology, and James Oakland, from psychology.

The Finch Symposium in Integration

One of the distinctive ways in which integration has been demonstrated at the school has been the annual integration lectureship which began in 1971. The faculty established an annual symposium at the instigation of Malony and entered into an agreement with Charles C. Thomas to publish the proceedings on a yearly basis. The lectures were named in honor of John Geoffrey Finch, whose inspiration and innovation was the prime force which led to the establishment of the school. An interfaculty committee composed of Professors Smedes (theology), Winter (world mission), and Malony designed a statement which became the foundation for the symposium. It read, "The John G. Finch Symposium on Psychology and Religion is sponsored by the Graduate School of Psychology of Fuller Theological Seminary. The series of addresses was established to deepen the understanding of man's religious behavior as seen in the light of social and behavioral sciences."

The format of the Finch Symposium has always included three lectures delivered by a visiting scholar, coupled with responses offered by a member of each of the seminary's three faculties—theology, world mission, and psychology. The rationale behind this format was twofold: One, the other faculties were intentionally included because of the desire to demonstrate integration among the three schools; two, this plan allowed the psychology faculty to invite persons whose convictions were not necessarily in accord with the seminary's theological orientation, yet who had some significant ideas to offer. For many years the lecturer was asked to affirm the seminary's Statement of Faith, but there was no theological examination conducted to assure exactly what was meant by such an affirmation. By having built-in responses, it was intentionally planned that there would be the opportunity to react to such presentations in print. This safeguarded the seminary's reputation. The possibility of such a situation arising was faced when the first person was invited to give the lectures.

Walter Houston Clark, professor emeritus at Andover Newton Theological Seminary in Newton Centre, Massachusetts, delivered the first Finch Symposium lectures on *Religious Experience: Its Nature and Function in the Human Psyche*.[15] Clark had been one of the nationally known figures with whom Fairweather and Finch consulted in 1961-'62 when they were seeking ideas about and approval of establishing the School of Psychology. He was teaching at the Hartford Seminary Foundation at that time and had been very supportive of the idea of Fuller Seminary's new school. Clark was known as a modern William James. In the 1950s he had written one of the books on the psychology of religion which indicated a revival of interest in the topic after its demise in the early 1930s.[16] The School of Psychology perceived Walter Clark as the dean of contemporary psychology of religion and a figure of notable reputation and deep insight.

The troubling aspect of these first lectures pertained to Walter Clark's well-known penchant for emphasizing the taking of psychedelic drugs as triggers for religious experience. It was his sincere conviction, expressed clearly in his volume *Chemical Ecstasy: Psychedelic Drugs and Religion*,[17] that modern technological society militated against the mystical experience of the transcendent. Feeling that reli-

Chapter 9 – Integration

gious experience was deeply needed by modern persons, he had become convinced that "triggers" were needed whereby the rational, technological world of the modern world could be transformed and people could experience the supernatural. He contended that the contemporary society had become so permeated by scientific technology that people were cut off from and suspicious of transempirical experiences. Psychedelic drugs were an ideal way for religious experience to be induced. He had come to feel it was the only thing that would work in the modern world. Clark had come to this opinion after participating with Timothy Leary in the early prison experiments using these drugs when Leary was at Harvard and Clark was at Andover Newton. He had been deeply moved by prisoners whose lives were changed by this type of religious experience.

Fuller Seminary faculty understood his analysis but were uncomfortable with his solution to the problem of the dearth of religious experience in the modern world. They thought that the idea of religious experience induced by psychedelic drugs would not be taken positively by those at the seminary. Caught in a dilemma, they felt that they should respect Clark's academic freedom and that they should not ask him to not mention this idea when he came. At the same time, they hoped that in his lectures he would refrain from mentioning his drug-related answer to the problem of diminished religious experience.

Thus, they decided to say nothing to Clark but pray that drugs would not be mentioned. They hoped he would have better social judgment than to mention this idea in his addresses. Their worst fears were confirmed, however. Clark mentioned drug-induced religious experience in every lecture! The seminary reaction was surprisingly mute. Perhaps not everybody realized what he was implying, although to those who knew what to expect, the ideas were perfectly clear. Responses to his lectures by missionary anthropologist Alan Tippett, biblical theologian Daniel Fuller, and clinical psychologist H. Newton Malony were included in the published manuscript. In each case, they addressed the issue of drug-induced religious experience but offered alternatives or critiques of the idea. The lectures were well attended and received without acrimony. The event passed with little comment one way or the other.

The second lecturer was Thomas A. Oden, professor of theology at Drew Theological Seminary in Madison, New Jersey. Oden had become well-known for his attempts to relate client-centered therapy and Barthian theology in such books as *Kerygma and Counseling* and *Contemporary Theology and Psychotherapy*.[18] Professor Neil Warren chaired the symposium and published the book *After Therapy What? Lay Therapeutic Resources in Religious Perspective*[19] which included Oden's addresses with responses by himself, theologian Calvin Schoonhoven, and missiologist Charles H. Kraft. A novel plan of organizing an integration seminar around the lectures started with the Oden lectures. Students taking the seminar attended the lecture, then took the following month to prepare response essays. Thereafter, the seminar met for dialogue weekly for the remainder of the term. The two student responses judged to be superior were also included in the published volume. These were written by Warren Walker, student in the School of Psychology and Kenneth B. Mulholland, a doctoral student in the School of World Mission. The practice of having an integration seminar organized around the yearly lectures has continued to the present, although responses are now seldom published.

Oden deeply impressed the seminary community. The faculty of the School of Psychology were seeking a professor whose main role would be to theorize about the integration of theology and psychology. They thought they had found the ideal person in Tom Oden. In the mid-1970s, he was offered the position of professor of integration, but declined. He seriously considered the offer but decided he wanted to stay at Drew, where he remains to this day a well-known professor of patristics. He has distinguished himself as one who feels that pastoral ministry should be grounded in the practices of the church fathers, yet he has remained an astute critic of trends in modern culture.

The third Finch Symposium lecturer was Richard L. Gorsuch, then professor of psychology at Texas Christian University. Gorsuch returned to the seminary as professor in the School of Psychology in 1976. The book titled *The Nature of Man: A Social Psychological Perspective* included Gorsuch's three lectures plus responses by Malony, missiologist Ralph D. Winter, theologian Paul K. Jewett, and students Douglas R. Matthews and Henry B. Venema.[20] This was a period shortly after the Communist attempts to brainwash American soldiers. Gorsuch presented a model of human nature as social, both in terms of the reflective nature of identity and the nature of social influence. He offered preventive remedies for ensuring that youth remained true to their ideals. He applied this to Christian education and recommended the use of social role-playing to prepare youth for attempts to change their faith.

The fourth and fifth integration symposia were delivered by psychiatrists. Orville Walters delivered the 1974 lectures on the topic "Christian Psychotherapy and the Legacy of Freud" and William P. Wilson, the psychiatrist who directed the Christian therapy program at Duke University Medical School, delivered the 1975 lectures on the topic "Christian Nurture, Life Adjustment, and Mental Disease." Donald F. Tweedie chaired the Walters symposium and Lee Travis chaired the Wilson symposium. Unfortunately, Charles C. Thomas decided to discontinue publishing the symposia because of poor sales of the first three volumes. Several of the subsequent symposia have been published, but it has been due to the initiation of the lecturer rather than of the school. In fact, the lecture fee was hereafter split and half the honorarium was given only when the lectures were published.

In June 1973, shortly after the third symposium, Malony wrote an article assessing the value of this type of integration. He wrote:

We are convinced of the value of these symposia and the integration seminars which are organized around them. The lectures have been thought-provoking and have provided much material for discussion in the seminary community. Of course, the format will improve with time—but the basic idea is a good one. . . . It [the Finch Symposium] is a unique contribution of Fuller Theological Seminary. At this time few, if any, other institutions are supporting such efforts."[21]

Malony was correct. To date there have been 25 integration symposia and no other institution has a record of such a noteworthy series focusing on the integration of psychology and theology. The titles and lecturers of symposia since 1975 are included in the Endnotes.[22]

The Goehner Award

The last but by no means the least important way that integration has been promoted at the School of Psychology has been by honoring significant student writing. This has been done in two ways; through the Goehner Award for the best example of integration in a dissertation and through the Travis Awards for the best theoretical and experimental papers in integration by students at the predissertation levels.

The Goehner Award was initiated in memory of Delbert Goehner who died in 1970. Goehner was the first person to die while a student at the School of Psychology. His death was traumatic for the faculty and student body as he was a young clinician with great potential. It was decided to keep his memory alive by recognizing dissertation-level integrative research and writing. The award was first given in 1972 and is given annually during the graduation ceremonies to the graduating candidate whose dissertation and past writing exemplifies the highest level of involvement in integrative thinking. Goehner award recipients are listed in the Endnotes.[23]

The Travis Awards were begun in 1978. Each year students submit papers they have written for courses and seminars. Judges from the three schools of the seminary read and decide which papers deserve first, second, and third place awards for the best essays in theoretical, experimental, and practical integration. These awards are made every year in the spring. Through the years numerous students have been recognized for their work.

ENDNOTES

1. John G. Finch and Paul D. Fairweather. "A Proposed Graduate School in Christian Psychology," *Christian Medical Journal*, spring 1962, pp. 9-11.
2. Hendrika Vande Kemp, *Psychology and Theology in Western Thought, 1672-1965: A Historical and Annotated Bibliography*, in collaboration with H. Newton Malony (Milwood, NY: Kraus International Publications, 1984).
3. Hendrika Vande Kemp, "Historical Perspective: Religion and Clinical Psychology in America," in Edward Shafranske, ed., *Religion and the Clinical Practice of Psychology* (Washington, DC: American Psychological Association, in press).
4. Clement's model can be seen in the lead article of the *Fuller Theological Seminary Bulletin*, Volume XVIII, March 1, 1968, titled "Integration of Psychology and Theology in Theory, Research and Psychotherapy." It is interesting that a statement within the article anticipates Malony's later model by stating that "We are attempting to integrate psychology and theology on at least three levels—personal, professional, and conceptual."
5. H. Newton Malony, *Integration Musings: Thoughts on Being a Christian Professional*, Revised Edition (Pasadena, CA: Integration Press, 1995): pp. 5-8.
6. The scientist/professional model was explicitly stated as the basis of School of Psychology's training approach in the "Self-Study Prepared by the Faculty of Fuller Theological Seminary's Graduate School of Psychology," December 1, 1973. This is often called the "Boulder model" after a conference on gradu-

CHAPTER 9 – INTEGRATION

ate training in clinical psychology held at Boulder, Colorado, in 1949. This conference set the norm for most programs in the United States. The conclusions of this conference was reported in V.C. Raimy, editor, *Training in Clinical Psychology* (New York: Prentice-Hall, 1950).

7. David Allan Hubbard, "Memo to All College and University Students Interested in Graduate Training in Psychology," spring 1965: p. 1.
8. Interview with John Finch by H. Newton Malony, fall 1993.
9. In the above-noted interview with John Finch by H. Newton Malony in September 1993, Finch shared some of the hurt he experienced over these interactions. When asked if he ever presented his ideas to the faculty for dialogue, he replied, "I was never asked to debate. Nobody has ever challenged anything that I said, actually confronted me, or even replied to my writings in writing. This has never happened. . . . I was never even invited to any faculty meetings. If I ever came, it was because I requested it." When Malony observed, "That must have been fairly awkward for you," Finch replied, "Very awkward. I felt unwelcome." Finch admitted he was disdainful of the situation and that he showed it in his demeanor. Unfortunately, I think the faculty was equally disdainful. The relationship remained a distrustful standoff for many years. I expressed this evaluation of the situation to Finch at the 1993 interview, "I think it's a continuing set of misperceptions on all our parts as to where any of us is and has been. Maybe it's the issue of style, as well as substance, that we couldn't overcome in one another. It's almost like we just wrote you off as a person. We felt that you had written us off, too. I remember saying to you more than once, 'You don't really know us.'"
10. H. Newton Malony, editor, *A Christian Existential Psychology: The Contributions of John G. Finch* (Lanham, MD: University Press of America, 1980).
11. Catalog of Fuller Theological Seminary, 1973-74 (Pasadena, California), p. 81.
12. Lee Edward Travis, "A Suggestion for Integration: A Memo to David Allan Hubbard," November 27, 1971.
13. The original curriculum had these "psychology-theology" courses beginning in the fourth year. The beginning curriculum can be found on the last page of the memo from David Allan Hubbard re: The New School of Psychology of Fuller Theological Seminary and its Ph.D. Program in Clinical Psychology, spring 1965.
14. Fairweather's negative interaction with George Ladd over the faculty dialogue about "image therapy" occurred after the teaching of this seminar with him. Ladd was known as a strong conservative thinker. It could be that the interaction with Fairweather in this seminar planted some concern in his mind which was expressed overtly later on when the idea of a faculty dialogue was presented. Fairweather has maintained an investment in the emphasis on "father-bonding" and on the influence of relationships with the father in determining a person's doctrine of God—both of which are essential to his "image therapy." These ideas were likely anathema to George Ladd. Some of these ideas are included in Fairweather's address at the opening of the Pasadena Community Counseling Center which is included among the Appendices to this volume.

15. Walter Houston Clark, H. Newton Malony, James Daane, and Alan R. Tippett, *Religious Experience: Its Nature and Function in the Human Psyche* (Springfield, IL: Charles C. Thomas, 1973).
16. Walter Houston Clark, *The Psychology of Religion: An Introduction to Religious Experience and Behavior* (New York: Macmillan, 1958).
17. Walter Houston Clark, *Chemical Ecstasy: Psychedelic Drugs and Religion* (New York: Sheed & Ward, 1969). The earliest book which brought the psychology of religion back into consideration by American psychology was Gordon Allport's *The Individual and His Religion; A Psychological Interpretation.* (New York: Macmillan, 1950).
18. Thomas A. Oden, *Kerygma and Counseling* (Philadelphia: Westminster, 1968);

    Thomas A. Oden, *Contemporary Theology and Psychotherapy* (Philadelphia: Westminster, 1967).
19. Thomas C. Oden, Neil C. Warren, Kenneth B. Mulholland, Calvin R. Schoonhoven, Charles H. Kraft, and Warren Walker, *After Therapy What? Lay Therapeutic Resources in Religious Perspective* (Springfield, IL: Charles C. Thomas, 1974.
20. Richard L. Gorsuch & H. Newton Malony, *The Nature of Man: A Social Psychological Perspective* (Springfield, IL: Charles C. Thomas, 1976).
21. H. Newton Malony, "Finch Symposium on Psychology and Religion: A Dream at Mid-Stream," *Theology, News and Notes*, June, 1973, p. 17.
22. Symposia Lectures after 1975 are listed below. Where the lectures became books, they are noted.

    Stanley R. Hopper, 1976, "Psyche, Logos, and the Human Spirit."

    Orlo Strunk, Jr., 1977, "Personal Religious Values: A Psycho-Theological Understanding."

    Gary Collins, 1978, "Psychology and Theology: Prospects for Integration" published as *Psychology and Theology: Prospects for Integration*, Edited and with a contribution by H. Newton Malony (Nashville, TN: Abingdon Press, 1979).

    David G. Myers, 1979, "Our Human Condition" published as *The Inflated Self: Human Illusions and the Biblical Call to Hope* (New York: Seabury Press, 1980).

    John G. Finch, 1980, "Can Psychology be Christian?" published as *Nishkamakarma* (Pasadena, CA: Integration Press, 1982).

    J. Harold Ellens, 1981, "God's Grace and Human Health" published as *God's Grace and Human Health* (Nashville, TN: Abingdon, 1982).

    Mary Stewart Van Leeuwen, 1982, "The Socerer's Apprentice: A Christian Looks at the Changing Face of Psychology" published as *The Scorcerer's Apprentice: A Christian Looks at the Changing Face of Psychology* (Downers Grove, IL: Intervarsity, 1982).

    David Moberg, 1983, "Wholistic Christianity: Sociological Interpretation."

    Vernon Grounds, 1984, "Unselfing the Self: A Pivotal Problem in Psychology and Theology."

Morton T. Kelsey, 1985 "Christianity as Psychology: Philosophy, Psychology, and Christian Faith" published as *Christianity as Psychology: The Healing Power of the Christian Message* (Minneapolis, MN: Augsburg, 1986).

Alvin Dueck, 1986, "Ethical Concepts of Healing" published as *Between Jerusalem and Athens: Ethical Perspectives on Culture, Religion and Psychotherapy* (Grand Rapids, MI: Baker Book House, 1995).

Donald M. Mackay, 1987, "The Pastor and the Brain Scientist" (presented by Warren Brown due to the death of Mackay).

C. Stephen Evans, 1988, "Psychology as a Human Science and the Prospects for Christian Psychology."

Lucy Bregman, 1989, "Death in the Midst of Life" published as *Death in the Midst of Life: Perspectives on Death from Christianity and Depth Psychology* (Grand Rapids, MI: Baker Book House, 1992).

Paul C. Vitz, 1990, "The Importance of Narratives for Christian Psychology" published as: "The Use of Stories in Moral Development: New Psychological Reasons for an Old Education Method," *American Psychologist*, 1990. 2, 709-720.

Rebecca L. Propst, 1991, "Christian Contributions to the Treatment of Clinical Depression."

Don S. Browning, 1992, "Love in America: Practical Theology and Family Decline."

Nicholas Woltersdorff, 1993, "Living with Grief."

Sydney Callahan, 1994, "Christ and the Unconscious."

Malcolm A. Jeeves, 1995, "Psychology and Christianity: Partners in Understanding Human Nature" to be published by Baker Book House (in press).

H. Newton Malony, 1996, "Brainwashing and Religion."

In 1993, the name of the symposium was changed to "The Fuller Symposium on the Integration of Faith and Psychology."

23. Goehner Awards to date include:

James A. Oraker, 1971; Clifford L. Penner, 1972; David C. Bock, 1973; Robert C. Richard, 1974; David A. Flakoll, 1975; William C. Weyerhaeuser, 1976; Claude P. Ragan, 1977; Peter L. Everts, 1978; William G. Bixler, 1979; Burley R. Howe, 1980; Aune J. Strom, 1981; no award was given in 1982; Quinn R. Conners, 1983; Alan C. Tjeltveit, 1984; Richard A. Blackmon, 1985; Timothy Kearney, 1986; Diane E. Bunker, 1987; Carolyn E. Kerr, 1988; James A. Tilley, 1989; Elmer Griffin, 1990; Terri J. Brenneman and Joseph J. Steigena, 1991; Charles A. Schaeffer, 1992; Ronald G. Rickner and Yung Soon Lee, 1993, Robert J. Voyle, 1994, Laura English, 1995.

CHAPTER TEN

Travis Retires—Warren Becomes Dean

In the fall of 1974, Lee Travis' title was changed. Formerly, he had been known simply as "dean." Now, he was to be known as "dean of the present." This change in title was to accommodate the fact that Neil C. Warren had been given the title "dean of the future." These changes in title and role had not been made hurriedly or haphazardly. When Travis became dean in 1965 he had already retired from a distinguished career of teaching at the University of Iowa and the University of Southern California. By 1974 he was over 78 years old. Although he moved with less agility and while he began to arrive later in the morning and leave earlier in the afternoon, his faculties were no less acute. He remained his warm, agreeable, affirming, alert, and nattily dressed self, even though he paid less attention to details than he had earlier in his deanship. He would often arrive at dissertation defense meetings, on which he sat as a committee member, without having read the dissertation. However, his questions always reflected acute appreciation for the issues even as he confided to his faculty colleagues, "I'm going to leave the details to you young squirts." At the dissertation defense committee meetings he would listen for a while, then offer a comment or make a query that reflected he knew full-well what was going on. He had an amazing grasp of contemporary psychology which often came out clearly at these times.

Concerns about Travis

Yet it was not so much these physical changes that caused President Hubbard to note as early as 1972 that "we have faced this transition since the day Dean Travis was appointed in 1964, when he was already past normal age of retirement."[1] His concern was with Travis' advancing age, which could not be denied. After all, in spite of the fact that he was still engaged in an active private practice in

Chapter 10 – Travis Retires – Warren Becomes Dean

the mid-1960s, Travis had already retired from teaching at the University of Southern California some years before he received the Fuller appointment. As much as Travis was admired, the passage of the years had to be acknowledged. The evidence for Hubbard's concern had prompted him to face the issue during the very same month that Travis had been chosen as dean. In fact, the letter of appointment had stated, "This appointment is not made for any specified length of time, but is to be considered permanent, conditioned, of course, upon your continued physical and mental vitality."[2]

At the same time Hubbard had written Lars Granberg inviting him to become director of academic affairs at the school.[3] In his letter to Granberg, Hubbard had forthrightly acknowledged that a successor to Travis would be needed, perhaps sooner rather than later. He had noted that the post to which Granberg was invited did not carry with it any automatic succession to the deanship, but that Granberg would definitely be considered.

No one disagreed with Hubbard, although many did not want to think that the exact day of Travis' retirement had arrived. Lysa, Travis' wife, never felt the day had come. She was always very protective and did not want "Lee," as she called him, to ever be embarrassed. Yet, the psychology faculty was becoming increasingly concerned that Travis' niceness and lack of attention to detail was putting the school at a disadvantage in interacting with the vigorous leadership of the seminary's new provost, Glenn Barker. Barker, who earlier succeeded Daniel Fuller as dean of the School of Theology, had become the seminary's first provost. Several among the psychology faculty felt that Barker looked at the School of Psychology as a second-class citizen; somewhat like a distant cousin to the main affair, the School of Theology. Barker had a way of filling every vacuum and finalizing every decision that was left undecided. The psychology faculty began to sense that Travis was not guarding their interests as vigorously as the situation demanded. Travis was beginning to come to the seminary only two or three days a week and sometimes would not be present at all at meetings with the provost.

The Travis Legacy

Nevertheless, in their evaluation of Travis, the faculty agreed with what Hubbard stated in his 1974 memo announcing the change from Travis to Warren, "It is impossible to conjecture where the program would be today without Dean Travis' leadership." Few if any would disagree with Hubbard's judgment that

> our successes in professional acceptance, in faculty recruitment, in academic stability, and in relationships with the Schools of Theology and World Mission are due in large measure to his leadership. He shared his lavish reputation with us. His highly personal style of leadership has made all of us—trustees, administration, faculty, students, staff, alumni—feel valued as members of his great family.[4]

That Lee and Lysa Travis had, indeed, made people feel part of their family was an understated truth. Beginning with the second year of the school's life, Lysa had invited all student spouses, all wives at that time, to meet weekly with her and Lee in a supportive group meeting.

At that time, many if not most of the students were former pastors who were disillusioned with parish ministry. They wanted to be in some form of religious work, but had experienced church leadership as traumatic. Their wives had lived through this disillusionment with them and had agreed to reenter graduate education with them long after they thought the days of professional religious leadership were over. Moreover, many of them were having to live with husbands who were learning new jargon and were dealing with new ideas. This was not easy. In fact, the experience was automatically stressful. Lee and Lysa met weekly and listened to their experiences. For many years, the group met in the building which occupied the place where the new Psychology Building now stands. Lysa called it "the building with the slanting floors." As time went on and fewer spouses of ex-ministers were in attendance, the character of these weekly meetings changed. Adjusting to life as student wives became more the central focus.

Lee and Lysa shared what it was like to be married to a psychologist as the student spouses began preparing for their future roles. These meetings are remembered by many wives as the time when they could share honestly about their lives and feel supported by others who were going through similar experiences. The support and concern expressed by the Travises became important ingredients in the graduate school experiences for many couples. The group often had as many as 12 in attendance and continued until the early 1970s—just before Lee became dean emeritus.[5]

Chapter 9 – Integration

The Travis home on Red Rose Drive in Encino was the site of many meetings—both formal and informal. It was a lovely spot away from the demands of graduate school life in an area of opulence and spacious living. The Travis home had a commodious living room, a swimming pool and an ample deck overlooking dramatic hills and valleys. It became a yearly tradition to have the opening celebration for new students there. Lysa was a gracious hostess who did everything "just right." The food was delicious and the welcome was genuine. The format was always the same: Lee would welcome the students and offer introductory words of encouragement. He would follow this with introductions of the faculty and staff. Marnie Frederickson was always present as a behind-the-scenes mastermind. After introductions, Annette Weyerhaeuser would tell the story of her healing through the help of John Finch. Finally, John Finch would speak. He would tell students about his concern that they base their counseling on a Christian view of human beings and encourage them to "be true to themselves relentlessly." After this everyone would enjoy a sumptuous lunch. After eating, each of the faculty would say a few words and there would be a time for questions and answers. New students came away with warm feelings, but a bit awestruck. Faculty knew what was going to happen but always looked forward to these yearly fall extravaganzas at the Travis home.

In between these yearly times of new student orientations, the faculty would gather in the Travis living room for serious dialogue about the integration of faith and practice and/or the design of the curriculum. Many important solutions to problems were reached in the comfortable ambiance of the Travis home. Never did anyone who attended feel unwelcome or uncherished. Not only did the Travises make persons feel a part of their extended family, but they also invited others into their personal lives. The relationship between the Travises and members of the faculty became very close. At one point, for example, faculty member Malony performed the wedding ceremony for the marriage of their son, Dwayne, to Penny, his fiancée.

Both on the job, as well as off, Lee Travis endeared himself to students and faculty alike. His door was rarely closed. Making an appointment with him was easy. He had time for people. He would roam the halls and stick his head into faculty offices. "How're you doing?" he would ask. And, to a person, faculty felt that he really wanted to know. He would stop and talk, if invited. Above and beyond his accomplishments, Travis was a man of stellar stature and Lysa was a woman of gentle and sophisticated love.

While both Lee and Lysa knew that the time would come when a change had to be made, neither wanted to acknowledge that time had come. Lee did not realize he was becoming less effective. He said, "No one has told me I'm slipping. Lysa tells me I'm as sharp as I ever was." Although it was apparent to many on the faculty, it was difficult for them, too, to state their perceptions directly to their beloved dean. There was one practical dimension to the drama, however. Lee had given up a fairly lucrative practice in Beverly Hills to come to Fuller. His salary at the seminary was never more then $20,000. The Travises spent most of what Lee earned. They had few resources for the time when Lee would fully retire. They were anxious about having to leave seminary employ because of the loss of income that would involve. Their anxiety was understandable. Their defensiveness was logical.

A Decision Is Made to Make a Change

Somehow the process came to a head when Paul Clement heard by the grapevine that the trustees had discussed the matter and decided that action should be taken. They voted that Travis was to be replaced as soon as possible. Clement asked Travis if this were true. Travis replied that he knew nothing about it. Clement then called President Hubbard, who confirmed that what Clement heard was true.[6] When Clement said that he thought the psychology faculty needed to know this, Hubbard insisted on telling the faculty himself. At the faculty meeting, Hubbard said that he wanted a person who had theological, as well as psychological, training. When Clement challenged the absolute necessity of this background, Hubbard became angry, slapped the table, and replied that the appointment of a dean without this background would be "over his dead body."

Hubbard conducted a national search and put several candidates before the faculty. Ken Shrable of Stanislaus State University, and John Stapert of the Reform Church of America, were among those considered along with Lars Granberg. Finally, he decided that the best candidate, Neil Clark Warren, was already at Fuller. He had strong qualifications. He had obtained an Master of Divinity degree from Princeton and was an ordained minister of the Church of

Chapter 10 – Travis Retires – Warren Becomes Dean

Christ. His doctorate in clinical psychology was from the University of Chicago. The choice of Warren to be dean met Warren's own need to take on a more responsible role. It also reassured the faculty that tradition would be maintained. Only Malony objected. He facetiously noted that he would be serving under someone who was younger than he was. Nevertheless, Warren debated about assuming the role. He returned from a European vacation determined to tell Hubbard he had decided not to do it. However, when Hubbard took him to lunch and offered the position once again, Warren acquiesced on the spot. Oakland advised Warren he should not have given in so quickly. Yet the relationships among the faculty, at this time, were unusually close and the cohesion around the choice of Warren as dean became very strong.

An agreement about the transition from Travis to Warren was reached in the late fall of 1974. Warren was appointed "dean of the future," and Travis retained the title "dean of the present." The plan was that Warren would function under Travis until the seminary graduation in June 1975. Warren would attend all meetings with the provost, the other two deans, and other seminary administrators. He would advise Travis on all decisions involving the School of Psychology. Travis reluctantly agreed with this plan. Hubbard did not want to offend or hurt Lee Travis. In fact, he had said in 1972, that two things were essential for a smooth transition: Travis' help and wisdom as well as Travis' blessing. However, as the fall gave way to winter, Hubbard and Barker began to feel the arrangement was not working out. They had difficulty knowing to whom to go to for decisions and whose opinion they could trust. On top of this, the seminary was going through a major financial crisis and agreement was needed on some important alternatives. The country was in a recession and faculty had agreed to take a five-percent cut in their salaries in order to help the seminary through the emergency. Chair of the Board of Trustees, C. Davis Weyerhaeuser, felt that the time had come for immediate action. In spite of his great affection for Travis, Weyerhaeuser felt that they seminary should put its needs before personal friendships. The situation came to a head in December, and Hubbard decided that the transition should be made January 1, 1995.

In an effort to ease the transition, John Finch made monies available for Lee and Lysa to go on a long-anticipated trip to Asia in January.[7] Travis was not scheduled to teach during the Winter

Quarter, so such a trip was feasible. Warren could assume the responsibility of the deanship while Travis was away. However, the Travises did not accept this offer. A decisive letter making Warren the dean was sent to Travis. It arrived, unfortunately, on Christmas Eve, 1994. This caused much consternation in the Travis household. It was felt that the timing was insensitive. Nevertheless, the act was considered necessary from Hubbard and Barker's point of view.

Warren Is Appointed Dean

The February-March, 1975 issue of *The Fuller Theological Seminary Bulletin* announced the change under the title "New Dean for School of Psychology." Hubbard stated in this publication,

> *I look forward to the growing influence and vitality of this program under Dean Warren's creative and enthusiastic guidance, as he builds on the strong foundation laid by the founding dean, Lee Edward Travis. The need for Christian psychologists is great, and Fuller's Graduate School of Psychology is uniquely equipped to meet this challenge.*[8]

In the psychology student publication *Stimuli*, newly appointed Dean Warren shared his hopes for the school. He said:

> *We have ten solid years under Dr. Travis' skilled leadership as a firm basis on which to build. The list of achievements for the school during those years is incredible. Now I sense that we are about to experience another growth spurt comparable to that dramatic explosion of the first few years.*
>
> *I see at least five specific goals toward which we will work during the coming few years. First, we must continue our struggle to be a community of true scholars. Research, reflection, and writing of the most solid quality will need to become a trademark of our school.*
>
> *Second, we must mobilize our resources to realize our unique mission as an academic community that is focused on the integration of theology and psychology. We are just beginning to scratch the surface in this area, and I am tremendously excited about the future if we keep our uniqueness well focused.*
>
> *We should never retreat from our goal of having the finest academic program in clinical psychology in the country. We will need to emphasize quality throughout every area of our general and clinical courses, as well as our research program.*

Chapter 10 – Travis Retires – Warren Becomes Dean

> *I believe our psychological center can become the model for the nation. I hope that we can have eight or ten facilities under a general administration, offering comprehensive psychological services to the community while providing excellent training for our students.*
>
> *Finally, I personally am committed to the creation of a learning environment which will help our students grow in a balanced way, with equal emphasis on a finely-tuned spiritual sensitivity, professional competence, and academic breadth and depth.*
>
> *We—the students, faculty, supporters and administration—are in a position to move forward together in the pursuit of our objectives. I am convinced that the special thing we are doing here at the Fuller Graduate School of Psychology is worth every ounce of energy we have to give.*[9]

So Neil C. Warren became the School of Psychology's second dean on January 1, 1975. He served in this position for seven years. During his tenure the endowment for the school was greatly increased due to Warren's outstanding effort and skill at fund-raising and the generous offer of a matching grant from alumnus William T. Weyerhaeuser. Further, under Warren's leadership, the Pasadena Community Counseling Center, the Church Consultation Center, and the Child Development Center were developed by Paul Clement into a full-fledged Psychological Center with 12 separate clinics. Warren obtained funding from the Irvine Foundation to assist in this expansion. At this time, the Psychological Center was probably the most complete training center in the nation for training clinical psychologist and was the first such center to be under the primary direction of psychologists, rather than psychiatrists. Warren was also the dean during the June 23, 1976, celebration at which Dean Emeritus Travis was presented the *festschrift, Psychologist Pro Tem: In Honor of the Eightieth Birthday of Lee Edward Travis.*[10] Admiring faculty members Tweedie and Clement edited the volume and planned the event.

Perhaps the most pleasant event of his deanship was planning for the retirement of Marnie Frederickson, the faithful executive secretary and administrative assistant to the deans of the School of Psychology. "Marnie," as everyone called her, had been with Fuller Seminary since 1959. She became part of the staff of the School of Psychology in 1963, a full year before the Pasadena Community Counseling Center was opened and two years before students came. She kept the records of all the planning that led up to the founding of the school and became the right-hand person for Donald Tweedie in the establishment of the Pasadena Community Counseling Center and deans Travis and Warren at a later date. She was deeply loved. Her gracious, affirming, yet thorough style endeared her to all who knew her. It was hard to think of the school without her. "The Marnie Frederickson Fall Festival" was held in her honor October 20 and 21, 1978.

In the morning of the first day, alumni held workshops.[11] This was followed in the afternoon by student presentations.[12] Also on that day, several faculty spoke on their current interests.[13] The second day of the festival, awards for the newly established Lee Edward Travis Prizes for the Integration of Theology and Psychology were awarded and Paul Clement and his assistants (Randy Miller, Kenneth Mathisen, and Jeff Prater) made a presentation on the APA Accreditation of Programs with Religious Requirements. Several alumni-led dialogues were also held.[14] After a service of Holy Communion, John Finch, Michael P. Maloney, and Leon Oettinger, all adjunct professors, made presentations. On the evening of this second day, a banquet was held at the Pasadena Civic Auditorium.[15] It was a wonderful time of celebration. The invitations said it well: "You are invited to share in expressing joy in knowing Marnie Frederickson, deep appreciation for her years of loving service, and heartfelt wishes for contentment in the next phase of her life."[16]

The most troublesome event of Warren's deanship was an episode that came to be known as "the Committee of Five." While the details of this event will remain for some future history of these years, it can be summarized by saying that five students protested the seminary's sexual standards and its religious criteria for student and faculty selection. They filed a grievance with the accreditation committee of the American Psychological Association. It took a great deal of Warren's energy during the late 1970s to salvage the situation and maintain the School of Psychology's accreditation.

Warren was an exhausted person when he went on sabbatical leave in the 1980-1981 academic year. Everyone knew he justly deserved this time away because of the energy it had taken to deal with the Committee of Five situation. However, no one realized how devastating the experience had been. So it was a surprise when he announced that he would retire from the deanship and enter full-time private practice at the end of the 1981-1982 year. He returned from Switzerland and spent the year in tying up the details. Warren moved his office two blocks away. He established his practice with Associated Psychological Services in Pasadena, where he had be a part-time psychotherapist for many years.

Warren Resigns, Hart Becomes Dean

Archibald D. Hart became the third dean of the School of Psychology in 1982. Hart had been assistant dean under Warren for a time before Warren went on sabbatical leave in 1980. He served as acting dean for the next two years and was elevated to the position of dean after a national search when Warren retired. Others considered for this position included David Benner of Wheaton College, John Powell of Michigan State University, Irving Severson of Pacific Lutheran College, and Richard A. Hunt of Southern Methodist University. Once again, as with Warren, the appointment of dean was made from within the faculty. Hart has served with distinction until June 1995. His tenure as dean has been the longest to date. Hart stated some of his vision in *Psychology News and Notes*, an in-house publication sent to all alumni and friends.[17]

Among many pleasant, as well as trying, events of his deanship was the celebration of Lee Travis' ninetieth birthday in June 1986.[18] During Hart's tenure, enrollment continued to increase to its present size of over 200 graduate students. A Doctor of Psychology (Psy.D.) degree was added to the Doctor of Philosophy (Ph.D.) degree the School of Psychology already offered. Further, in 1989 the seminary program in Marriage and Family Counseling (MFC) became part of the School of Psychology. Offering both master's and doctoral degrees, this program was headed by Dennis Guernsey until Thomas Needham was appointed associate dean in the early 1990s. Under Dean Hart, the faculty was increased to 20 full-time and a number of adjunct professors. American Psychological Association accreditation was maintained through Hart's and the faculty's assertive action in behalf of "Footnote 3" which allowed exceptions to guidelines regarding selection of students and faculty for religious institutions.

The most newsworthy accomplishment during Dean Hart's deanship was construction of a new three-story, steel and stucco edifice for housing administrative, teaching, clinical, and research facilities for the Graduate School of Psychology on Oakland Avenue. Hart, a trained civil engineer before becoming a psychologist, participated actively in designing the building as well as overseeing its construction. This new building for the school, though long-hoped-for and much-needed, was made possible only through the generosity of anonymous donors. The building was named the John Geoffrey Finch Hall in honor of the Tacoma psychologist who first conceived of the school and whose tireless efforts contributed so significantly to its beginning. Some years later, after indiscretions provoked the state of Washington to revoke Finch's license, the seminary trustees changed the name of the building to the Psychology Building. The 300-seat auditorium was named in honor of Lee Travis, the founding dean. The new building was dedicated on October 3, 1986.

In the late fall of 1994, Hart announced his decision to step down from the deanship and return to teaching as of June 1995. Hart has become widely known for his public presentations and writing of over 15 widely read volumes addressing many current concerns. He went on a one-year sabbatical leave in the fall of 1995, after which he indicated he would return to teach and to carry on his extensive public ministry to the nonseminary world.

Hart Announces His Retirement; Guy Appointed Dean

After an extensive search process in late fall and winter of 1994-1995, James D. Guy, Ph.D., vice president for university services at Biola University, was recommended by provost Rob Johnson to become the fourth dean of the School of Psychology. Dean Guy is a 1981 graduate of the school, was a student assistant to Dean Neil Warren. Guy brings to the role a wealth of administrative experience, a career as tenured professorship in the Rosemead School of Psychology and provost of administration at Biola University, and a distinguished publishing record.[19] The school is, once again, in good hands.

This history ends with the appointment of Guy as dean. It has recounted in detail only the deanship of Lee Edward Travis. These were the early years of the School of Psychology. In a sense they ended with the appointment of Lee Edward Travis as dean emeritus and distinguished professor of psychology at the June 1975 seminary graduation at which Travis was awarded an honorary Doctor of Science degree.[20] The end of an era, however, occurred with the death of Lee Travis in October 1987 at the age of 91 and the sale of the home on Red Rose Drive, Encino, and the move of Lysa to Encinitas, California, in January 1995. Donald Lindsley, eminent professor at UCLA who took his doctorate under Travis at Iowa, wrote an obituary of Lee's life for *The American Psychologist*.[21] As the scriptures report David's lamentation over Saul and Jonathan, we who knew the Travises now say of them, "Oh, how are the mighty fallen" (2 Samuel 1:19, RSV).

I hope this volume has provided a firm basis for future historians to take up where this account leaves off. Much has happened that is yet to be told. At the time of this writing, there have been nearly 500 graduates in clinical psychology and in marriage and family therapy whose careers are spread throughout the United States and in several foreign countries. As was stated in the preface, it is to the faithful service of these Christian mental health professionals that one should look to find the real history of these 31 years of one of the more innovative endeavors in modern Christian higher education. In words of Johann Sebastian Bach, "To God be the glory."

ENDNOTES

1. David Allan Hubbard, "The Deanship of the Graduate School of Psychology: Some Observations," November 1, 1972.
2. Letter from David Allan Hubbard to Lee Edward Travis, December 8, 1964.
3. Letter from David Allan Hubbard to Lars Granberg, December 16, 1964.
4. David Allan Hubbard, "New Dean for School of Psychology." *The Bulletin of Fuller Theological Seminary* (Feb.-Mar., 1975): 1.
5. This tradition has been continued by the wife of the third dean, Kathleen Hart. Up to the time of Dean Hart's resignation, she continued to meet weekly with spouses from all three schools for prayer and support. Her concern and care were deeply appreciated.
6. Paul W. Clement, in personal interview with H. Newton Malony, December 1994.
7. David Allan Hubbard to Lee Edward Travis, December 5, 1974.
8. Hubbard, "New Dean," *Bulletin of Fuller Theological Seminary* (Feb.-Mar., 1975).
9. _____ "Warren Appointed Dean." *Stimuli* (January, 1975): 1.
10. Donald F. Tweedie and Paul W. Clement, editors, *Psychologist Pro Tem: In Honor of the Eightieth Birthday of Lee Edward Travis* (Los Angeles, CA: University of Southern California Press, 1976).

11. The alumni who conducted workshops were as follows:
    David C. Bock—Integrating Psychology and Theology as a Private Practitioner
    Gary L. Brainerd—Basic Marriage Communication Training
    John P. Davis—The Enhancement of Self-Esteem
    William O. Evans—An Approach to Change in the Prison System
    Thomas J. Malcolm—The College Teaching of Psychology
    Clifford L. Penner and Joyce Penner—Team-Teaching and Team-Counseling Sexual Adjustment
    Edward B. Rettig—Behavior Modification in Business and Industry
    Robert C. Richard and David A. Flakoll—Establishing a Psychological Center Serving the Christian Community
12. The students who made presentations were as follows:
    John W. Fantuzzo and Richard C. Josiassen—Pedophilia Treatment Using Multi-stage Aversion Therapy and Social Skills Training
    Richard W. Raney—Stages in the Development of Moral Reasoning and Theology Come of Age
    Randolph K. Sanders—The Motivation Toward Competence and Integration of Psychology and Theology
    Scott R. Scribner—What Is Integration and Is Gary Collins Doing It?
    Sue Folk Smith—Church Member Recruitment/Involvement as a Function of Leadership Role Expectations
    Raymond L. Towne—The Problem of a Rigorous Psychotheology
13. Faculty who spoke were as follows:
    Archibald D. Hart—Current Feedback Procedures
    Clinton W. McLemore—The Status of Clinical Interaction Research
    Hendrika Vande Kemp—New Developments in Family Therapy
14. Alumni who led these dialogues were as follows:
    Bruce M. Bakeman—Military Psychology
    David A. Cater—Clinical Psychology in Large Hospital Settings
    Thomas A. Elkin and Walter W. Becker—Functional Integration: A Christian Psychological Center
    William N. Kennemer—Developing a Private Practice
    Claude P. Ragan—Christian Faith Commitment and Psychology
    Roy E. Shearer—Establishing a Counseling Center in a Church
    Martin E. Shoemaker—Psychological Aspects of Chronic Pain
15. H. Newton Malony was master of ceremonies. Special music was provided by Freeman Davis, bass soloist, and the choir of La Cañada Presbyterian Church. Tributes were given by Dean Emeritus Travis, President Hubbard, alumnus William O. Evans, seminary colleague Inez Smith, student Joe Verga, staff member Janie Elson, and faculty member Paul Clement. Highlight of the evening was an old Young Life skit performed by alumnus James R. Oraker. Dean Warren closed the evening by speaking on "Where Do We Go From Here?"

Chapter 10 – Travis Retires – Warren Becomes Dean

16. As usual, institutions go on after the retirement of even their most treasured staff. This has been no less true of the School of Psychology. Marnie Frederickson has been followed by two outstanding and equally appreciated administrative assistants to the dean. These have been Dorie Lott, 1978-1983, and Bertha "Bert" Jacklitch, who continues to hold this important position to the time of the publishing of this volume. Without question, their names will appear prominently in the volumes to follow which will recount the history of Fuller's School of Psychology since the deanship of Lee Travis.
17. Hart statement.
18. The celebration of Lee Edward Travis' ninetieth birthday was held in the Barker Commons of Fuller Seminary, June 13, 1986. Louis H. Evans, Jr., the pastor under whom Lee had his religious experience, gave the Invocation and John Crowley presented Lee a key to the city of Pasadena in his role as mayor. Tributes to Travis were paid by William O. Evans, the first graduate; President Hubbard; Donald McGavran, dean of the School of World Mission; John Finch; Professors Clement and Warren; and Douglas Umetsu, the last graduate chaired by Travis. Christopher Rosik presented to Lee a copy of *The 1983 Travis Papers in the Integration of Psychology and Theology* which he and Professor Malony had recently edited. Dorie Lott, successor to Marnie Frederickson paid tribute to Lysa Travis, and Dean Hart gave an appreciation. Travis delivered the following poem to his wife:

    At midnight in the winter, we were married
    May we never be without but always within each other
    Beginning now and ending never
    May we always be together
    I live only and constantly in relation to you
    Together we stand in awe of one of the other and in need one of the other
    In what I do to you I see the image and hear my echo
    In what I think of you I stand naked before myself
    Nothing is more precious save what is I in you and what is you in me
    Will I fare well when you search me out
    And will I fare well when I search you out
    May I come to you defenseless knowing that nothing stands between us
    That in your presence I stand fully revealed
    I long to be one with you and to have you at one with me
    That through our oneness we may find oneness with all others.

    Lee Edward Travis died at the age of 91 on October 9, 1987. He taught a class at the School of Psychology until a few weeks before his death.
19. His best-known publication is *James D. Guy, The Personal Life of the Psychotherapist* (New York: John Wiley & Sons, 1987)

20. The Citation for Lee Edward Travis at the awarding of the honorary Doctor of Science degree was as follows:

    Lee Edward Travis
    This is a Salute to a Pioneer.
    You linked technology to psychology
    in a way that baffled and
    astonished your peers in your
    early researches in electroencephalography.

    This is a Salute to a Pioneer.
    You took struggling stutterers
    and pointed the way for them to become
    world class therapists.

    This is a Salute to a Pioneer.
    You found an infant discipline
    and nurtured it to a maturity that has
    released the gift of speech in
    countless thousands of children and adults.

    This is a Salute to a Pioneer.
    You seized an idea about
    Christian training of competent
    clinical psychologists and shaped it into
    a plan, a program, a faculty,
    a curriculum, a student body and a national force.

    In the days of space pioneering
    someone remarked that with the
    scientists we should have sent to space
    a theologian to see what is happening
    and a poet to tell us about it.

    Though a speech pioneer,
    not a space pioneer,
    Lee Travis, you could have been sent
    on such a mission alone.
    You are a man who can see human behavior,
    human need, human potential
    through the eyes of faith.

Chapter 10 – Travis Retires – Warren Becomes Dean

You are a man who can describe your
special blend of Christian commitment.
Your pioneering has been made less lonely
because you have the uncommon gift
of taking the rest of us with you.

In recognition of what you have given
through technical achievement in speech pathology,
through scholarly supervision of nearly
two hundred doctoral theses,
through the decade of visionary
leadership of the Graduate School of
Psychology as founding dean,
we wish to honor you with the seminary's highest tribute.

On nomination of the faculties of
Fuller Theological Seminary
on approval of the Board of Trustees,
and by virtue of the authority vested in
me by the state of California,
I hereby confer on Lee Edward Travis
the honorary degree of Doctor of Science
with all the rights and privileges
appertaining thereto.

> David Allan Hubbard
> Fuller Seminary Graduation, June 1975

21. Donald B. Lindsley, "Obituary: Lee Edward Travis (1896-1987)" (*American Psychologist*, 1989,44) p. 1414.

Appendices

The Importance of a View of Man

John G. Finch

(The first of three lectures delivered by John Finch at Fuller Theological Seminary in the spring of 1961)

The pervasive influence of psychoanalytical perspectives is apparent everywhere. Plays, such as Arthur Miller's "Death of a Salesman," and theological works, notably the works of Emil Brunner and Paul Tillich, as contrasted as they appear—have been deeply influenced by psychoanalytical motives. Courts of law are increasingly influenced in their judgments by whether or not the lawbreaker should be punished or hospitalized. The psychoanalytical motif directly and indirectly constitutes the basis for much television entertainment. This implies a new of understanding of the nature of man. The response of the audiences appears to be significant enough to warrant a continuation of this perspective from a purely financial viewpoint. It also indicates an increasing measure of self-awareness through identification and thus audience participation. Essentially, the question is: What is man?

A view of man is basic to any psychology, just as to any theology. Man is the focal point at which these two, among other disciplines, meet. Therefore, some clarification of the nature of man as defined by psychoanalysis is important. While it is true that each of the above-named disciplines adheres to its own presuppositions, each inevitably arrives at a view of man. The question pertinent to this discussion is: What is the psychoanalytical view of man? Unless one is able to clarify this in terms of the basic assumptions of psychoanalysis, and unless one is able to arrive at a coherent view of man, the concepts which emerge are impossible to compare. Thus, the concept of sin implies value judgments. Psychoanalysis professes not to be concerned with value judgments. It speaks of neurosis, etc. How then can a valid comparison be made between sin and neurosis without standing on the same platform? This platform is the nature of man.

The Importance of a View of Man

Statement of the Problem

This study attempts (1) to survey the criticisms of Freud's view of man, as brought by some of his main dissenters and (2) to analyze them from the standpoint of their implications for a Christian anthropology.

In doing this, Freud's view of man will be summarized, then the criticisms of the dissenters will be summarized. Finally, we will draw some generalizations and make some observations. This discussion limits itself to a concept which appears to protrude as a common factor in the writings of all these early associates in the development of psychoanalysis. This concept is the notion of "spirit." Now, of course, we are quite aware of the fact that this *spirit* is a difficult and elusive word. The temptation to coerce its meaning is ever-present. Moreover, since the word is used almost loosely and lightly by some and not at all by others, more specifically Freud, one is aware of the hazardousness of this undertaking. In order then to follow a circumspect path, our procedure will be to first determine whether or not the individual psychologist's assumptions will permit consideration of such a dimension as *spirit*. Having passed this test, the next step will be to determine what characteristics are ascribed to this dimension. The third step will consist of correlating and comparing the characteristics of *spirit* as it is seen by the psychologists under consideration.

Having arrived at some comprehensive outline of the nature of spirit in the writings of the psychologists, an attempt will be made to compare the notion of spirit in psychology with the notion of spirit in some Christian theology. This last attempt is indicated because when two disciplines with different presuppositions talk about something, it is necessary to determine whether or not they are talking about the same thing, or whether they even can be talking *of* the same thing. The problem of communication between the disciplines of psychology and theology is a most difficult one, but a most urgent one. The subject matter of both, i.e., man, is the same.

Obviously some attempt to understand man from a common point of view is most relevant. If a common viewpoint is achieved, a vital step forward has been taken. But even if one does not arrive at a common viewpoint, at least some ground has been gained by eliminating some confusion. Therefore, the underlying question that will guide this discussion is: To what extent, if any, do their assumptions converge?

A. Introduction

The prolixity, the novelty, and the constant revision of their own concepts leaves them open to the criticisms of ambiguity, inconsistency and, at times, contradiction.

B. *The Physico-Chemical Premise—A Mechanistic View*

In the autumn of 1895, just before the writing of his magnum opus, *The Interpretation of Dreams* in 1900, in his project for a scientific psychology, Freud outlined the theoretical framework for his future research into the nature of man. In the Introduction, Freud states:

> *The intention of this project is to furnish us with a psychology which shall be a natural science: Its aim, that is, is to represent physical processes as quantitatively determined states of specifiable material particles and so to make them plain and void of contradictions.*

To run through the section headings of the project is sufficient to acquaint the reader with the strong physico-chemical bent of mind which was set to wrestle with the facts of human experience and the human organism. In Section 8, speaking of consciousness and basing his findings on the foregoing sections of the project, Freud writes:

> *Only by means of these complicated and far-from-self-evident hypotheses have I so far succeeded in introducing the phenomena of consciousness into the structure of qualitative psychology.*

Attention is drawn to three ideas in the foregoing quotations: (1) Freud's physico-chemical intention and objective; (2) his attempt to reduce even consciousness to a physico-chemical quantity; and (3) the "far-from-self-evident hypotheses" building up to this conclusion.

Now it must be said, in fairness to Freud's work, that as early as 1896, he was losing interest in the problem of representing the psychical apparatus in terms of neuropsychology. Years later, he alluded to the failure of his efforts in that direction in the following words:

> *Research has afforded irrefutable proof that mental activity is bound up with the function of the brain as with that of no other organ. The discovery of the unequal importance of the different parts of the brain and their individual relations to particular parts of the body and to intellectual activities takes us a step further—we do not know how big*

a step. But every attempt to deduce from these facts a localization of mental processes, every endeavor to think of ideas as stored up on nerve-cells and of excitations as traveling along nerve-fibres, has completely miscarried.

While this appears to reverse Freud's physico-chemical approach to an understanding of man, it must be noted that many years elapsed between the formulation of the project in 1922 and its repudiation, and that during these years some of his most basic writings came into existence, for instance, *The Interpretation of Dreams*, and the all-important *Introductory Lectures on Psychoanalysis* in 1922. It must be noted further that there is never a repudiation of the method of natural science. As James Strachey suggests in the Editorial Note for Freud's *Interpretation of Dreams*, Freud "certainly never gave up his belief that ultimately a physical groundwork for psychology would be established." It seems characteristic of Freud that he never repudiated anything openly; rather he became silent about certain issues and proceeded to introduce new ideas and new terms. To understand the nature of man, it would appear proper to begin with Freud's own starting point, viz., a discussion of the instincts and the libido.

According to Freud, "there can be no question that the libido has somatic sources, that it streams into the ego from various organs and parts of the body." Or, as he elsewhere puts it:

The source is a state of excitation within the body, and its aim is to remove that excitation; in the course of its path from its source to the attainment of its aim, the instinct becomes operative mentally (No explanation of how this change takes place is given.) The aim can be attained in the subject's own body but as a rule an external object is introduced in which the instinct attains its external aim; its internal aim is always a somatic modification which is experienced as satisfaction.

Before the full impact of these quotations can be assessed, some attention should be given to the development of instincts in Freudian psychology. The theory of instincts reached its present state in four steps: Freud's first step was to set up two groups of instincts—the sexual and the ego instincts. His early work emphasized interest in the concrete description of the sexual instincts. The ego aspects of the instincts were left ambiguous. Here the dualistic nature of the instincts is encountered. In the second step, Freud introduced the concept of narcissism into libido, which led to the postulation of a libidinal component of the ego instincts. The third step is described by Freud in the last sections of his paper on "Instincts and Their Vicissitudes" (1915), and discusses the relation between love and hate, in which hate is regarded as a nonlibidinal reaction of the ego. It is only in the fourth step that the confusion clears, due to a growing knowledge of the structure of the mental apparatus as a whole and its division into a vital stratum (the id), and an organized part (the ego) and, more specifically, to a study of the unconscious regions of the ego—the superego. The substance of this view is that aggressive trends are no longer regarded as the primary attributes of the ego instincts, but as independently existent instincts of aggression and destruction existing side-by-side with the sexual instincts in the vital strata of the mind. The ego instincts cease to be independent entities and are derived partly from the libidinal and partly from the aggressive instincts.

In his posthumous work, *An Outline of Psychoanalysis* in 1949, Freud adds a final note: "After long doubts and vacillations we have decided to assume the existence of only two basic instincts, eros and the destructive instinct.

This is the history and development of the theory of instincts. Now, according to the most general definitions, instinct is an energy arising from the vital stratum of the body and having a direction which is determined inherently. This indeed appears to be the most prominent feature of Freud's theory of instincts. It has the merit of locating "the instincts in the organs of the body" and, in turn, of facilitating an "understanding of the more constant biological roots of behavior" (Edward Bibring, 1941).

Bibring, upon whose work the outline of Freud's theory of instincts partly rests, says that "Freud's theory of instincts (was) built directly upon clinico-psychological data and problems. It was a biological theory of instincts, since it rested almost entirely upon biological considerations." And again, "as we know, psychoanalysis has always had a biological orientation."

Here, then, emerges the first article of Freud's doctrine of man. Man is composed of and governed by the instincts. The locus of the instincts is the id. "The id remains the reservoir of instinctual needs which press toward immediate fulfillment. Its origin is somatic and it is the major source of the drive energy" (Munroe, 1955). Freud described the manner in which the latent and completely unconscious drives of the id find expression through his term ego. Ego is the experiencer of outer reality's demands and the regulator of the flow of energy from the id. This drama of suppression and expression all takes place in terms of the unconscious demands of the superego which, as it were, provides the rules of the game.

Now analyzing this a bit further, and bearing the biological emphasis carefully in mind, it might be observed that the ego controls the untamed impulses of the id in terms of the gratification or security of the organism, in relation to the unconscious demands of the superego. Indeed, it was his need to discover a motif that caused Freud to set up the two basic instincts of *eros and thanatos*. Thus, to clarify the nature of the organism, the following depicts, it would appear, how the drama of life (on a Freudian level) would proceed.

The human child is born completely helpless. In its helplessness, the id finds gratification of its impulses. Through the process of approval and disapproval, the ego mechanism of the id begins to thwart or encourage free gratification in strict relation to a feeling of well-being—the "pleasure-unpleasure principle"—in terms of preserving the organism alive. Thus does Freud attempt to develop the conscience out of the fact of the biological helplessness of the infant. So, in easy steps, violating the demands of the superego would produce disapproval and insecurity. Insecurity would be a threat to the very existence of the organism. Thus the ego would assert itself and restore the equilibrium. In this manner, too, Freud accounts for all anxiety states. Thus, to quote Ruth L. Munroe, who notes this same biologism as characteristic about Freud, "It is characteristic of Freud that he could not accept even anxiety as a simple fact but felt that it must be biologically explained."

C. Another Possible Interpretation—A Dynamic View

The Ego and the Id, first published in 1923, could be used as the possible point of departure for what has been termed the dynamic view as against the mechanistic view in Freud's view of man. The use of the word "against" in the preceding sentence attempts to draw attention to the substantial difference between the mechanistic and dynamic conceptions. As Franz Alexander, a staunch Freudian, points out, "The dynamic principles of psychoanalysis are independent of theories concerning the ultimate nature of instincts."

Thus, a sort of split is implied in Freudian principles. Man is viewed on the one hand as a biological entity no different from any other organism and, on the other, as a dynamic being capable of transcending himself with a different point of purchase. Of course, this is the age-old problem: Which impinges on which—spirit or flesh? Only in Freudian research and with his presuppositional premises as already outlined, there appears to be no concept of spirit.

Nevertheless, the impingement of this transcendental quality does not appear to be altogether lacking. Thus, for example, in *The Ego and the Id*, Freud makes his first attempt to outline the total structure and functioning of what he calls the "mental apparatus." He distinguishes three structurally different parts: the id, the ego and the superego. He represents the id as the original powerhouse of the mental apparatus; it contains the inherited instinctive forces which at birth are not yet organized into a coordinated system. The ego is taken to be the emergent adaptive mechanism which plays the homeostatic role mediating between the instincts among themselves and the environment. The superego, in the main unconscious, is the precipitate of adaptation. Included in it are the accumulation of parental, social, and cultural standards. The question which is not answered in so many words is: Is the ego physical or psychical? Where does the physical begin, and where does the psychical leave off? Or vice versa? In assigning a homeostatic role to the ego, obviously some independence of both the id and the superego must be necessary. Yet it is likewise true that the ego is inextricably and indissolubly intermingled with, influenced by, and influencing the id. It is in this work specifically that Freud grapples with the homeostatic function of the ego. Here he makes mention of the mental function beyond his previous brain psychology. Moreover, the mental functions have relevance to the total organism. The ego's function, according to Freud, is to coordinate and regulate rational behavior—behavior not in violation of the superego and the id needs. Thus the function of the ego is geared to the maintenance of a constant condition (level of excitation) within the organism (stability principle). In short, the ego functions very much like the radar device in the nose of an airplane which anticipates all the variations in the weather and attempts to maintain the equilibrium of the plane. This equilibrium is, of course, preyed upon by the biological drives within the organism no less than by external stimuli and also by superego demands. It was

The Importance of a View of Man

through Freud's ingenuity that he discovered the principles by which the ego performs this homeostatic task. These principles, four in number, are: (1) internal perception of existing needs; (2) external perception of existing conditions; (3) the integrative faculties by which the ego coordinates instinctive urges with one another and with the requirements of the superego and adapts them to the environmental conditions; and (4) the executive faculty by which the ego controls voluntary behavior.

In the performance of its duty of homeostasis, the ego frequently runs counter to the urge of the id to seek immediate gratification—the "pleasure-pain principle." It is the duty of the ego to ensure that immediate gratification of id impulses will not lead to the ultimate ruin of the organism. Thus, the ego learns such tactical and strategic maneuvers as will enable it to ensure the greatest happiness and security of the organism. The results of the techniques which the ego uses may be called "rational behavior." Rational behavior is arduously learned through the process of experimentation and habit formation with the objective of expending a minimum amount of energy—the "economy principle." Of course, with the growth of the organism and changing circumstances, the ego is forced to new reckoning all along the line. But because of the economy principle, the "principle of inertia" sets in. That is, such factors as "fixation"—the tendency to retain previously acquired patterns; "regression"—the tendency to return to earlier successful patterns whenever the ego's integrative ingenuity is threatened, or "repetition compulsion"—the tendency to repeat previously acquired patterns in accordance with the general principle of economy (inertia)—are brought into play instead of rising to the challenge and working at the task of finding new ways of behavior, of finding new solutions to new problems instead of trying to use old solutions for new problems.

Another device which the human being uses to handle problems is "identification." This is a process by which the growing child incorporates the behavior patterns and attitudes of adults. The manipulative or homeostatic function of the ego is never at an end, according to Freud. It is this factor that prompted Freud's structural conception, differentiating the ego from the id. The id, he assumes, continues to be noncooperative and keeps seeking isolated gratification. It is this turmoil of the id whence arose such psychological phenomena which are not rational or coordinated, such as dreams, fantasies and impulsive behavior. Whenever the id threatens the ego's homeostatic function, the ego reacts with anxiety, and in turn brings into play one or more of its arsenal of defense mechanisms. The first and principal of these mechanisms which Freud notes was "repression." Repression, according to Freud, is the simple technique of excluding from consciousness the psychological content of that which it cannot absorb or include harmoniously in its framework. Or, another defense mechanism is overcompensation, i.e., conformity to cover up hostility, exhibitions of superiority to cover feelings of inferiority. There are numerous other defenses that ego uses to maintain equilibrium in the organism. Thus, rationalization, identification, substitution and displacement, conversion, self-rejection, regression, projection, provocative behavior, isolation, sublimation, and guilt feelings are among some of the most important.

The point being made is that in the dynamic conception of Freud's discoveries, were it possible to forget the strong biological basis with which he started and which he emphasized and insisted on, a view of the human could be outlined which would remove some of the obstacles to his presuppositions as seen by the dissenters and perhaps to his scientific naturalism. To see the incisiveness and precision with which Freud describes the homeostatic role of the ego, almost creates "guilt feelings" for not being able to include him among the phenomenologists. For the way the ego functions in the Freudian system, it is quite easy to see it in a transcendental role. It appears as the self (the ego) which rises above itself (the id). The ego quite clearly takes an objective view, stands aside from itself and dominates and controls persons in the sense of growing them beyond what they are. According to this dynamic conception, it is entirely possible to see a more dynamic freedom than the strictly causalistic, naturalistic assumption will warrant. It is not difficult to see the creative and recreative, the free and responsible aspects of such an ego as Freud describes. Indeed, this dimension of man as seen by Freud, if his presuppositions and biologism be discarded or modified, could with his permission be called with the dissenters, the dimension of *spirit*.

It would be a quite congenial task to place Freud altogether in the camp of the dissenters and make a phenomenologist out of him. It would be no less profitable from a psychological point of view to do with Freud what so many of the so-called nondissenters have done, viz., emphasize his later discoveries, underplay his premises and biologism, add to him from Jung and Meyer et al., and create what Franz Alexander and the "Chicago school" have produced—a "dynamic psychiatry"—or assign him a place of eminence as the non-Freudians have done and then modify and edit his views a la Fromm, Horney, and others. But this leads to numerous problems. First, there is Freud himself. Freud nowhere repudiates his presuppositions nor his naturalistic assumptions. It may be said that his later discoveries repudiated them automatically, but even this statement denies what he put forth in his posthumous work, *An Outline of Psychoanalysis,* in 1949, in which he endeavored to return everything to the life-and-death instincts on a biological plane. Second, it would be difficult to reorient Freud. That was what the dissenters failed to accomplish and hence their dissent.

To further implement the limitations of the Freudian presuppositions and premises, attention is drawn to the development away from biological Freudianism in the writings of those who have not chosen to repudiate Freud altogether, but who have modified and edited his findings to a substantial and important degree. Even the New York Psychoanalytic Society, which is the largest organization of analysis in that city, is moderately classic or eclectic. The tendency is definitely in the direction of a more dynamic view. This point is noted to bring to focus the varying and, if necessary, contrary views of Freud's findings. Of course, it is the liberty of each person to select his or her own material, and in Freud this may be done to real advantage. However, when those closest to him, the dissenters, found it necessary to withdraw on the grounds of his scientific naturalism and limited presuppositions, as will be seen in the next lectures, that is only one more reason for being cautious to interpret Freud from a phenomenological point of view. Freud's biologism will be further considered from the standpoint of his early orientation and stated objectives.

D. *The View of Man*

Now the question may be raised: With this as the fundamental basis of Freud's view of man, what can be the sum and substance of the matter?

First, man is a biological organism on a plane with other biological organisms and is capable of being understood on this basis, viz., a naturalistic scientific basis. Man is void of ontological or eschatological dimensions.

Second, the objective of man's existence is the instinctual need to continue to exist. To this end the eros principle, under which Freud included the instincts of self-preservation, and the reality principle aided and abetted. Or, as Freud states, "The phenomena of life (biologically) would then be explicable from the interplay of the two and their counteracting effects on each other."

Third, if the question is asked: What kind of man is this? Freud's answer would be: He is driven by the impulses of the id and the unconscious. The unconscious is "disfigured by a gigantic hypocrisy." It is as dark and dismal a canyon of hate as can be found anywhere.

Fourth, what is Freud's view of man as a moral or religious being? At this point, as at all points, man as a moral being can only be defined by implication and in conformity with Freud's naturalistic, scientific biologism. Religion is an illusion, while at the base of all morality and good deeds is the instinct of self-preservation. The finest expression of altruism is only an accommodation of the instincts for purposes of self-preservation.

Fifth, what of the old problems of free-will and determinism in relation to Freud's man? Since man is set in a naturalistic milieu and driven by the instincts, freedom is another illusion. Of course the gospel of Freud has been summed up in his words: "Where id was, there shall ego be." But as far as man's being a creature of the unconscious, Freud's view was bleak and black with pessimism. For instance, in writing to Lou Andreas-Salome, a former fellow-student of his and one who had a "remarkable flair for great men," Freud wrote:

> *I do not doubt that mankind will surmount even this war, but I know for certain that I and my contemporaries will never again see a joyous world. It is all too hideous, and the saddest thing about it is that it has come out just as from our psychoanalytical expectations we should have imagined man and his behaviour. Because of this attitude I have never been able to agree with your blithe optimism. My secret conclusion was: Since we can only regard the highest civilization of the present disfigured by a gigantic hypocrisy, it follows that we are organically unfitted for it. We have to abdicate, and the Great Unknown, he or it, lurking behind fate, will sometime repeat such an experiment with another race.*

The Importance of a View of Man

At this point it must be stated that absolute consistency and clarity without ambiguity are not to be expected of Freud. His was a developing and creating mind. While he established the premises upon which he intended to proceed, there are indications that he wandered from his objectives. This is not intended as a criticism of him, but merely as a precautionary note to the reader. Freud's view of man as summarized above is in reasonably strict conformity with the main outlines of his thought. Other indications have been omitted so as not to fog the issues.

It is also to be noted that not a little of the detailed analysis of Freud's view of man is seen by inference from the basic outline of his psychology.

E. Influences that Molded Freud's Thinking

To see the influences that played an important role in the thinking of Freud is to further stabilize the view of man abstracted from his writings. Thus, if it can be shown that Freud followed in a certain tradition, it will help to identify his position. No exhaustive attempt will be made at this point, but only a bare outline of those influences which molded his thinking.

In this connection, perhaps a personal psychoanalysis of Freud would be most revealing. This cannot be undertaken. In his work *The Death and Rebirth of Psychology* in 1956, Ira Progoff has done quite an admirable job of this very thing. However, such an analysis must be quite highly speculative and therefore subject to serious differences of opinion.

For purposes of this paper, some assistance will be sought in Freud himself and in the findings of his official biographer, Ernest Jones (1952, 1955, 1957).

Freud's orientation on the naturalistic, scientific level appears to be weighted with a predisposition to see the organism "not only as a part of the physical universe, but the world of organisms itself as one of the family." Freud was a devout admirer of Ernest Brucke. Brucke (1819-1892) was a neurophysiologist whose death preceded any of Freud's publications on psychopathology. Brucke and Du Bois-Raymond

> pledged a solemn oath to put into effect this truth: No other forces than the common physical-chemical ones are active within the organism. In these cases which cannot at the time be explained by these forces one

has either to find the specific way or form of their action by means of the physical-mathematical method or to assume new forces, equal in dignity to the chemico-physical forces inherent in matter, reducible to the forces of attraction and repulsion (Jones, 1952).

Still another influence in Freud's youth was Hermann Helmholtz (1821-1894), who was referred to by Freud as one of his idols. Helmholtz was one of the most outstanding members of the group to which Brucke belonged. Helmholtz had started a scientific movement which became known as the Helmholtz School of Medicine. He did a great deal of work in physiological reactions to stimuli. He is one of the discoverers of the Law of Conservation of Energy, the inventor of the ophthalmoscope, and is best known to physiologists for his great work on the senses of sight and hearing. Jones, in his biography of Freud, gives an account of these men and then writes:

These men formed a small private club which in 1845 they enlarged to the Berliner Physikalische Gesellschaft (Berlin Society of Physicists). *Most of its members were young students of Johannes Muller, physicists and physiologists banded together to destroy, once and for all, vitalism, the fundamental belief of their admired master.*

Freud's sympathies lay quite clearly in the direction of the Berlin Society of Physicists and, on his own admission, he accepted their apparent bias against vitalism, and was for the physiologizing of all phenomena including mental phenomena.

The following account of the physical physiology that captivated the student Freud is abstracted from the introductory pages of Brucke's lectures on physiology, published in 1874:

Physiology is the science of organism as such. Organisms differ from dead material entities in action—machines—in possessing the faculty of assimilation, but they are all phenomena of the physical world; systems of atoms, moved by forces, according to the principles of the conservation of energy. Progress in knowledge reduces them to two—attraction and repulsion. All this applies as well to the organism man.

Does this not clearly adumbrate the sense and spirit of the project in 1922?

In 1926 (12 years before the death of Freud), Jones points out that "in spirit and content" the words Freud used of psychoanalysis characterize the words of Brucke. "The forces assist or inhibit one another, combine with one another, enter into compromises with one another." Evidently, though in 1915 Freud renounced the project (in *The Origins of Psychoanalysis*, 1956) as having miscarried, its premises and motivations had not been eliminated from his work.

Freud also seems to have imbibed Brucke's high regard for Charles Darwin. "In this evolution of life, no spirits, essences or entelechies, no superior plans or ultimate purposes are at work. The physical energies alone cause effects—somehow."

If specific attention is drawn to Freud's devotion to a "physical-mathematical" method, it is merely to emphasize that this was the viewpoint from which Freud attempted to understand man. Several references to Darwin are noted in Freud's *Totem and Taboo* (1955—first published in 1913), while in his *Moses and Monotheism* (1939) he acknowledges that the argument in *Totem and Taboo* "started from some comments by Charles Darwin." And later on he says, "I made use of certain theoretical reflections of Charles Darwin and Atkinson, and especially Robertson Smith." These references help sketch the bent of mind and the framework of reference to which Freud was to bring his research data.

Jones quotes a paper of Freud's in which the latter attempted to establish himself in the line of the Polish astronomer Copernicus (1473-1543) and the English naturalist Charles Darwin (1809-1882), a contemporary of Freud. Copernicus had ushered in a cosmological revolution. Darwin introduced a biological evolution. Freud believed he was in their line by creating a psychological revolution.

Yet another significant insight is brought out by Jones in a letter Freud wrote to Karl Abraham in which he says, "Our intention is to place Lamarck (a French naturalist, 1744-1829) entirely on our basis."

But there was another kind of influence that appears to have left its mark on Freud. Being heir to the product of such minds as Nietzsche (1841-1900), Darwin (1809-1882), Schopenhauer (1788-1860), Goethe (1749-1832) and Lamarck (1744-1829) gave Freud a bent of mind that almost inevitably began by equating the scientific method with a naturalistic philosophy. Albert Outler emphasizes this suggestion:

> It has never been sufficiently noticed that from Freud to Fromm and Alexander, the men who have made psychotherapy were themselves heirs of a curious double legacy from the eighteenth and nineteenth centuries. They are direct descendants of the eighteenth century

> *'Enlightenment,' that tremendous secular revolution against Christianity. . . . Even a cursory examination of psychotherapeutic literature will show how deeply this secularist, humanist worldview and commitment has entered into its outlook and main conceptions.*

In the light of Freud's working hypothesis and assumptions, in the light of his scientific and philosophical forebears, the view of man that has been adduced from his work appears reasonably consistent. If, as has been observed in Section C of this chapter (Another Possible Interpretation—A Dynamic View), the phenomenological possibilities in Freud stand out, in the interest of internal consistency, as also consistency with his orientation and stated objectives, this must be seen as a strain on his presuppositions and a consequent criticism of his own methodology. The question that arises from this analysis and which will receive attention in a later lecture is: How defensible are Freud's presuppositions, and hence his view of man?

Freud and the Dissenters

John G. Finch

*(The second of three lectures delivered by John Finch at
Fuller Theological Seminary in the spring of 1961)*

Time is a limiting factor in pursuing in any great detail our discussion of the dissenters and their reason for dissenting from Freud. But it would give us some of their feelings if we could at least sample each of the dissenters. It would also add significant weight to our contention that by adhering rigidly to a preconceived naturalistic theory, Freud mutilated the nature of man on a procrustean bed. But, without further comment, let us hear the dissenters themselves voice their objections, bearing in mind that they started out being admirers of, and collaborators with, Freud.

In his Introduction to *The Neurotic Constitution* (1926), Alfred Adler (1870-1937) says:

Less for the purpose of following a critical bent than for the purpose of making clear my own position, I beg leave to separate from the fruitful and valuable contributions of Freud three of his fundamental views as erroneous, inasmuch as they threaten to impede progress in the understanding of the neurosis. The first objection is directed against the view that the libido is the motive force behind the phenomena of the neurosis. On the contrary, it is the neurosis which shows more clearly than does normal psychic conduct how by means of this neurotic positing of a "final purpose," the apperception of pleasure, its selection and power are driven in the direction of this final purpose so that the neurotic can really only follow the allurement of the acquisition of pleasure with his healthy psychic force, so to speak, while for the neurotic portion only "higher" goals are of value . . . the libido, the sex impulses, and the tendencies in accordance with this guiding principle, no matter whence they originate.

Here a quite fundamental difference is made. Whereas in Freud the etiology of the neuroses is purely biological, resulting from a frustration of libidinal energy, in Adler the trouble is teleological. Or it may be put this way: for Freud, neuroses are propelled from behind; in Adler they are propelled from in front. For Adler, neuroses result from an attempt to overcompensate by attaching oneself to an excessive goal. For Freud, sex is the prime cause. In Adler, there is a hint that sexual perversions are symptoms and not causes. It is used or abused to the end of attaining mastery over the situation.

This readily anticipates Adler's second objection which "is directed against the sexual etiology of the neuroses":
> It is strange that Freud, a skillful connoisseur of the symbolic in life, was not able to discover the symbolic in "sexual apperception," to recognize the sexual as a jargon, a "modus dicendi."

He then goes on to his third objection to Freudian dogma, which is the rejection of the idea
> that the neurotic is under the influence of infantile wishes, which come to life nightly (dream theory) as well as in connection with certain occasions in life. In reality these infantile wishes already stand under the compulsion of the imaginary goal and themselves usually bear the character of a guiding thought suitably arrayed, and adapt themselves to symbolic expression purely for reasons of thought economy.

Additionally, Adler does not see a neurosis as arising
> out of any sort of biological or constitutional primitive force, but (it) has received direction and motivation from the compensatory superstructure and the schematic guiding principle. Its emergence took place under the pressure of uncertainty, its tendency to personify itself is the doubtful success of the craving for security.

Here there appears to be a clear expression of his differences with Freud. There is no sexual emphasis in Adler. Sex is just one of the by-products which may lend themselves to a need for compensation and therefore the creation of an improper goal. Adler states:
> Freud assumes a sexual constitution as the basis of the neuroses and psychoses, under which terms he understands a qualitatively and quantitatively varying arrangement of partial sex impulses. The development of perverse inclinations and their unsuccessful repression into the unconscious furnishes, according to him, the picture of the neurosis and in itself forms the primary cause for the neurotic psyche. We shall see from our considerations that the perversion, so far as it reaches development in the neuroses and psychoses, is not dependent upon a connate impulse, but that it arises from the striving toward a fictitious goal in connection with which the repression takes place as a by-product under the pressure of the self-consciousness. That which is to be taken cognizance of biolog-

ically in an originally abnormal sexual conduct, namely, the greater functional valency as well as the compensatory psychic superstructure indicates directly as I have shown in my "Studie" a congenital defect of the sexual organ.

Here, note the place Adler assigns to the role of sex. Its primacy in the etiology of the neuroses is set aside, its relevance appearing only when there is "a congenital defect in the sexual organ." Once again he turns to purpose, end, or *telos* as the prime cause for neuroses.

It must be noted at this point in the discussion that while Adler was basing his theory on empirical facts as they appeared in his patients, more justice is done in the interpretation of both Freud and Adler when it is remembered that Freud was attempting to subsume all the activities of the psyche under the biological drives, while Adler was unable to limit psychic activity to purely biological drives and was trying to give expression to something more comprehensive. His complaint was against Freud's reification ("thingification") of man. Adler was attempting to understand man as a totality.

This becomes even more apparent when Adler's use of the evolutionary hypothesis is noted. By and large he accepts this hypothesis, his exception at this point being similar to Jung's. He sees a psychological fact in the idea of God, though he treats it with a guarded reserve. More important to this discussion is his consideration of selectivity in evolution.

Speaking of the compensatory mechanism, Adler bases his doctrine on the evolutionary hypothesis of selectivity:

With the release from the maternal organism there begins for those inferior organs or systems of organs the struggle with the outside world, which must of necessity ensue and which is initiated with greater vehemence than is the more normally developed apparatus. This struggle is accompanied by greater mortality and morbidity rates. This fetal character, however, at the same time furnishes the increased possibility for compensation and overcompensation, increases the adaptability to ordinary and extraordinary resistances and assures the attainment of new and higher forms, new and higher accomplishments. Thus the inferior organs furnish the inexhaustible material by means of which the organism continuously seeks to reach a better accord with the altered conditions of life through adaptation, repudiation, and improvement.

Here, the instinct of self-preservation appears to receive attention, or the techniques which ensure the survival of those who adapt themselves. But it is significant that Adler does not confine his doctrine to a mere biological survival, he does concern himself with the psychic results of this attempt at survival. It would appear that he is more perceptive than Freud at this point. For whereas Freud makes a somewhat similar transition, he does not quite seem to recognize what he is doing, i.e., converting the biological into psychological data.

Assia Abel, in 1951, quotes Freud's *The Origins of Psychoanalysis* and points out that it was Freud's purpose in that "draft" to furnish a scientific psychology. Freud sought to describe psychic processes as quantitatively determined states, having demonstrable material parts, and thus to make them visible and free of contradictions. Abel further notes that Freud was attempting to merge brain physiology with psychology.

As we read further in Adler, we find him advocating the concept of selectivity in the evolutionary process together with his emphasis on "purpose," "a guiding principle" which leads to the concept of self-preservation for survival, the aspect of self-transcendence.

For Adler, self-preservation is more than survival of the biological organism. The objective is more than seeking pleasure and avoiding pain. Self-preservation in Adler is: "a complex of moving powers . . . which strive for the consummation of a single goal. The organism continuously seeks to reach a better accord with the altered conditions of life through adaptation, repudiation, and improvement."

It seems apparent that in Adler, there is a hint toward self-preservation. The organism is not propelled by blind biological drives of libidinal energy or instincts. The organism is a psychic whole which moves forward with a purpose, a telos, a goal. It is this concept of totality which separates Adler from Freud.

The Freudian emphasis on the biological aspects of self-preservation seems not to be based on empirical data, but on speculation founded on nonexistent experience. As John Layard, the Oxford anthropologist, has pointed out:

> *Freud's hypothesis, as advanced in* Totem and Taboo, *is that a primitive horde was led by an aged patriarch, who possessed all the women, and whose sons finally rebelled against him and married his wives, thus giving birth to the Oedipus complex. This has done more to discredit Freud among anthropologists than any of his works, for there is no evidence whatever that such a condition ever existed (Abel, 1951).*

Freud's position seems to result from the limited mechanistic, individualistic, reified view of man upon which his work is founded.

The conclusion of the matter *vis-a-vis* Adler's dissent from Freud appears to be that the former saw a dimension in man which Freud either did not or could not see. Adler could not accept Freud's reification of man. Adler's data acquainted him with facts which called forth the use of such terms as "spiritual" and "God," and he makes such statements as, "Through the great being that surrounds and penetrates us, there is a great becoming which strives toward a completed being." For Freud, these categories had only a biological orientation. Therefore, for reasons of presuppositions which appeared too limiting and specialized, and therefore unable to account for a dimension beyond the biological, Adler found it necessary to dissent from Freud.

Turning to James Jackson Putnam (1846-1918) we may classify him as a dissenter mainly because, while he fully appreciated the genius and contributions of Freud, and even introduced him to this continent, he objected to Freud's theoretical assumptions. As he was an eminent professor of neuropsychiatry, his objections give us valuable information. Putnam could not bring himself to accept the limitations of the methods of psychoanalysis and was constantly attempting to broaden its scope. This major dissent is referred to by Freud in the following words: Putnam demanded that psychoanalysis

> *as a science—should be linked on to a particular philosophical system and that its practice should be openly associated with a particular set of ethical doctrines.*
>
> *So it is not to be wondered at that a mind with such preeminently ethical and philosophical tendencies as Putnam's should have desired, after he had plunged deep into psychoanalysis, to establish the closest relation between it and the aims which lay nearest his heart.*

Ernest Jones seems to have assessed the intention of Putnam more accurately when he notes that Putnam desired

> *to widen the psychoanalytical principles by incorporating into them certain philosophical views, especially concerning the relationship of the individual to the community at large and to the universe in general. He regarded this not as a criticism of psychoanalysis, but as a proposed enrichment of it, indeed it was rather a quarrel with science as a whole*

than with psychoanalysis, though for obvious reasons it came more to the front in the case of the latter.

Both Freud and Putnam seem to feel that psychoanalysis is an adequate instrument for the understanding of the total man. They appear to stress the need to understand man in terms of a purely empirical scientific method. It is at this point that some questions must be raised. Is the purely scientific, mechanistic, causal method capable of providing a full understanding of man? Is it possible to understand man in isolation from the community on the one hand and the universe on the other? Was Freud as thoroughgoing in his empiricism as he wished to be? Are his conclusions based entirely and exclusively on empirical data? To all of these questions, Putnam returned a negative answer, as will be shown.

Fay B. Karpf, in her book *The Psychology and Psychotherapy of Otto Rank*, in 1953, speaks to this question thus:

Since . . . experiences could be recalled under proper conditions, it seemed logical to assume that they were present somewhere and this somewhere Freud called, by contrast to consciousness, "the unconscious." It is clear, however, that the unconscious, the foundational concept of psychoanalysis, is not a matter of observation, in fact, cannot in the nature of the case, be a matter of observation. It is an interpretive or inferential concept based on observation, with all the possibilities of error that may, as we know from the history of thought, creep into such a process. The same may be said of the concept of "repression."

Repression similarly cannot be observed. It, too, is an inferential concept which Freud found indispensable in the formulation of his doctrine of the unconscious.

Or, as Putnam points out, "Psychoanalysis should not make light of inferential forms of reasoning, for it is on this form of reasoning that the value of their own conclusions largely rests."

To put it in different words, we seem to see Freud slip rather easily from empirical data to theoretical conclusions where the need arises. But in consideration of larger philosophical issues, he seems to be either unwilling or unable to make a similarly necessary transition. This is one of Putnam's major dissents with Freud.

Next, an attempt will be made to outline those areas of differences between Freud and Putnam significant enough to justify placing Putnam among the Freudian dissenters. These differences lie in three general areas: First, Putnam notes repeatedly that the scientific method is an inadequate instrument for a comprehension of the nature of man. The second area follows logically from the first. Besides frequent reference to the need for metaphysics in order to implement the scientific view of man, Putnam devotes a special lecture to the subject which he calls "The Necessity of Metaphysics" (Chapter XV in his *Addresses on Psychoanalysis*, 1921). The third area emphasizes aspects of the nature of man omitted by the limitations of the Freudian method.

Putnam points out that the analytical approach (in scientific method), which focuses its gaze on particulars, is incapable of evaluation of the whole and therefore misses the meaning of the whole. When the relationship of the part to the whole is considered, he contends, this is metaphysics, and while this is taken for granted, "instead of doing it tacitly and implicitly, we should do it openly and explicitly." So he continues:

The study of human nature should, in short, begin at the top (in terms of functional meaning), rather than at the bottom (in terms of structure); just as, if we had to choose what phase of a symphony one would choose in order to get an idea of its perfection, one would take some culminating moment rather than the first few notes simply because they were first. To be accurate, one could not do justice to the symphony except by studying it as a whole, and similarly one should study the man as a whole, including his relations to the universe as a whole. . . . It is as a whole that each and every human life, standing as it does as the representation of the body of the universe, on the one hand, and the spirit of the universe, on the other, should implicitly be viewed.

Putnam calls psychology a relational and relative science and its findings must be viewed in relation to the knowledge provided by the anatomist and the physiologist, no less than by the philosopher and the metaphysician who "point to the bonds between the individual and the universe."

A summary of Putnam's position *vis-a-vis* Freud indicates that Freud was clearly impaled on a too-restricted approach for a full comprehension of man. Putnam notes this other dimension in man constantly defying and breaking out of his narrow scientific confines. To this other dimension Putnam ascribes such qualities as self-transcendence, freedom, creativity, a genesis outside the mundane and a goal and destiny beyond time. "It begins in the unseen but real and infinite world of the spirit, the psyche generatrix, and consists in a series of attempts to express the life of the spirit in finite form," says Putnam. This appears to adumbrate rather accurately the Christian notion of the *imago Dei*: its origin, its nature, its destiny.

Moving to the next dissenter, Otto Rank (1884-1939), we encounter much the same objections to Freudianism. Rank's main criticism of Freud devolves upon two basic issues. First, Rank rejected the "mechanistic theory of life according to which all mental processes and emotional reactions are determined by the unconscious" as invalid for a comprehension of man. Second, Rank was aware of a dimension in man which he calls "will" which is "beyond psychology," i.e., the methods of psychology do not facilitate its understanding. To Rank, the psychological rationale is incapable of accounting for life. To quote him again on his difference with Freud, "My main thesis which was derived from a crisis in psychology . . . lays bare the irrational roots of human behavior which psychology tries to explain rationally in order to make it intelligible, that is, acceptable." Thus, more specifically, Rank was taking issue with Freud's methodology, and for that matter, with the methodology of all psychology. It is not without significance that Rank notes that both Adler and Jung dissented at the level of Freudian methodology because they saw its limiting effects:

It was not valid for all races, Jung pointed out; that it did not apply to different social environments, Adler emphasized, but that it did not even permit individuals of the same race and social backgrounds to deviate from the accepted type led me beyond these differences in psychology to a psychology of difference.

As it happens, these spontaneous reactions within the psychoanalytic movement itself provide an excellent illustration for that development. Freud's tendency to absolutize his psychology was countered at an early date (before World War I) by two diametrically opposed reactions.

To quote Rank further:

Freud tried to apply the strict determinism of natural science to psychic events, and to demonstrate the principle of causality in mental life from which it previously had been barred.

In a footnote at this point Rank says:

In the Interpretation of Dreams (Traumdeutuing) *which appeared in 1900, Freud attempted to establish strict determinism in the realm of mental phenomena; and in* Three Dissertations on Sexual Theory (Drei Ashandlungen zur Sexualtheorie), *he tried to establish biology* as the causal basis for psychic events. About a quarter of a century later, philosophers and physicists themselves began (Bergmann's "Gifford Lectures" in 1907; S.A. Eddington in "The Nature of the Physical World" in 1928) to develop the epipstemological implications of the new physical worldview, and to regard the principle of causality as threatened by "chance" events. In ignorance of this movement, I was questioning the physical causality of Freud's determinism, and opposing "freedom of the will" to such causality.

And again, Rank states:

I sensed a crisis in psychology which approximates quite closely the collapse of the scientific worldview. Only in this connection I went a step beyond the crisis in physics, since I conceived of the psychological attitude itself which determines the meaning of facts, as an interpretation of the human microcosm based on the ideology of consciousness and will. However, I still find myself on a common footing with physics, since I did not simply hypostatize freedom of will out of subjective experience or deduce it philosophically, but was rather driven to it as the physicists had been driven to "chance," by a too-strict application of determinism, to mental phenomena, in this instance. I have pursued to its ultimate consequences (especially in The Trauma of Birth, 1924) *the principle of causality which Freud applied to psychic events in a naive "physical" way, and have been led inexorably to a point where I simply had to derive mental phenomena from a "causality of willing" in order to understand them. My conception was not that the principle of causality was false, but that it no longer sufficed for our current level of awareness because its psychological meaning had undermined its heuristic value.*

Rank's chief contribution to our discussion lies in the fact that with the most cogent reasoning and careful documentation, he points out the dilemma of the scientific method among the physicists themselves. Even the physical sciences are compelled to admit "chance" into the chain of cause and effect! What does this do to so-called determinism? And if this is obvious and true in the physical sciences, can this be omitted from a study of man as psychology attempts to do? Following the scientific evidence adduced by Heinrich Gompe, who arrives at a "spontaneity theory" according to which material elements disclose certain individual and transitory peculiarities of behavior, Rank continues:

It appears, then, that in psychology as in physics there is greater freedom the more one advances from masses to elements, and the smaller and finer one conceives these elements to be. Psychologically, that means that the more completely one analyzes his elements, the more difficult it becomes to justify strict determinism and causality, and the more freedom one must grant the ultimate individual elements. This corresponds in the psychological realm to the so-called normal psychology which derives laws of "average events" from observation, but is unable to explain the behavior of an individual in a particular situation. . . . For the individual simply lies beyond lawfulness, and cannot be fully comprehended or explained by the causality either of natural or social science. In my opinion, the only rewarding approach lies in a will psychology which includes both ways of considering the individual and yet does not attempt to understand him principally or solely on the basis of himself alone. For in the realm of psychology, too, a correct formulation of the problem seems to me more important than any attempts to solve it.

Much could be added to this point which further delineates Rank's differences with Freud, but this is not required. It is sufficient first to show that Rank rejected the methodology of Freud as inadequate to an understanding of man, and second, to follow the arguments on which Rank based his rejection. Both these aspects of the case have been considered. The basic reason underlying Rank's rejection of Freudian scientific naturalism, as in the case of the other dissenters, is that man is too great and diversified a being to be comprehended thereby. When this method is applied, man's uniqueness somehow slips through the mechanism, and what is left is little more than a caricature of man. The aspect of man which evades comprehension by the scientific method, according to Rank, is man's conception of himself as spiritual.

We need do little more at this point than to indicate once again that Rank, like the other dissenters, found Freud's assumptions too limiting to allow for any comprehensive view of man. Man is a "spirit," according to Rank, and any method that misses man's autonomy and free will and ability to transcend himself is little more than a caricature.

When we turn to Carl Jung (1875-1961), essentially the same objections to Freudianism are raised. He sees Freudians as participating in the scientism of the nineteenth century which believed that

everything that could not be seen with the eyes or touched with the hands was held in doubt. . . . Nothing could be considered "scientific" or admitted to be true unless it could be perceived by the senses or traced back to physical causes.

This, he further intimates, was
> the popular attitude of unreasoned, not to say emotional, surrender to the all-importance of the physical world. Let no one suppose that so radical a change in man's outlook could be brought about by reasoning and reflection, for no chain of reasoning can prove or disprove the existence of either mind or matter.

To explain mental phenomena in terms of glandular activity is acceptable to scientism. To
> explain the break-up of the atom in the sun as an emanation of the creative weltgeist. We shall be looked down upon as intellectual freaks. And yet both views are equally arbitrary and equally symbolic. From the standpoint of epistemology, it is just as admissible to derive animals from the human species, as man from animal species.

Thus, it appears that Jung is not only critical of Freudian scientism, but he is also at odds with biologism which is the same misapplication of principles to an area where they cannot possibly apply, viz., the principles of biology are not applicable in all their details to "psyche-ology."

Jung attributes a positive value to biology, and to the empiricism of natural science in general, in which "I see a herculean attempt to understand the human psyche from the other world." Jung does
> not doubt that natural instincts or drives are forces of propulsion in human life, whether we call them sexuality or the will to power; but I also do not doubt that these instincts come into collision with the spirit, for they are continually colliding with something, and why should not this something be called spirit? I am far from knowing what spirit is in itself and equally far from knowing what instincts are. The one is as mysterious to me as the other, yet I am unable to dismiss the one by explaining it in terms of the other. . . . Instinct and spirit . . . are terms we allow to stand for powerful forces whose nature we do not know.

Because Jung sees the instincts as colliding with spirit, the hopelessness of Freudian determinism is relieved. "Incest with the past and incest with the future—there is nothing that can free us from this bond except that opposite urge of life, the spirit.

Jung's contention is further pointed out by the fact that while it is possible for an observer to observe material objects, he cannot disentangle himself from observing himself because there is no

Archimedian point outside, "since only the psyche can observe the psyche . . . (these) necessary limitations" are intrinsic to a study of psychology, and to attempt to deny it is to try to leap over its shadow. This pitfall might have been avoided by Freud if he had examined his philosophical presuppositions.

We have seen Jung, then, moving away from scientism, making it quite apparent that he is a phenomenologist. He cannot construe man in a purely "organic-zoological" sense. He refuses to reduce man to a product of biological phenomena. To further anticipate his meaning of phenomenology, he sets the dimension of *spirit* as a self-transcending formative power of the organism.

A relevant question at this juncture then, is: What does Jung mean by *spirit*? Here, caution is advised. Jung speaks as a phenomenologist and not as a theologian. We can not expect either dogmatics or absolutes. It is our feeling that in attempting to bridge the gap between psychology and religion, we need a *via* media so that at least a conversation may be begun between two disciplines hitherto diametrically opposed. This, indeed, is the crucial point. Until we can demonstrate, from the psychologists themselves, that the naturalistic, scientific, materialistic presuppositions are inadequate for a full understanding of man, these two disciplines are as far removed as East from West, and never the twain shall meet. Our labors are expended in demonstrating that while East and West are necessary points of demarcation, we must not miss the fact that "this is our Father's world," and as he holds the whole world in the hollow of his hand, East and West, psychology and religion, are merely two highly specialized ways of viewing the same man.

So to answer our question, Jung sees three things that are characteristic of the spirit dimension: (1) It cannot be identified with matter and the laws governing matter are inapplicable to it; (2) spirit is free and unpredictable and beyond the bounds of determinism; and (3) spirit, therefore, is that aspect of humans which enables them to transcend themselves in terms of goals and ideals.

A somewhat latecomer to the Freudian dilemma is Ludwig Binswanger (1881-1966). His inclusion among the dissenters is more on the grounds that he differed in method than that he was with that group and subsequently left. It is also appropriate to include Binswanger in our discussion because he represents the existential approach to psychology. While this school is open to all the data that can be amassed toward an understanding of man from every discipline, its insistence that the logical, positivistic, biological, piecemeal approach does not give us a view of the whole man is not only highly significant for our purpose, but at the same time it points out the loopholes in Freudian assumptions.

Binswanger questions the aprioristic view of the human psyche which imagines that it can understand man analytically with causally reducible (mechanical) processes, observable in a field of which the observer's vantage is independent. In other words, he suggests that Freud's reification or *thingification* of man arbitrarily chops off self-transcendence which is present in the very process of all self-knowledge. Freud's method has the appearance of getting a bird's-eye view of man, but then attempting to coerce the view into the snail's viewpoint. Now both viewpoints are valid, but quite obviously the snail cannot possibly comprehend as much of the totality as the bird sees. Man is made up of parts, but functions as a whole—and the scientistic, biological, materialistic approach is a "part-ial" view.

This is why Binswanger suggests that Freudian therapy is inadequate. "The subject's world, in the particular way in which it matters to him, is structured by values—valences, demand qualities." These values are transcendental. They cannot be reduced to or understood by an immanentist approach. "Conflicts in the patient, then, which at their roots are always value conflicts . . . cannot be reduced to needs and drives." To confine oneself to empirical data in the Freudian manner is to miss the transcendental element and therefore to limit the scope of the therapy. As Sonneman states:

"'*Full psychological understanding*'" then is never full enough psychological understanding if it strives to be merely that the "value problem" is inescapable and occurs at practically every step in theory and therapy. Freud avoids it, as he avoids "philosophy," yet he evaluates as well as philosophizes constantly and not even implicitly.*

When psychoanalysis produces insight, for this insight to be effective, it must have meaning for the person as a whole. Now, Binswanger asks, Why cannot this insight be produced by any other existential encounter? Again, why does this insight have to be attributed to any strata of the psyche? For indeed, Sonneman adds:

True insight assesses the self in the light of norms transcending the self, (religious, erotic, ethical, aesthetic) viewing it against a background inaccessible in principle to psychoanalytic objectification.

This constant bursting of the bounds of naturalistic immanentalism by the attempt to absorb all the dimensions of the personality within it leads to a "kind of conceptual seasickness as the inevitable result."

Binswanger's third objection to Freudianism is that Freud, for the first time in modern psychology, sees the whole subject matter—man—but misses out on his most unique and constitutional characteristic, his quality of self-transcendence, his "psyche." The psyche indeed is the one and only source of integration; the one and only source of wholeness which man is! It is this source of wholeness, this soul, if you please, which gives to the parts a unity that can no longer be reduced to any one of them or to their sum total. Freud made very much the same error that Descartes made. Descartes adduced the whole man from one aspect—his thinking, *cogito, ergo sum*—but exactly the reverse is the truth. Man exists, and, then and therefore, thinks.

In a word, then, Binswanger observes the same characteristic of soul or psyche in man. He is driven to it as the most unique factor which indeed flows out beyond Freudian biologism and is incomprehensible aside from a noncausalistic, nonmaterialistic, nonmechanistic method.

As we have followed the thinking of the dissenters—Adler, Putnam, Rank, Jung, and Binswanger—certain factors have emerged which I feel certain are apparent. First, they are unanimously opposed to Freud's mechanistic, naturalistic, materialistic, scientistic view of man. For them, man cannot be confined and therefore cannot be understood in such terms. They were aware of a dimension which kept transcending the Freudian mold. They gave this dimension various labels, i.e., Adler called it the "soul;" Putnam saw it as "spirit" and the *imago Dei*; Rank described it as a dimension "beyond psychology" as it was practiced, and also called it *soul* or *spirit*. When we attempt to identify this characteristic in Jung, he too uses the term *spirit*. In Binswanger we find a similar transcendence of Freudian mechanistic psychology as he demonstrates the psyche to be the "one and only source" of wholeness and integration.

Now we find a similarity in phraseology, in argument and in description of this other dimension beyond mechanistic psychology which also is full of significance. For we find all the dissenters converging at a point where they see this dimension as characterized by

(1) self-transcendence, (2) freedom and, therefore, (3) an inability to be understood in biological terms.

The question that remains is: How closely does the dimension of spirit, discovered by psychologists, compare with the dimension of spirit as characterized by Christian theology? Are these psychologists moving in the direction of seeing man as made in the image of God as spirit? Is man spirit? The answer to this question is highly relevant. Because if man is nothing more than a biological organism, if instincts and drives are geared to self-preservation as the ultimate goal of man's existence, then what are God and heaven for? But if psychologists of the caliber we have examined have been forced to abandon materialistic psychology and to keep being confronted by this other dimension of the soul, then two things of note have been accomplished: (1) The psyche has been restored to psychology, and (2) the Christian dimension need no longer be ruled out as illusory but is, on the contrary, germane to the understanding of man.

Spirit and Psyche

John G. Finch

(The third lecture delivered by John Finch at Fuller Theological Seminary in the spring of 1961)

The point to be discussed here is a somewhat more definitive description of the nature of "spirit." The notion of *spirit* in man is discussed rather fully in at least two distinctly different spheres. In one sphere, as has been shown, the notion of spirit is seen psychologically as that something in man which eludes scientific methodology. Similarly, in the second sphere, as there will be occasion to see, the notion of spirit—as seen in Christian writers such as Emil Brunner, Nicholas Berdyaev, Søren Kierkegaard, Reinhold Niebuhr, to name only a few—is likewise elusive. However, these two areas in which a discussion of the notion of spirit falls have a rather hard and fast line of demarcation. Psychology considers itself an empirical science on a plane with the natural sciences. It encounters the dimension of spirit almost by default, and much to the undoing of its presuppositions and methodology. In the context of Christianity, the notion of spirit is a basic assumption of its anthropology. According to Christian dogma, man is made in the image of God, and this image of God in man is what is most generally identified with *spirit*.

Now the question that shall employ the remainder of this series is: Is the dimension of *spirit* which the psychologists encounter almost inadvertently, and to which their investigations lead inexorably, akin to or identical with the notion of *spirit*, the *imago Dei* of Christian dogmatics? In our judgment the identification of these two notions is not advisable at this time. First of all, psychology is committed to no particular religion, while the *imago Dei* concept is a distinctly Christian notion, even though it did receive some instruction from Greece, as Brunner so well points out in his *Man in Revolt*. Second, psychology finds it necessary to limit its researches to the here-and-now, and therefore does not consider ontology its field. The notion of the *imago Dei* is an ontological problem. Third, the presuppositions of religion and the presuppositions of psychology are too divergent to be able to identify concepts that appear alike. Nevertheless, given a Christian anthropological viewpoint, it would appear not without good results to seek some similarities between the Christian and the psychological notions of spirit, particularly if the two notions do concur in several characteristics. Furthermore, it might not be entirely irrelevant or ill-advised to undergird scientific psychology with a Christian foundation without setting arbitrary barriers against the findings or pronouncements of either discipline.

To begin with, it is important to emphasize what has already been pointed out several times—that the notion of spirit in the dissenters is a dimension "beyond psychology," that is to say, causalistic, naturalistic, mechanistic psychology. In noting this dimension all of them repudiated the exclusively biological approach to an understanding of man. Man to them was more than an animal, more than a biological organism. Man was a "spiritual" being.

What are the characteristics of this spirit dimension in man according to the psychologists?

First, there is the quality of self-transcendence. This quality has already been discussed as being possibly latent in Freud's notion of the instinct of self-preservation. It was also noted as a necessary foundation for therapy. With Adler, it appears to be that quality in man which draws the biological and psychic qualities into a totality, a wholeness, "a great becoming which strives toward a completed being." With Binswanger, self-transcendence is a characteristic unique in man, and consists of his ability to stand aside, as it were, and see himself, though this aspect of him which stands aside is not capable of comprehension. This capacity for self-transcendence is "structured by values—valences, demand qualities, conflicts—(which) cannot be reduced to needs and drives," as Sonnemann notes. He continues, "Self-transcendence is the one and only source of integration from which this 'object' entity itself can draw." Spirit appears as something that dominates and controls man in the sense of growing him beyond what he is.

In the thought of Putnam, these metaphysical tendencies are so acute that there is grave variance with Freud at this point. Putnam describes this self-transcendent quality in man as something of an awareness in his patients that they "ought or ought not to do this or that," and this, suggests Putnam, somewhat adumbrating Kantian thought, "will lead (the patient) to see his obligations in the light of his origin and destiny." Thus Putnam notes the quality of self-transcendence which is native, unable to be grasped by the methods of scientific naturalism and capable of directing the individual beyond himself to higher and better goals—"the transcendency of the mind over the brain." It is difficult to read Putnam without coming to a clear awareness of the dimension of spirit and its exhibition in self-transcendence.

As far as Rank is concerned, the phenomenological viewpoint is similar to Binswanger's and Putnam's and Jung's. This third dimension in Rank is characterized by self-transcendence which he further describes as a "will to power," as a "creative" and "free" impulse. The point being made is that in Rank, too, the characteristic of the dimension "beyond psychology" is self-transcendence, the irrational factor that cannot be rationalized as psychoanalysis attempts to do.

Finally, in Jung there is perhaps the clearest description of the notion of spirit. As has been noted in the discussion of Jung, he describes himself as a phenomenologist, and assumes the self-transcendent character in man to be intrinsically wrapped up with the dimension of spirit.

A second characteristic of spirit in man—and one which is intimately tied in with the characteristic of self-transcendence, as has already been noted by the phenomenologists, particularly Scheler, Binswanger, Jung, and Rank—is that while the spirit is capable of objectifying, it is itself incapable of objectivization. This is precisely the downfall of Freud's psychology. The spirit cannot be an object. *Thingification* is only applicable to things, not to the spirit.

Again, intimately associated with self-transcendence, as a characteristic of spirit, are the twin qualities of freedom and responsibility. All the dissenters, and indeed Freud himself (in spite of his causalistic determinism, he appears to have allowed for freedom; otherwise how would therapy be possible?), are clear in their recognition of this aspect in man, and they all tie it in with that distinctive quality of self-transcendence which is unique in man. The ability of the self to transcend itself, to be something other than itself, assumes a quite nonbiological dimension in man, and this dimension anticipates freedom, and freedom logically posits responsibility. For if it is the native capacity of persons to be better than they are, then (to use the logic of Kant) they feel responsible to achieve it.

Thus, from a psychological point of view, it would appear that spirit can be defined as that quality unique to man which is able to objectivize but incapable of objectivization, has the characteristic of self-transcendence, and gives man a quality of freedom and responsibility which ascribes to man powers of creatorship. In this sense then, in essence, man is spirit.

At this point, some consideration will be given to the notion of spirit as outlined by certain Christian anthropologists. As Niebuhr puts it:

The Christian view of man is sharply distinguished from all alternative views by the manner in which it interprets and relates these aspects of human existence to each other: (1) It emphasizes the height of self-transcendence in man's spiritual nature in its doctrine of "image of God." (2) It insists on man's weakness, dependence, and finiteness in his involvement in the necessities and contingencies of the natural world, without, however, regarding this finiteness as, of itself, a source of evil in man. In its purest form the Christian view of man regards man as a unity of Godlikeness and creatureliness in which he remains a creature even in the highest spiritual dimensions of his existence and may reveal elements of the image of God even in the lowliest aspects of his natural life. (3) It affirms that the evil in man is a consequence of his inevitable though not necessary unwillingness to acknowledge his dependence, to accept his finiteness and so to admit his insecurity, an unwillingness which involves him in the vicious circle of accentuating the insecurity from which he seeks escape.

Niebuhr then proceeds to outline the biblical and Christian notion of "the image of God," going through Gregory of Nyssa, Origen, Thomas Aquinas, Augustine, Calvin, and Luther. He sets Origen aside because of his Platonism, and also Aquinas because of a too-close identification in his thought which all but makes the *image of God* man's "intellectual nature." The one point that comes clearly into focus in the others, according to Niebuhr, is the quality of self-transcendence in the nature of the *imago Dei* or spirit. Thus Niebuhr points out:

Even in the most Platonic and Aristotelian forms of Christianity, some suggestions of the imago Dei *as an orientation of man toward God, some hint of the Christian understanding of man's capacity for indeterminate self-transcendence are given.*

"Augustine is primarily interested in the capacity of transcendence to the point of self-transcendence in the human spirit. This power of transcendence places (man) . . . outside of everything else." So Niebuhr proceeds to quote from Calvin, who writes:

> Though the soul is not the whole man, yet there is no absurdity in calling him the image of God with relation to the soul. . . . The image of God includes all the excellence in which the nature of man surpasses all the other species of animals.

Niebuhr is careful to point out that "by reason of the soul (Calvin) means capacities which include the self-determination of the will and the quality of transcendence." Then he suggests by way of summary that the biblical conception of *image of God* has influenced Christian thought, particularly since Augustine (when not under a too strong Platonic or Aristotelian influence), to interpret human nature in terms which include his rational facilities but which suggest something beyond them. The best nontheological analysis of human nature in modern times, by Heidegger, defines this Christian emphasis succinctly as "the idea of transcendence, namely, that man is something which reaches beyond itself—that he is more than a rational creature."

At this point, interestingly enough, Niebuhr uses Max Scheler's thought to implement or further define the nature of spirit. Scheler suggests a possible similarity in the nature of spirit and some seemingly repressed elements of Freud's thinking with regard to self-transcendence. This quotation from Scheler which Niebuhr uses is of particular value insofar as it appears further to augment a possible identification of self-preservation and self-transcendence:

> It is the quality of the human spirit on the other hand to lift itself above itself as a living organism and to make the whole temporal and spatial world, including itself, the object of its knowledge.

In this quality of self-transcendence, Niebuhr sees with Scheler a certain freedom. Thus he says:

> Man is self-determining not only in the sense that he transcends natural process in such a way as to be able to choose between various alternatives presented to him by the process of nature but also in the sense that he transcends himself in such a way that he must choose his total end. In this task of self-determination he is confronted with endless potentialities and he can set no limit to what he ought to be, short of the character of ultimate reality.

Niebuhr then quotes from Kierkegaard to stress the aspect of freedom in self-transcendence. "But what is this myself? . . . It is the most abstract and yet at the same time the most concrete of all realities. It is freedom."

Thus far there is little reason for quarreling between Niebuhr's concept of the nature of spirit as self-transcendence, freedom, and as incapable of *thingification* or objectivization, and the position of the psychologists discussed. But from here on, the difference is profound and impossible to relate. For from this point on, Niebuhr sees both the origin and destiny of man as being grounded in God, whereas, as has been pointed out, questions of ontology and eschatology are not considered by the psychologist, who is mainly concerned with the here-and-now. Niebuhr is right in feeling that the doctrine of spirit or *imago Dei* inevitably raises ultimate questions with reference to reality, and it is not without importance to question the validity of a psychological methodology which, while escaping scientific naturalism, moves on to phenomenology, recognizes man as spirit, and stops there. As he points out:

> Implicit in the human situation of freedom and in man's capacity to transcend himself and his world is his inability to construct a world of meaning without finding a source and a key to the structure of meaning which transcends the world beyond his own capacity to transcend it. The problem of meaning which is the basic problem of religion, transcends the ordinary rational problem of tracing the relation of things to each other, as the freedom of man's spirit transcends his rational faculties.

So Niebuhr depends on Scheler to define this distinction more clearly:

> A problem of reason would be the following: "I have a pain in my arm. Where did it come from and how may I get rid of it?" To determine that is a task of science. But I may use the pain in my arm to reflect upon the fact that the world is tainted with pain, evil and sorrow. Then I will ask: What is pain, evil and sorrow essentially and of what nature is the ground of all existence, making pain as such, without reference to my particular pain, possible?

The psychologist stops at the first part. And this, as has been indicated *vis-a-vis* Freud, produces a partial view of man, and an attempt to understand him as an object, a thing. The phenomenologists go beyond Freud in rejecting his *thingification* on the grounds of the spirit dimension, but insofar as they note this spirit in the here-and-now only, their view of man from an ontological viewpoint and from a logical viewpoint appears to stagnate too.

Now when the concept of freedom is given closer scrutiny, there can be no doubt that the psychologist (Freud, it has been suggested, encountered it in spite of his presuppositions) runs into this "elusive" aspect of man's spirit. But again, from the Christian anthropological viewpoint, this freedom can only be fully comprehended in relation to God. For, as Niebuhr states, this "freedom is obviously something different from the necessary causal links of nature." So again, in further explication of this theme, he writes:

> We have previously alluded to the fact that the human spirit has the special capacity of standing continually outside itself in terms of indefinite regression. Consciousness is a capacity for surveying the world and determining action from a governing center. Self-consciousness represents a further degree of transcendence in which the self makes itself its own object in such a way that the ego is finally always subject and not object. The rational capacity of surveying the world, of forming general concepts and analyzing the order of the world is thus but one aspect of what Christianity knows as "spirit."

The nature of freedom in relation to God is of course different from the elusive thing which the psychologist calls freedom. Nicholas Berdyaev, in his *Slavery and Freedom* in 1944, emphasizes this same characteristic about freedom. He opposes freedom to materiality. "Nature in this sense is the world of objectivization, that is to say, of alienation, determinability, impersonality." This is where the breakdown of the naturalistic scientific method is anticipated both in relation to understanding or comprehending man in the spiritual dimension, and therefore in its full understanding of the notion of freedom. For "freedom presupposes the existence of a spiritual element, not determined either by nature or society."

It is impossible to elaborate a logical and positive concept of freedom which is capable of completely elucidating its mystery. Freedom is life which can only be grasped in the experience of life, for in its inner mystery it eludes the categories of reason (and science). Rational philosophy involves a static view of freedom, while the latter is dynamic in its very essence and can only be conceived dynamically.

This may perhaps offer some clue as to why Freudianism failed to understand the nature of man in freedom while the dynamic, existential viewpoint of the phenomenologists, although not grounding freedom in God, nevertheless did come to a fuller appreciation both of this spirit dimension in man and also of the aspect of freedom.

Thus, as Berdyaev points out:

All these theories contain elements of truth: Man is a rational being and a bearer of values. He is an evolving being, a social being, a being suffering from the conflict between conscious and the subconscious. But none of them expresses the essence of human nature as a whole. The biblical and Christian doctrine alone deals with the whole man, with his origin and destination. . . . The Christian conception of man is based upon two ideas: (1) Man is the image and likeness of God the Creator and (2) God became man, the Son of God manifested himself to us as the God-man.

Thus, while there are differences between Berdyaev and Niebuhr, at this point they seem to concur. Man is free. Freedom is spirit. But spirit cannot ground itself in itself. The ground of spirit is Spirit, as Hopper points out. And, apart from such a ground, apart from such an ontological admission, while there may be premonitions of the spirit dimension in man—"He (God) did not leave himself without witness" (Acts 14:17). The fullest dimensions of the nature of man is impossible. If this be true in relation to the phenomenological psychologists, then the naturalistic scientific methodology of Freud is evaluated accordingly.

When an examination is made of the notion of spirit in the thought of Emil Brunner, the same general theme is encountered. More specifically, Brunner identified spirit in man with the notion of the *imago Dei*. He notes that the characteristics of spirit are (1) self-transcendence; (2) the ability to objectivize but not be objectivized; and (3) freedom. Similarly, he is at one with Berdyaev and Niebuhr, with Kierkegaard and Augustine, in pointing out that the nature of spirit regresses logically into Spirit, and cannot be understood apart from man's origin and destiny; that is, man's position as a creature made by God and for God. So he sums up his position in relation to psychology in these words:

But that means with reference to the situation in psychology, that Christian psychology can indeed give the reason why man can only understand himself in several irreconcilably antithetical aspects, and thus at the same time cannot understand himself. It can so far correct the one-sidedness of each separate school by reference to the source of

> the crisis, but it cannot itself unfold the synthetic psychology which might take the place of this one-sided one. Its task is rather to expound those fundamental concepts in the knowledge of faith, in which the contradiction of man is recognized as essential, and to offer them as regulative or connective ideas to all psychological study. But it does not admit of being built up as a psychology with a character of its own which might take the place of those one-sided "natural" schools of psychology. Christian psychology is thus not to be understood as constitutive, but merely as regulative, and must in consequence remain in constant fellowship with the work of all other psychological investigation.

Brunner appears further to summarize his position through a quotation from Hamann which appears in his work *Man in Revolt*:

> From this we see how necessarily our self is rooted and grounded in him who created it, so that the knowledge of our self does not lie within our own power, but that in order to measure the extent of the same, we must press forward into the very heart of God himself, who alone can determine and resolve the whole mystery of our nature.

This notion of spirit has been carried forward with such subtle insight in the work of Søren Kierkegaard that he has often been acclaimed the greatest Christian anthropologist and psychologist. In Kierkegaard, *spirit* is basic to his psychology. Its transcendence and synthesizing qualities put man in a category qualitatively different from any other creature. Thus he says:

> Man is a synthesis of the soulish and the bodily. But a synthesis is unthinkable if the two are not united in a third factor. This third factor is the spirit. . . . So when the spirit is present, it is in one way a hostile power, for it constantly disturbs the relation between soul and body. . . . On the other hand, it is a friendly power which has precisely the function of constituting the relationship. What then is man's relation to this ambiguous power? How is spirit related to itself and to its situation? It is related as dread. It cannot do away with itself. Neither can man sink down into the vegetative life, for he is determined by spirit. He cannot flee from dread, for he loves it; really he does not love it, for he flees from it.

If at this point it be asked: What is dread? Kierkegaard's answer is that "dread is a qualification of the dreaming spirit . . . dread is the reality of freedom as possibility anterior to possibility." Thus two aspects emerge. First, spirit in self-transcendence, and second, freedom. But Kierkegaard goes further and seems almost to speak directly to the problem of the scientific methodology and its limitations when he suggests that "science cannot explain such things. Every science has its province either in immanent logic, or in an immanence within a transcendence which it cannot explain."

This theme is treated somewhat more definitively in a later work by Kierkegaard, *The Sickness Unto Death* (1849). Here, in a passage that is almost a classic in depth psychology, he says:

Man is spirit. But what is spirit? Spirit is the self. But what is the self? The self is a relation which relates itself to its own self, or it is that in the relation (which accounts for it) that the relation relates itself to its own self. Man is a synthesis of the infinite and finite, of the temporal and the eternal, of freedom and necessity. In short, it is a synthesis. A synthesis is a relation between two factors. So regarded, man is not yet a self.

In the relation between two, the relation is the third term as a negative unity, and the two relate themselves to the relation, and in the relation to the relation; such a relation is that between soul and body, when man is regarded as soul. If, on the contrary, the relation relates itself to its own self, the relation is then the positive third term, and this is the self.

Such a relation which relates itself to its own self (that is to say, a self) must either have constituted itself or have been constituted by another.

Such a derived, constituted, relation is the human self, and in relating itself to its own self relates itself to another.

By relating itself to its own self and by willing to be itself, the self is grounded transparently in the Power which posited it.

Thus, to summarize the position of Kierkegaard, the same factors pertaining to spirit appear to emerge as were noted in the other Christian apologists. Kierkegaard's anthropology is clearly based on the assumption that man is *spirit*, that this spirit is characterized by self-transcendence, and that it is capable of objectivization and possessed of freedom. He likewise concurs with the interpretation of freedom which was outlined under Berdyaev and Niebuhr, etc., and in this sense which stands in contradistinction to that of the psychologists. And finally, he notes that spirit cannot ground itself in itself, but only in that "Power which posited it." In other words, where naturalistic science breaks the relation with that Power, it is incapable of comprehending man and man's problems. And insofar as phenomenological psychology sees the dimension of spirit, "it cannot explain" it because it sees spirit trying to ground itself in itself.

What then is the conclusion of the matter vis-a-vis the dimension of spirit in man as seen by the psychologists and the Christian anthropologists?

The dimension of spirit of the *imago Dei* is a *sine qua non* of Christian anthropology. As far as the psychologists are concerned, Freud attempted to eliminate it by his naturalistic scientism, but was forced to go beyond his methodology into a recognition of what might legitimately be strained to represent a likeness of spirit in his speculative concept of *eros* through his assumption of the instinct of self-preservation. The dissenters broke with Freud's methodology which was too limited and limiting and were compelled to a phenomenological viewpoint by the *subject* man, saw the dimension of *spirit* as possessed by self-transcendence, incapable of being objectified and having freedom, but in attempting to ground spirit in itself, failed to comprehend the full dimension of the nature of man as a being made by God and for God. This having been said, it must be noted that Adler, Jung, Putnam, and Rank are not altogether lacking in a religious dimension, and they must be given credit for at least leaving that area open—unlike Freud who attempted to seal it off. However, as Kierkegaard noted, they have apprehended the spirit dimension without fully comprehending it, because of the self-imposed restrictions of their methodology.

More particularly, the relation of the spirit dimension in the psychologists to the spirit dimension in Christian thought, as identified with the notion of *imago Dei,* cannot be consummated because what the Christian anthropologist insists on, viz. the creation of man by God, for God, the psychologist, lacking a clear ontology, fails to reckon with. It would almost appear as though, starting from radically different points of view—psychology from the standpoint of man and Christianity from the revelational standpoint of God—have converged toward the same point, spirit, and then diverged to a sort of hiatus. It would appear to this writer that any attempt at rapprochement between religion, or more specifically the Christian faith, and psychology will have somehow to go through this wicket gate. Or, if that time does not come, the regulative discipline of Christianity will be a valuable informant for the efforts of psychology to understand man.

Findings in Summary

The objective of this discussion was to examine the nature of man from some psychoanalytical perspectives and to examine the nature of man from a theological point of view and then to evaluate these in terms of their own premises and methodologies.

Sigmund Freud was taken as basic to the study because he was the father of psychoanalysis. Freud's view of man was found to be capable of two interpretations: (1) a biological view based on his scientific naturalistic methodology and (2) a more dynamic conception which emerged in spite of his methodology. In consistency with Freud's own "choice" set out in the "Project," we grounded our arguments against Freud on the basis of his biologism. Freud did not altogether miss the more dynamic conception of man, but in attempting to explain man in terms of biology, crippled his own findings on such a procrustean hypothesis, and the net result was that Freud emerged with a view of man that was limited and inadequate.

Freud's biologism, carried over into psychology, was the target of criticism by those who were his most intimate associates. It was demonstrated that they dissented from Freud on two grounds: (1) the limitations of his methodology and (2) the empirical evidence of another dimension of man—*spirit*—which unduly and unsuccessfully coerced Freudian biologism.

The dimension of spirit noted by the dissenters and not altogether absent in Freud—provided his premises could be enlarged—offered the stepping stone to an evaluation of the nature of man from Christian perspectives. The comparison of the nature of man in psychology with that of Christian anthropology appeared to suggest some rather exciting possibilities. Were psychology and theology speaking of the same thing when they had reference to *spirit* in the first and the *imago Dei* in the second? Several substantial similarities were noted: self-transcendence, the nature of spirit was incapable of objectification, and the characteristic of freedom. At this point the comparison terminated. The unique and necessary methodologies frustrated any hope of intimate and open rapprochement. Nevertheless, each had curiously substantiated the findings of the other to a rather remarkable degree. Scientific naturalism had proved abortive for a complete evaluation of the nature of man. Christian theology could look forward to a valuable ally in phenomenology as it unfolds man's nature. The regulative discipline of Christian anthropology might be a valuable informant for the efforts of psychology to understand man.

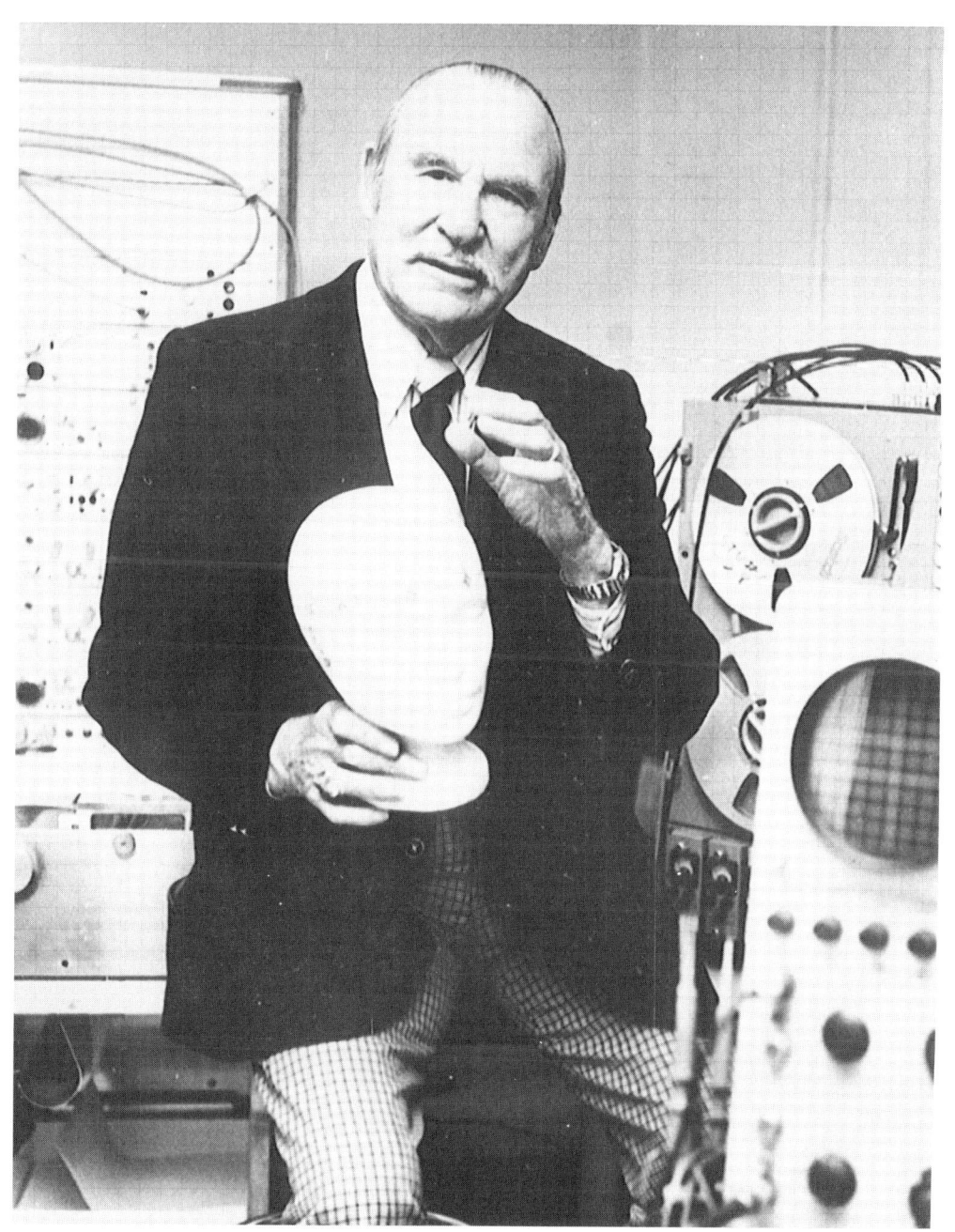

Lee Edward Travis in lab

Lee Edward Travis with student Steve Meyer

Top: Lee Edward Travis with John G. Finch
Above: From left: Annette Weyerhaueser, Lysa and Lee Travis, Honey and Charles Fuller

Top: Bill Evans (first graduate), Lysa and Lee Travis
Above: Edith Munger (first woman graduate)
Right: Symbol of the School of Psychology: Christ in the heart of psychology

Top, from left: Harold J. Ockenga, (president of Fuller at the time the School of Psychology was established), Donald C. Weber (director of development at time School of Psychology was established)

Left: Daniel P. Fuller (dean of the School of Theology at the time the School of Psychology was established)

Above: Jay Umetsu placing lei on Travis at his 90th birthday celebration in Barker Commons.

Right: Lee and Lysa Travis at 90th birthday celebration.

Far right top: Mayor of Pasadena presenting a key to the city to Travis at his 90th birthday celebration.

Far right below: Lysa Travis with artist Stephanie Beazley at the presentation of the bust of Travis she sculpted.

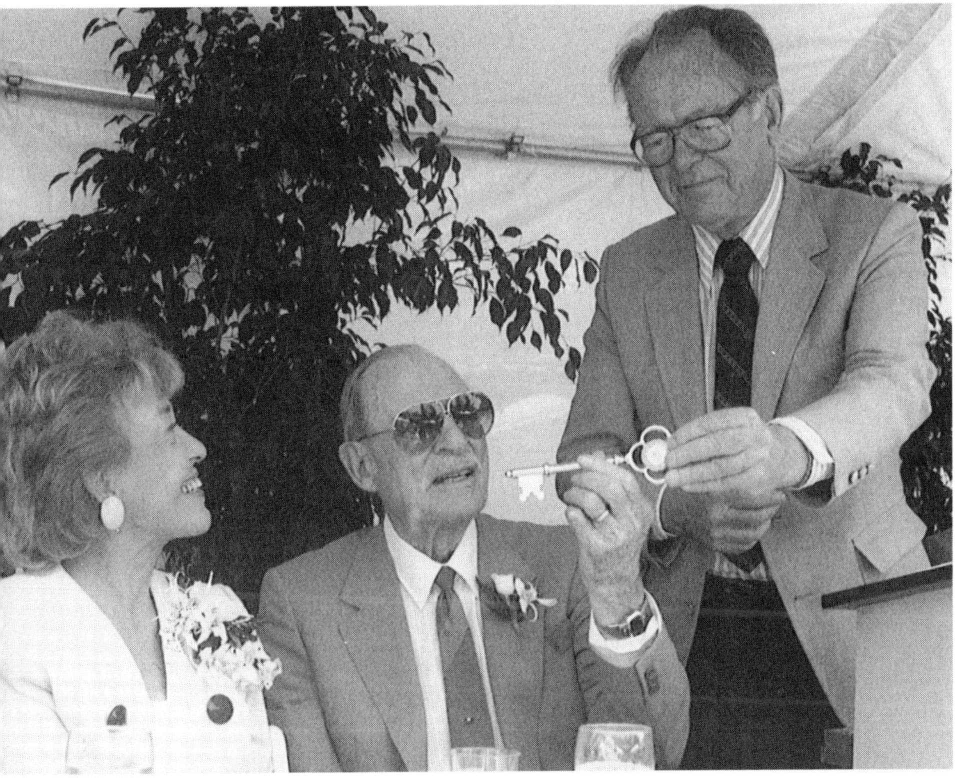

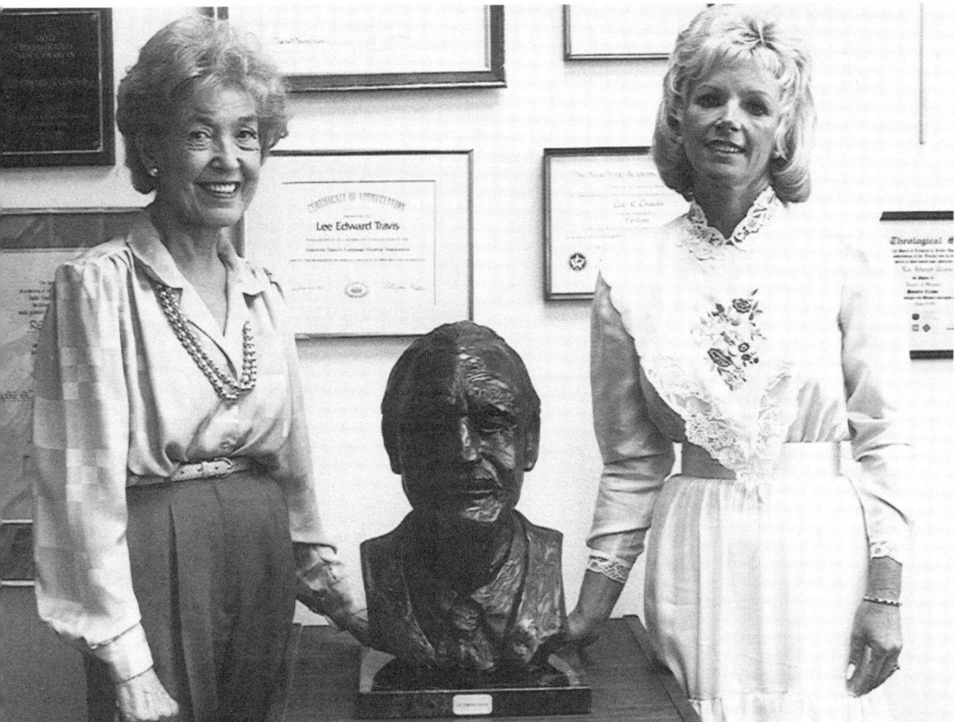
Lee Edward Travis

Top: New building at 180 No. Oakland Avenue
Inset: Old building at 177 No. Madison Avenue

A Proposed Graduate School of Christian Psychology

(Published in the Christian Medical Journal, Spring 1962, pp. 21-24)

A new development has emerged in theological education. This came as a result of a proposal offered to the faculty and board of Fuller Seminary. The proposal envisages the founding of a graduate school in psychology in relation to and under the aegis of the Fuller Theological Seminary. The proposal recommends the training of theologically oriented persons for the vocation of Christian psychotherapy to a point of competence necessary to function at the professional level. This proposal fills a hiatus in the needs of the Christian community, in that the church is missing its opportunity to minister to the rapidly increasing problem of emotional ill health in our time. This omission has left us with a very serious problem. Since apparently the church did not communicate the answer to emotional ill health, a non-Christian approach has developed to meet some of the most cogently Christian needs of the individual. In a real sense, our culture is challenging the church to fulfill its total mission. Out of a welter of confusion this school is proposed to attempt to find a distinctive Christian answer. Premised on this need of the church to meet the problem of emotional ill health, the following philosophy, objectives, and economics of a proposed graduate school were outlined.

1. The unique objective of this school is to provide for the Christian community an adequately integrated theo-psychological conceptual framework within which to conduct Christian psychotherapy.
2. This school will be devoted to conducting the necessary research from which may be developed a theo-psychological conceptual framework.
3. This school will produce psychologists who will have professional recognition and who, at the same time, will have the necessary theological understanding.
4. The school practicum activities will be so related to the church community as to provide the necessary data upon which an adequate conceptual framework may be developed.

5. The school will be so related to the seminary B.D. program as to provide appropriate instruction and counseling for seminary students.
6. The school will provide a broad base for related disciplines. One half the training is to be in related fields through arrangements with a university or graduate school such as Hartford's arrangement with Yale, which is 70 miles away.
7. The time of graduate study beyond the B.D. degree will be about three years for the Ph.D. degree. The program will be somewhat shortened by evaluating areas of competency attained through a total B.D., plus Ph.D. effort.
8. The finances for this school will require approximately $150,000 per year for faculty, research, and operating expenses. Other financing for building, equipment, library, etc., must be added to this figure.

Using these principles as a point of departure, it was decided to reap the wisdom of outstanding professional psychologists and educators who recognize the religious dimension in man. Therefore, a committee of two was authorized by the Board of Trustees to communicate the above-outlined ideas. All those interviewed felt this venture had the merit of uniqueness. The consensus was that the need was so great that something more must be done and that only a sound educational program of high competency can meet the need. Some of those interviewed, however, were not prepared to speak to the uniqueness of the proposal and some offered alternative solutions.

The committee, after close scrutiny of all alternative suggestions, decided that neither these nor other present solutions begin to touch the root of the problem. There is a Christian psychology. This is not psychology plus Christianity nor Christianity plus psychology. But, there is a need for the clarification of such Christian psychology as was expressed rather adequately by an administrator in a large Christian hospital. He said, "Throughout the years our staff and others in this field have sought for an adequate expression of principles in the area of psychiatry and psychology. We look forward to gaining some of the results of research which would quite naturally form an important part of your program. We also would like to assure you of our cooperation in every way possible. From the proceedings of this organization, the Christian Association for Psychological Studies, it has been difficult to come to an acceptable statement of our distinct approach to the human personality. There are many views and various members have their ideas and operate in their specialized fields on the basis of their own Christian viewpoints." What the administrator of this hospital is saying is that there is a crying need for synthesis, implying a specific theological point of view, to which psychological data may be related. This does not mean coercing one discipline in terms of the other but rather an affirmation of the necessity for scientific inquiry on a scientific level.

As a result of the many interviews, the committee formed certain conclusions in regard to the establishment of the proposed school. These are as follows:

1. The Christian must see his responsibility to fathom all mysteries and bring them into captivity to Christ. The area of the study of human behavior in the formulation of a Christian answer to mental illness is intrinsic to this responsibility. The school projected herein is necessary to serve as the medium to make the Christian answer evident. Other efforts simply have not been adequate.
2. The bifurcation of the function of minister and psychologist implies the relegation of the spiritual aspects of therapy to a minor role and denies the church its healing ministry. Since we believe the basic problem of mental illness is "spiritological" rather than psychological, such bifurcation in terms of training and therapeutic effort is considered contradictory.
3 In order to communicate with the field of psychodynamics, the church must accept its vocational responsibility for competence.
4. Seminaries, as educational arms of the church community, must make themselves responsible for this critical educational need of the church.
5. It is no longer possible to suggest that makeshift programs of academic training can serve as a substitute for the assumption of full responsibility for Christian scholarship. Training for those who are to function at this level must be thorough enough to create within the individual a theo-psychological integration, because the solution to the problem transcends the purely empirical approach of logical positivism.
6. This program should be of paramount interest to all serious minded Christians and can best be conducted in a setting which transcends artificial barriers of narrow prejudice or entrenched

ecclesiastical positions. For this effort, the school should be open to the contributions of all denominations. The faculty of the school should possess both theological and psychological training and experience.
7. It is essential that some such institution be established to serve as a focal point of research and reference. Leaders were concerned about the lack of such a centralizing agency to serve as the unity from, to, and through which their contributions could be evaluated and advanced. Another aspect of the research reference is the necessity for a community of scholars organized to give themselves in research and clinical practice to the development of an adequate theo-psychological conceptual framework.
8. The school also should serve as a valuable resource for the development of theological educators who are more adequate in the field of pastoral counseling.
9. The school is designed to provide graduates who are professionally competent to serve in the vocation of Christian psychotherapy. This is indeed its central objective. The values of such training are many. Some of them are as follows:
    a. They will be able to better serve the emotionally ill Christian person because of their adequate comprehension of the Christian dimension of the patient.
    b. They can function within the organized church without being a charge on its economic structure, which, at the present time, it would be unable to bear.
    c. Christian psychotherapists professionally recognized can function in private practice and bring a sense of Christian stewardship into the therapeutic profession.
    d. They can act as acceptable liaison persons interpreting the church to the profession.
    e. They can help restore to the church its rightful role in the healing ministry,
10. The objective of the school should be to secure accreditation and recognition by appropriate professional and legal bodies such as the APA and state certification boards.
11. The unanimous feeling is that the high merits of this endeavor should not be endangered by inadequate finances. The singularity, uniqueness, and pertinency of this school all point to a need for sufficiency of funds. Since the effort is new, a very compe-

tent faculty is primary. The need for research and clinical facilities involving the latest developments is essential. It is not recommended to proceed otherwise in light of the seriousness of this endeavor.

A Christian Approach to Psychology

Paul D. Fairweather

(Address delivered at the opening of the Pasadena Community
Counseling Center, November 1964)

The age through which we have passed has been titled by some as the age of the "twilight of the gods." Victor White, eminent psychologist with Christian perspective, states that it was felt, even widely welcomed, as something final and definitive.

God was dead and done with or very soon would be; dead ignominiously and almost imperceptibly, and never to be replaced. He was slain, moreover, not by other and more powerful divinity, but by the apparently triumphant march of science, by man's all conquering brain, his own head emancipating him from the delusions and superstitions which had enslaved his heart. The pure thought of philosophers had destroyed the reason for his existence; now anthropology, comparative religion, biblical criticism and the physical sciences were held to have shattered all grounds for faith in him.

At the apex of all this rationalizing came the science of psychology, as Victor White says, "to drive the last nails in the coffin of divinity." Such dramatic statements as those of the eminent psychologist Raymond Cattell characterized its expressions of omniscience. In his writings one can read statements to this effect, "The psychologists have jostled each other to be the first in routing the shattered remnants of religious forces from the battlefield of human thought. The situation is considered to be that since the physical sciences have shown how illusory religious notions are, psychological science will show through what flaws in the human mind the illusion is created and sustained." In particular, depth psychology and Freudian psychoanalysis have been credited with singular success in this achievement which is believed to have proved that God and gods and demons are but projections of the unconscious; delusional personifications of unconscious complexes. These are illusory by-products of the conflict between instinctual drives within man and the demands of the social environment. Freud is well known to have proclaimed that religion is the universal neurosis of humanity. Dumas, a Freudian psychologist, writing on the supernatural and mental illness, indicated that religion (i.e., a belief in the supernatural) is an alien and hostile element peculiar to the psychotic and that this fact invalidates religion and shows the unreality of that with which it is concerned. Depth psychology thus, in its classical psychoanalytic character, proclaimed a new salvation from man's [sic] emotional dilemmas; a salvation not through religion, but from religion, in the name of science. Its aim was to enlighten man in regard to his attempt to "escape to religion" to avoid reality. By making him aware of his nonscientific or nonobjective behavior, and by informing him of the block religion was to his ascertaining the meaning of truth, it was believed man could be freed from neurotic behavior. As Cattell and others indicated, religion basically was dangerous for society, involving as it did, "boredom and misuse of energy, vacillating loyalties, false goals, fruitless conflicts, and despair." Cattell indicated that the only course of action left to man was to follow science stoically into its bleak altitudes, that man may yet "reach something as valuable as all that was lost in religion."

But for all these allegedly scientific notions, god-substitutes in their demonic manifestations would not desist and would not lie down and die for the observing psychologist, and particularly for many perceiving psychotherapists. The science of psychology can change the name of the deities or demons whose reality they meet, but the problems they create continue. Psychologists may even reveal the problems inherent in an unenlightened faith, culticly organized religion, the irrationalities of a particular theological system, or the neurotic emotional manifestation and distorted perceptions obvious in some religious activities. But man will have his god, or gods, and the person cannot begin to be understood unless it is accepted that he will become aware of the true God, or he will fashion and worship one of his own contrivance. So-called scientific efforts to explain God away by postulating that such thinking grows out of delusions, which in turn forms the substance of the god-illusion, will not satisfy the quest of the human soul for the realities of need underlying his delusion, i.e., the experience of the true and living God of history and the acceptance of his image in man. It is one thing to believe that a person can be deluded in his understanding of his spiritual nature as a human being, and another thing to contend that the delusion is rooted in the irrationalities and secret wishes involved in mere biological propagation and survival. Thus, in inspecting the roots of religious behavior, the psychotherapist has been brought to the frontiers of a realm traditionally held by theology, the realm of ultimate meaning and values without which understanding of the person is impossible. Psychology and theology can no longer exist in isolation one from the other in their search for truth. Some may say no synthesis of meaning can be reached. Some may even say they do not care whether synthesis of meaning can be reached; but synthesis of meaning must be shown to be possible unless both disciplines are to starve and die in the land of a uselessness to man in terms of his spiritual nature and needs. This is the right of psychology to be part of the theological task.

This need for the understanding of the meaning of the spirit dimension in man's behavior is discussed by Sidney M. Jourard, professor of psychology at the University of Florida, in a paper titled "Body Image and Cultural Norms" presented at the APA in September 1959. He says "a nagging and persistent problem to psychologists is spirit. For centuries, nonscientific man has insisted that spirit is real, and that it is the essential part, the truly human part of man." Carl Jung states in an article written in 1952, "the problem of neurosis extends from the disturbed sphere of the instincts to the ultimate questions and decisions of our whole "worldviews." Neurosis is no isolated, sharply defined phenomenon. It is a reaction of the whole being. Here a purely symptomatic therapy is obviously even more definitely prohibited than in the case of purely somatic illnesses, although these also invariably have a psychic component or syndrome, even though they are not psychogenetic. Modern medicine has just begun to take account of this fact which the psychotherapists have been emphasizing for a long time. In the same way, long years of experience have again and again taught me that a therapy along purely biological lines does not suffice but requires a spiritual completion. Jourard, in speaking of the spirit dimension of personality, says, "I think we may be on the brink of a conceptual breakthrough." Certainly the theological Christian community has a responsibility to contribute to the effort that is needed to facilitate breakthroughs along these frontiers of thought. Victor White says, "The psychologist can no longer bypass in the name of illusion those (spiritual) realities which underlie such immense demonstrations of love, hate, passion, devotion, wrath, fear, wonder, beauty, joy, horror, cruelty, ecstasy, self-denial, inspiration, thought, intelligence, power, weakness, tears, laughter, guilt, and repentance." It is up to the Christian community in its educational effort to make as certain as possible that such realities of experience be not bypassed and that their spiritual-psychic roots be appreciated.

Dr. Carl Jung and Dr. Earle Biddle perceive the entire problem of authority in human affairs as due to the ascription of omnipotence and omniscience to inappropriate aspects of human experience when such omnipotence is not ascribed to the character of God. Under such conditions persons unconsciously substitute or deify the nation or state, a leader, a party, a relation, even a religious leader, or themselves. Under such a denial of the spirit in human affairs, the gods which remain to be worshipped are diseased and sick and cause oddities of the professional office so that they find release in mental epidemics. "When God is not recognized, selfish desires develop and out of this selfishness comes illness," states Jung.

A major handicap to overcome in understanding the person in Christian psychological perspective is the accurate assessment of the traditional psychological position on the nature of man as compared to the contemporary mood of many psychologists who perceive man as a spiritual being. Traditional psychology, contrary to much popular opinion, should not be identified with a deep appreciation for the total person in both his [sic] conscious and unconscious dimensions. Traditional psychology has been significantly concerned to evaluate and measure conscious function on the one hand, or on the other hand, as via Freud, to describe the processes of the unconscious in limited terms that define away much of its true meaning for the person so that much of its spiritual significance is bypassed. The purely scientific reductionistic approach to the person assumed the unconscious was basically the enemy of rational man; a refuse-bin of the mind, a receptacle into which noxious material had been passed. It was identified with instinctual wishes and their repressed by-products. Actually, psychology, in the name of Freud, became concerned with the unconscious when it had handed to it a structure which assertedly could explain and encompass and thus control for scientific observation, the deeper recesses of the personality. Thus, rational explanations could be given for all man's moral and spiritual dilemmas.

This interpretation of the unconscious in terms of instinctual wishes coupled with the aggressive drives associated with them, fits in very well with naive theology and the tendency in man in his sinfulness to rationalize religion and cut off its meaning for the whole person. Our Christian faith can become a mere set of cultic norms to be used defensively against the unconscious when the unconscious is seen as a lower order of being.

Modern man has developed a mental-spiritual paralysis in his attempt to intellectualize himself, and split off from the deeper reaches of his spirituality, has begun to become ill. He has more and more given himself over to a denial of all that he is, and his need for God in a more than intellectual way. Out of touch with himself and with God, he is lonely and divided within. He is a victim of his fears, "hanging on," possessing a faith which more and more amounts to intellectual discussion. It is certain that the spiritual needs of man require a psychology that goes in a different direction from that of Freud. The effort of most modern psychology to keep man's psyche a closed system, all of whose contents can be explained according to some set system, must be transcended.

This leads us to posit that the Christian psychological stance must relate itself to theology and philosophy if man is to be understood in the totality of his being. Man simply cannot be understood only in terms of the measurable, or even in terms of an overly simplified naturalistic-biologistic explanation of his being. Man as spirit must have the meaning of his being revealed to him as a spiritual being. What needs to be determined is the way that which is measurable is compatible with that which can be given only by revelation. This is the heartbeat of the psychology department at Fuller. Dr. John Finch, in a series of lectures given at the seminary, made it abundantly clear that psychology had its roots in philosophy. With the Enlightenment and consequent development of logical positivism, however, psychology separated itself from philosophy to study man as an object, a biological-naturalistic phenomenon. This attempt was summarized by Peter Koestenbaum in the *Journal of Existential Psychiatry*:

In sum, the general features of the positivistic position are: (1) that meaning is tied to method of confirmation; (2) that confirmation is ultimately based on the observable characteristics of physical objects, and (3) that a proposition to be confirmable, and consequently meaningful, must be capable of precise and preferably measurable formulation."

This article demonstrates that this positivistic position eliminates phenomenological data which is incapable of being forced into this scientific mold. Dr. Finch has stated that "it is this incapacity to accommodate the phenomenological data which has forced the study of psychology back into philosophy in order to be able to understand its subject—man." The American Psychological Association has recognized this move in its establishment of the Committee on Philosophical Psychology involving such psychologists as Rollo May, Carl Rogers, etc. Theological psychologists likewise have been busy this year establishing a National Pastoral Counseling Association designed to bring theology and psychology together on a level of more adequate communication. In regard to counseling and therapeutic concerns in this relationship to theology, much more they realize is needed.

It is believed that a positivistic approach to man and his true needs contains the seeds of neurosis because, in an attempt to understand himself along and within such lines, if man is truly spirit in nature, he must become less reasonable with himself rather than more reasonable with himself as a spiritual being. His attempt to hide the spiritual realities of existence under a cloak of scientific knowledge about himself can easily cut him off from an awareness and experience of himself as a spiritual being. The essential meaning of anxiety, guilt, and fundamental conflict-laden emotions will be misinterpreted in light of their true significance. In turning his gaze from himself as a needful spiritually dependent person who can exist meaningfully only in humble acknowledgment of these needs to a defensive scientific intellectualizer who knows a great deal about himself but has little experience of himself, man has cut himself off from the spiritual meaning of his anxiety and has lost himself in attempting to evade the call of God upon his spirit. Such "hip-pocketing" of the universe, the broad reaches of his own selfhood and the meaning of God has left man being very unreasonable with himself. A psychology which relates itself to the study of man along more adequate dimensions is certainly called for. Man needs to be reasonable with himself in his spirituality.

Theological systems and the cultic expectancies of the church have further exaggerated this psychologically defensive posture against man's basic spiritual needs. Christian congregations often have compromised their own conscience and conviction and thus traded their spiritual integrity for the potage of temporary social security among other Christians. Members play roles and hide their true opinions from each other and even themselves. But, that this does and can happen, in no way vitiates the significance of man's dealing with himself and being responsible to himself and God as a spiritual being. Man in his sinful state ties himself to his neurosis whenever he is encouraged to accept his responsibility for himself. Christian psychology must foster understandings on this dimension rather than to negatively focus on the problems of the neurotic expectations of the Christian community as if something outside of man himself is responsible for his loss of spiritual integrity. Christian psychological understanding of personality must proceed along lines of theological conceptualization. Such understandings as the Trinity must be duplicated in psychological conceptualization in terms of their meaningfulness for man within his own psyche. The Father God of love, reason, and guidance, the Holy Spirit of God who succors, helps, sustains, nurtures, calls into spiritual life and sustains that life, and the Son of God who identifies personally with us as captain of our salvation in our efforts to relate to the Father as obedient children, need to become a focal point for studying the meaning of the image of God for the Christian. Important theological concepts such as sin and salvation must be understood in terms of man's self-integrity or his relationship to himself, and his spiritual-personal needs, as well as in terms of his relationship to God. It is the task of Christian psychology to go beyond present means of personality assessment to an investigation of personality related to needs developed by revelation and theology. Christian psychology must study the unconscious processes from the standpoint of the image of God in man. Man's behavior, emotional structure, and the pursuits of his intellect must be studied in terms of his basic spirithood.

Christian psychology of the self will take as serious projects for a study of the unconscious the realities underlying the illusions and idols of religion with the aim of helping man toward behavior more responsible in terms of the true and living God. As important a concern for psychology as it is for theology is the meaning for man of both subjective and objective reality. Christian theological perspective at this point must be accepted as having real meaning for an adequate understanding of man's psychological dilemma. The significance of revelation for psychology must be integrated with psychological concerns. A brief statement of the Christian psychological problem in this regard has been stated by Dave Donaldson: "Modern man is torn between this objective-subjective dilemma. Part of his conscious mind wants to believe in religious reality, that he is made in the image of God, that his inner life is objectively real; while part of his conscious mind wants to believe that truth can be found only in reality which is outside himself." But truth's criteria are both objective and subjective. Objective data finds meaning only within the self. Objective fact can reveal the link between the conscious self, the unconscious self within, and the Spirit of God which is both imminent and transcendent. The Scriptures show how this can be done. They show that there is a transcendent quality to the images man possesses within his own psyche of God and himself. These transcend consciousness in other than purely rational ways. Man's self-image and God-image point to something unknown in many of their ramifications, but inherently valid. Man needs to be interpreted in such a way that his outward acts are seen as consistent symbolically with his spiritual, or image state. Psychological defenses involve the projection of denied, bad images of God and self onto the external world. Man's drive to contact inner reality and become whole is self-defeating whenever he is not made aware of this. When the bad image of God and self which man has is absolutized, his behavior is idolatrous; i.e., false absolutes are substituted for the true absolute and served in self-defeating ways. A study of the conditions of man's psyche in its idolatrous states should be undertaken as a serious task by those psychologists perceiving the importance of man's spiritual nature.

A problem which harasses the contemporary study of psychology is the persistent one of values. Freud and modern psychology generally treat the conscience of man superficially although in a very complex manner. Nevertheless, the conscience of man presents psychology with the most stubborn and intractable elements of the human psyche. In the act of treating God as an illusion among the other illusions of religion, i.e., man's psychic idols, psychoanalysis has dealt with God himself as an unconscious projection of irrational instinctual wishes. It is just here, however, that it has been faced with the unyielding demand of human nature in its spiritual dimension. Man's basic psychological problems must be dealt with at this point, the point of differentiating his neurotic idols from his desire and need for trust in the true and living God.

This makes the place of values in the psychological effort much more significant because they pass out of the realm of the relative into the realm of the absolute. It is relativity of all values that has made entering into dialogue with a client of psychotherapy outside the prerogative of the psychotherapist until recent years. It was argued that to introduce any external frame of reference would damage the client's own value system and produce a conflict. There is an increasing awareness that this position is untenable, but there is no answer to the dilemma which does not involve for man some absolutes. Values now are known to have been passing into the psychotherapeutic effort unconsciously and are now having to be recognized. As for the Christian psychological commitment, he must recognize that for legitimate psychological help to be given a person, ultimate truth must be involved in the therapeutic or healing ministry he performs. This means the goals of psychology and theology are very similar in some areas. Legitimate theology and legitimate psychology can never be at variance. Man's concept of truth cannot be related to the mere fad and circumstance of each generation, but must rest on that which is eternally true. Psychological truth must be consistent with that which is ultimately true about God. Psychology which is Christian must indicate how man in his self-delusion has tried to evade and deface the divine image within. God must be communicated to us through the experience subjectively of his Son who is the truth. The revised image of God which we experience must be evaluated against the revelation given us in Scriptures.

By means of the concept of self-realization, secular psychology has come close to admitting that man is a spiritual being. Man, the classical approach asserts, is not in rebellion against God, he is simply an instinct-driven animal. The higher values and achievements are viewed in terms of reaction formation, sublimation, etc., as if the higher spiritual motivations and aspirations could be based upon irrational instincts and biological drives. Attention is turning to the areas of values, and spiritual motivation has produced such terms as self-actualization, self-realization, ortho-psychology, orthogenesis, psychosynthesis, and many others. The direction these new theories are taking is helpful to a Christian perspective, but it must constantly be held in mind that man cannot be seen as an already unified personality. There are powerful forces within man which make him try to go against himself. The drive toward spiritual integration is a normal human urge, but this must be seen as different from the illusion of an already unified personality. A true Christian psychology must steer clear of the course of identifying altogether with such psychological movements and identify rather with the need for utilizing man's need for God in order to gain a commitment of faith and to recognize in the revelation of Jesus Christ, the final answers to those needs. In this way he can believe that with God's help he can work with his dividedness rather than being its victim. From this perspective man can be seen according to the depths of his predicament, but always in terms of a basic need, however distorted and sinful, to find the true God. Such an approach to personality can help us understand theological concepts more in terms of states of being described in Scripture by such terms as "deadness", i.e., the attitude of man in his defensive posture. Man can be understood best when need is not confused with state of being. Man in his sinful inner-dividedness psychically fights that which is good with all his strength because he misperceives it as bad, and that which he needs most as a spiritual being he fights until he dies unless he finds the grace of God to make him aware of his need and state of being. This demands that psychotherapy can, and rightly conducted will, make place for an inner conversion, a spiritual experience, a calling forth into life, and into the wholeness and integrity of the spiritual being. This is psychological growth and spiritual maturation which goes in the direction of self-actualization theory but goes far beyond mere self-awareness into growth toward spirithood. Self awareness is a necessary step toward the goal of man as a spiritual being but it is not the goal. The goal is the "new person" in Christ; anything else is not psychological growth any more than it is spiritual growth.

    The psychotherapeutic task can be stated in terms of its understanding of man as a spiritual being in different ways. One way is as follows: Man is made in the image of God. Because of his spiritual nature he has an inner need and drive to become good or whole in his person, i.e., holy; to act consistent within the meaning of his spirithood. In his bad image of God and himself as God's creature due to his sinful state of being, he constantly tricks himself, calling the good bad, and the bad good, because his need for wholeness or holiness is too frightening for him to face within the bad concept of God he possesses. He eventually comes to the deluded state of acting as though his defenses against God were good. He thus dooms himself to fulfilling the drive to wholeness in badly deluded ways. His sin is treating a good God and his creation badly and calling his own actions good. He ends up fighting God in the name of goodness. The person must be "untricked"; he must have his blindness to God's goodness removed. He must have eyes that see spiritual truth and ears that can hear spiritual truth. Man must be turned around and admit he has acted against himself, his basic nature, and the God who created him. He must perceive God as good, and recognize he needs him.

In the person of Christ, man is able to see what God is really like. Having seen in Scripture and experienced his presence in other Christians, we can go about correcting his distorted image and conforming it to the image of the true God revealed in Jesus Christ. Man in his illusion has attempted to destroy the true God by the use of a bad image of God called good. This is what happened when men crucified Jesus. In this central crisis point in history, man did his utmost to find the good Father by destroying his bad image. Man projected on to the perfect Son of God his worst image of God, i.e., the God of blasphemy and deceit. He then tried to destroy him in the name of goodness or religion, but the good God did not permit man's bad imagination to be victorious at the cross. He demonstrated to men that though they truly knew not what they did, the good God would continue to frustrate man's efforts to see him as bad. Christ truly paid the price for sin on the cross and salvaged the truth about God for man though it cost him his very life. In this act, God frustrated man's efforts to confirm his delusional thinking by making him bad. He brought into objective reality the absolute truth of his goodness as well as the truth that man's need for relationship with the good Father can be fulfilled, that man cannot frustrate God. The Word was made flesh and dwelt among us, and we beheld what God is like. And that alone can change man and make him psychically whole. Faith is the act of belief in the good image. The good image is mediated through our lives and in psychotherapy if it is to heal. This is therapy. This is love. This is the gospel. This is life. Peace becomes the ability to walk within awareness of our tensions and fears, which are the tendencies to reestablish within us a bad image of God and self. This ability is possible because life can be seen as having ultimate meaning when our images are not distorted. In inauthentic existence, when man's image of God is bad, he must evade anxiety by panicking himself, or confusing himself so he will not have to face anxiety which has within it no meaning. He experiences a kind of hell. He feels he can't believe when his very being calls for faith. Repentance is his return to his idols, his false gods, his bad images, facing them and turning to the true God.

In Summary

There are spiritual laws conveyed in revelation which predetermine the way man's unconscious processes function. We do not understand enough about these processes, but we know they are both integrative and disintegrative, depending upon the way they are understood in terms of spirithood.

Since man is made in the image of God spiritually, the unconscious must be understood according to the spiritual adequacy of the image of God he holds.

Man perceives the world around him according to spiritual laws operating in both the conscious and unconscious aspects of his experience. All objects and persons possess intrinsic, symbolic, spiritual value for him as well as extrinsic or concrete value. Unless this is understood, the person is interpreted concretely rather than spiritually.

Maturation is in terms of unconscious attempts to integrate spiritually. Behavior of individuals needs to be understood for its symbolic value in attempting to readjust the world in terms of spiritual harmony.

Images of the unconscious must be understood in terms of the individual's attempt at spiritual integration.

The image of God, man, and self is the way in which man relates to all ultimate meaning and value. It determines his symbolic use of objects and persons and the quality of his faith.

Misinterpretation of the meaning of the unconscious and conscious image of God and self lies at the root of all mental ills.

Man's moral behavior is rooted in his symbolic behavior according to the images of God and self he holds rather than in terms of cultural expectancies. The culture reflects the way in which basic images affect symbolic behavior.

Theological concepts are understood and used according to the image of God and self.

Man: In Search of Him

by
Lee Edward Travis

Dean of the Graduate School of Psychology, December 6, 1965

There are Lysa and our four children, who have given us four more children, their spouses, and 11 grandchildren. Thirteen of these 16 beloved ones are here with us tonight. There are also our two younger brothers and their wives.

There is our pastoral family, Lou and Coke Evans, Donn and Carol Moomaw, Tom and Nan Carr, and Ted and Joy Nissen. All of these loved ones except Ted and Joy are here now.

There is our Bel Air church family, our psychology and speech family, our Gibraltar family, our new Fuller family, and our vast family of dear friends who defy categorization.

Finally, may I honor particularly our very first class of students, some two dozen young men and women who have joined us in this great adventure.

My generous and constructive critic, President Hubbard, says that I am addressing myself more to the scientific establishment than to the theological community, that this is good—but I should challenge the theologians to dig in and help us carry out our task of integration.

May all of you read into my utterances our need for your help.

We are gathered here tonight to celebrate the substantiation of an idea, the metamorphosis of thought and feeling into land, buildings, books, equipment, curriculum, and people, in short, into a school, a graduate school of psychology. But still, hovering over the boards and iron, the blood and bones, is an ideal, the ideal of a center of learning, of inquiry, of search and *not* the ideal of a movement. The accepted task is to work at the growing edge of inspiration and revelation, pushing the knowledge of man into ever retreating perimeters. Not only will man's [sic] behavior, both simple and complex, be detected and recorded, but also his feelings and attitudes, beliefs, commitments, and values, will be studied by currently acceptable methods of research. Not only will we use proudly the distinctive scientific approach by which we may come to an increased understanding of man, but we will use the several other ways—common observation, intuition, and self-inquiry, reflection and philosophizing, creative and artistic expression, and revelation. All of our problems of study abound in a multiplicity of interdependent variables. We cannot employ the prescientific notion of simple cause and effect. We must utilize procedures that can identify and measure several variables operating simultaneously.

Our great challenge, as well as our great trouble, is the study of ourselves. Whatever we may do, and however we may do it, always we will be standing in our own shadow. And then, too, you and I can never really observe the same thing, because never at the same time can we be at the same place of observation. There will always be two centers of the universe, yours and mine; and physically they can never become one common observation post. But we will note well that man is able to dwell in one place physically and in another place spiritually, at the same time. Only in the spiritual dimension, then, can there ever be oneness in observation. Only in the spiritual dimension can there really ever be identity of report!

Soul to soul can never teach
What unto itself was taught.
CHRISTOPHER P. CRANCH

May we ask, "Why is this school at this place at this time?" You must have read in the program before you that Dr. John Finch had an idea of a school of psychology at Fuller Seminary, that the Board of Trustees and the faculty expressed confidence in the idea, and that Mr. Weyerhaeuser subscribed funds to encourage the realization of the idea. There are many, maybe even plenty, of universities with accredited programs educating graduate students in clinical psychology to deal with people's problems. Strong faculties, adequate research programs, and extensive clinical facilities abound all over the United States. So why Fuller Seminary? I have been asked this question often by my fellow psychologists, theologians, and ministers, by prospective students; yes—even by myself. Is there in this time of plenitude, when so many people lack nothing materially, a repeated dirge to man's hopeless existence? But is there also, at this very same time when so many people lack nothing and have nothing left, a soundless shedding of man's separate and lonely estate and the swelling appreciation of living in explicit consciousness of being a citizen of the universe? Are not ever-increasing numbers of us feeling that by the humblest work of our hands we are assisting in the completion of the creation? Are not ever more and more of us sensing that all our creaturely energies derived from God's universe amplify their source through our efforts?

The founding fathers had moments of doubt of the uniqueness of the school. They struggled, not only with its right to come into being, but with articulating that right to the field, both of theology and psychology. The theologians say that man as creature is made in, and contains, the *imago Dei*, the liberty to create. The psychologists say that man as creature is conditioned to the passivity of determinism. The theologians are ever so much more respectful of themselves and of others. Philosophically, the psychologists are disrespectful of man. Religion says that people, through decisions, make history, and that nature, apart from persons, simply passes through change.

Is the best to be done a *psychology* of religion, the explanation of the *queen* of sciences by the infant of the sciences? Maybe we could have a "religiosity" of psychology. I do not think that either one of these views matters particularly. Man lives and dies by a symbol, by a word, an idea, a feeling; by something that stands for something else that in turn may stand for still something else; by a way to tell another one about something that has no material substance at all.

Our psychology faculty members will communicate a view of man that has an abiding concern for values of ultimate significance. They will teach that the universe becomes drenched with significance by passing into man's consciousness, that man in a sense is outside nature, even though he lives in it. They will convey a conviction of the existence of resources that transcend their own. They will reveal a belief that in the smallest task, one is contributing infinitesimally to the creation of some absolute. And they will display a discerning openness to all viewpoints and approaches to the understanding of man and to fresh experiences by which they continue to move forward in the understanding of themselves and others.

So long as he lives, man moves in an environment that is not merely physical. Whatever else it is, he can seldom verbalize it easily and well, *but* of the presence of something else, he is certain. He senses his own being aside from his bodily sensations; and he senses the being of others aside from their physical dimensions. At this period in our human development, there is no point in asking about the real nature of the nonphysical milieu. It is correct to state, however, that man senses it enough to believe in its existence, and that this belief is a key determinant of his behavior and, therefore, most worthy of devoted psychological research. To date psychology has limited itself to a study of the influence of the physical and of the social environment upon the individual's behavior, It has not concerned itself with the influence of a third environment upon his behavior, the *sensed essence of being* in himself and in others. As the person continues to sense this essence of being and to grow in its import, he will develop end values that constitute the supreme motivation of his life.

In a related vein, we may contemplate the three great unions in human existence. For the individual person, life begins with the *organic* union with another, the mother one. The soundness of this union will determine the soundness of his physical equipment. Through semipermeable membranes, nutrient substances from the mother's blood enter the child's blood, and waste products from the baby's blood enter the mother's blood. In this exchange between the maternal and embryonic bloodstreams, there is the first union, the physical or biochemical. May we note importantly that there is no channel for the transmission of feelings and intentions, moods, memories, or ideas from the mother to her infant. No nervous tissue connects the two, the *only* tissue that subserves the mind. Her mind cannot get to his mind in this stage of organic union. The interaction of minds has to wait upon the second union, the *social* one.

Man takes about 25 years to reach full stature, longer than any other creature; and the bulk of this time is spent in one form or another with others. Poor interpersonal relationships with a significant parent ends in an irreversible reduction in natural intellectual, language, and emotional development of the child. Learning of all kinds occurs best under conditions of a warm and close social union between child and parent, pupil and teacher. Identification with another person and acceptance or rejection by him constitute the most important single ingredient in maturation. In every conceivable way, modern man's problems are social. His main trouble and his main help, both, are people. Horizontal relationships are capricious and ambiguous. The ultimate in social rapture results in the ultimate in mental illness, in a condition commonly known as autism. A degree of autism characterizes every variety of emotional disturbance.

The third or *spiritual* union is born in man's discontent with his lonely and transitory station. He cannot maintain a unity between the *knower* and the *known*, between himself and *every other one*. He is terribly aware of the split between the subject and the object. A chasm exists between man's act of thinking and the objects of his minding. Every single conceivable earthly union, at times and in ways, fails him. In his struggle against illness, insanity, and evil, only an impelling appropriate role in the scheme of creation will sustain him. And in the cosmic creativity, buried deep within his own resources, man may find his place in a harmony much wider than himself or anybody else. He will experience a total shedding of his awareness of his separate existence and a sublime realization of his oneness with all others. A unitive consciousness will displace his usual self-regardful separateness. An experience of *allness* abides in the submersion of his individual person into all else. He will become at one with himself only when he is overwhelmed with the sense that he is not self-containing and was never meant to be, but just a channel of the life and energies of the universe. He will become particularized in the infinite, where the whole is both the song of creation and the singer himself, without beginning and without end. Is this mysticism? And if so, is it bad? Certainly it need not be, but instead it can be a continuing experience of the divine presence in the encounter and activities of daily living. No escape from reality whatsoever needs to follow upon the consummation of spiritual union. Instead, the demands of the here and now become acutely relevant and joyfully welcomed.

We will search man out organically, mentally, socially, and spiritually. We will search him out by every means of study possible. We will not assume now or ever that we will or can know all of the meaning of the revelation of the nature of man. We can only hope to grow in knowledge and understanding from whatever source possible. May we here note the poet, our own reflective selves, and the scientist as helpmates in our search.

Man: In Search of Him

The poet can most assuredly enrich our insights with the extra-rational character of revelation in imaginative vision, symbols, and metaphors.

*Any man's death diminishes me
because I am involved in mankind;
And therefore, never send to know
for whom the bell tolls. It tolls for thee.*
                                    John Donne

*True language of life is always a monologue.
All that I verbalize is naming what I am.*
                                    John Dorsey

*Whither shall I go from Thy Spirit?
Or whither shall I flee from Thy presence?
If I ascend to heaven, Thou are there!
If I make my bed in Sheol, Thou are there!
If I take the wings of the morning
and dwell in the uttermost parts of the sea
Even there shall Thy hand lead me
and Thy right hand shall hold me.
If I say, "Let only darkness cover me
and the light about me be night,"
Even the darkness is not dark to Thee;
The night is as bright as the day;
For darkness is as light to Thee,
For Thou didst form my inward parts,
Thou didst knit me together in my mother's womb.*
                                    Psalm 139:7-13

*See ever so far, there is limitless space outside of that
Count ever so much, there is limitless time around that
My rendezvous is appointed, it is certain
The Lord will be there and wait till I come on perfect terms
The great Camerado, the lover true
for whom I pine will be there.*
                                          WALT WHITMAN

*I have memories of joy between the tears
of yesterdays and tomorrows,
Moments of perception and passion and
black trees against an endless sky.
Children play games of make believe,
for only in darkness does dreaming run its course.
Make believe dreams until faith, or death—
Until the moments become eternal.*
                                          PAUL BERGEN

*By night and by day
From afar and from near by
He was without a secret.
His soul was open for all to see.
And when they looked, as many as could venture the risk,
They saw the purified countenance of themselves.*
                                          LEE TRAVIS

We, all of us, have at our ready disposal for the deepest insights into human nature, man's most cherished possession, self-reflective consciousness. It is both creative and evaluative. Through its creations it speaks unto its existence as personal, quantal, and nonfragmentable. Among its masterpieces of creation is a universe of inconceivable proportions. The path from body to mind is strewn with an ever-increasing fragility of substance. At the end of the trail the tissue serving consciousness is like delicate and sheer lace ensured against damage and tear by placement in the strongest of lock-boxes, the cranium. From this tissue, in this vault, consciousness rules the world. Man, its proud owner, man the timid and frail one, equipped with creation's crowning glory, can span the space-time binding of his senses and his muscles and, quicker than a flash of light, encompass the whole universe. From the beginning this was the purpose of the creation of life. All human living is purposed to furnish this self-minding with a supply of material for its enjoyment and censoring. This self-minding is *not* a conglomerate of heterogeneous functions, but a *given*—one and indivisible.

Many have proclaimed that all observation is self-observation, and of the nature of an appraisal. Knowledge of the external world is no more in the final analysis than a perception of our reactions to outside stimulation. Knowledge cannot be of anything but of ourselves, of the resonance of our organisms to changes from without and from within. All labeled mental illness is a diminution in the capacity to know, that is, in a lowering of the level of consciousness. So long as the normal level of self-reflective awareness is not reduced by either psychological or physiological forces, we keep fast our contact with the external world which is public and common to us all, and do not submerge ourselves in our interior and private worlds. The one demand made of us in remaining normal is to discriminate and differentiate sharply between an internal and an external event. And the key to the distinction is an awareness of self, the necessity for one to sense himself as a subject capable of dreaming and of doubting. In a loss of self-consciousness, doubting is lost and the individual is plunged into the darkness of the immovable security of a psychosis. So long as one can doubt, there is hope for his sanity.

The current high level of self-minding is still not high enough. The human being is still living in incomplete self-illumination because his ability to own himself is not yet fully developed in nature and because, as he grew, he willed out of his mind some painful living. Until now there were some dark corners in his selfhood. To make himself more consciously mindful of his totality should be his only concern. He can help himself by letting his mind have its wayward course and then observing its revelations. He can improve by loving his helper as his very own loving and by recognizing that he is the sole originator of his own distress. His solution lies entirely within himself as both the perpetrator and the victim of his troubles. For at strategic moments in his living, he chose sides.

The third helpmate, the scientist, uses a procedure that is essentially the persistent and repeated testing of an idea, a hunch, an hypothesis. When he finds any correspondence between his guess and the facts of observation, he feels he may be getting at the symptom of the truth—not the truth itself, and certainly not the whole truth. Controlled step by controlled step, he searches for ever-deepening and widening correspondence. Without a sustaining faith in the unity of all things; without an intuitive recognition of the universal beauty in harmony and in oneness, I just do not believe he would continue his patient labors. Bridgeman has written that "the scientist is perhaps only a passing phase in the evolution of man; after unguessable years it not impossible that his work will be done, and the problem of mankind will become for each individual the problem of best ordering his own life." And, too, it is to be remembered that there are no objective data. All data belong to a subject and are, therefore, subjective.

In a significant sense the scientist is compelled both logically and emotionally to accept the planner in the planned, since actually he, the scientist, finds intelligibility in the whole universe to meet his own craving for this correspondence to his own human intelligence. Attesting to the certainty of God's existence is man's ability to create him in order to meet man's need of him. The creation of man included in the process a need of God and the *ability* to meet the need.

The fact that we have scientists who are so dedicated and make such heroic efforts to recreate in the mind the unity of the universe in all its dimensions is what is significant, and not what they find. The idea common in certain circles that science has nothing to do with values is erroneous and unfortunate, if not damaging. Science itself is no more materialistic than religion, and is just as much concerned with the ultimate meaning of things, whether matter or mind. In my humility, I feel that there is no barrier beyond which inquiry cannot be pushed. If science enters the world of the spirit, so much the better for the scientist, and the spirit cannot possibly come off the loser. Truth can *never* suffer from scientific inquiry. And if theology enters the field of the scientist, the theologian may develop in wanting to know *why* and *how* and to be able to prove it.

A man is both body and soul, and to be a good man his body and soul must live together in peaceful union. *Man: In Search of Him.* Can we face in innovative endeavor, scientific or otherwise, uncertainty and recurrent disappointments? Can we fulfill the dream and pursue the goal that one day man may be found and revealed more understandably in his true significance?

Thou wouldst call, and I would answer thee
Thou wouldst long for the work of Thy hands
JOB 14:15

The Graduate School of Psychology
A Faculty Genealogy for the Travis Years

Anniversaries often spur us to reflection on the past, as we recall shared memories and anticipate a shared future. Families may use such anniversaries to reflect on their ancestors and their extended kinship network. Academic psychologists may also benefit from such reflection, as their research, teaching, and scholarship is rooted in the work of those who served as research mentors or clinical supervisors. The faculty genealogy illustrated in this chapter was prepared in honor of the twenty-fifth anniversary of the Graduate School of Psychology but was unfortunately not published at that time. It provides the research-related roots of the first-generation faculty who served under Lee Travis' deanship. The research was conducted primarily by students in the required course on History and Systems of Psychology and a related research seminar, after I had tested the research procedures and library resources on several branches of my own "family tree."[1]

Working together in small groups focused on their academic advisor, students began by identifying the chair, and sometimes the committee members, for their advisor's dissertation, as well as the title of the dissertation.[2] They then repeated these procedures, identifying the dissertation chair (and sometimes committee members) for their advisor's chair, and so on, back to the first generation of psychologists (both American and European). This exercise was relatively easy for the most recent generation of psychologists, since the information is in most cases easily found in *Dissertation Abstracts International*. It was also relatively easy for the first generation, for whom the information often appears in standard textbooks. Intervening generations were more difficult to trace, forcing us (mostly me!) into the realms of archival research that generated extensive correspondence and phone calls.[3]

Initially this project was simply a way to make historical names and events a part of the students' personal history and to teach them the rudiments of historical research methods. Eventually, we realized that there were many interesting personal stories to tell as we explored this part of our history. We asked living Fuller faculty to look over their personal genealogies and to write a reaction. I added other comments from my perspective as a historian of psychology and of the task of integration. The sections that follow blend my commentary with personal reactions, taking the faculty in alphabetical order.

PAUL F. BARKMAN (1964-1970)*

> **Paul F. Barkman**
> Ph.D. 1959, New York University
> *A Study of the Relationship of the Needs for Belonging and Conformity to Religious Beliefs and Values in a Christian College*

> **Dan William Dodson**
> Ph.D. 1941, New York University
> *Protestant Church Trends of New York City 1900-1936—Causes, Correlates, Consequences*
> (dissertation chair)

* Note: For all charts, the Fuller faculty member's name is in a box with a solid rule. The names of those who chaired the faculty members' dissertations or were members of the doctoral committees are enclosed in a box with a dashed rule. When scholars who influenced these persons are known, they are also noted.

Barkman's roots as a psychologist are very recent. His dissertation was chaired by the sociologist Dan William Dodson, who was the director of the Center for Human Relations and Community Studies and a member of the Society for the Psychological Study of Social Issues (now Division 9 of APA). Barkman offers the following reflections on his roots:

> When I chose a college major in psychology there was no defined profession of clinical psychology. So my professional roots are rather like a Florida cypress—coming from all directions to nurture one resulting entity.
>
> In my first breathtaking course in psychology, Peter Schellenberg asked questions that provoked thought without attacking faith.
>
> At the Biblical Seminary in New York, inductive Bible study was done so intimately that one felt the dust of Palestine on one's shoes. I

became more at home in the Word than in the structures built upon it. And my integration of psychology has been more with the Bible than with theology.

Dan W. Dodson, who guided my doctoral studies through an interdisciplinary department (anthropology, sociology, and psychology), had recently persuaded Branch Ricky to hire Jackie Robinson for the Brooklyn Dodgers.

My first clinical supervisor, Newell Schmalzreid (Ph.D., Purdue) was a "lay" psychoanalyst with such honesty, insight, and caring that I persuaded him to change roles and become my analyst, which opened another new world.

At Reiss-Davis Clinic for Child Guidance in Los Angeles, Rudolph Ekstein, Freud's last pupil (who was for many years on the staff of the Menninger Foundation), taught the psychoanalytic theory of psychotherapy in an engaging style, with solid footing in practical human affairs (his degree was in social work), an Old Testament kind of wisdom, and the ability to integrate it all in a warm, empathic person. His teaching, Mortimer Meyer's lucid instruction and supervision of projective techniques, and Anna Freud's booklet, "Ego and the Mechanisms of Defense,"[4] together with my own psychoanalysis, became integrated with my evangelical Christianity and my interdisciplinary education to give a psychodynamic orientation to my subsequent eclectic clinical style. With time I came to realize that what I had absorbed was not so much classical Freudianism as my teachers' personal integration of it. Looking at it through their eyes made sense.

Significant about these diverse mentors is that each of them was as much a convincing person as a source of knowledge or skill. They all seemed to draw a breadth of resources into their specialized concentration, and each put it together in the kind of being that made their theories plausible, their skills relevant. Knowing them, I could listen to what they taught. They were good models.

A Faculty Genealogy for the Travis Years

Robert K. Bower (1958-1978)

> **Robert K. Bower**
> Ph.D. 1956, University of Chicago
> *Curricular Factors in the Selection of Organizing Principles for a Course of Study*

> **Ralph W. Tyler**
> Ph.D. 1927, University of Chicago
> *Statistical Methods for Using Personal Judgments to Evaluate Activities for Teacher Training Curricula*
> (dissertation chair)

> **Douglas Waples**
> Ph.D. 1920, University of Pennsylvania
> *An Approach to the Synthetic Study of Interest in Education*
> (committee member)

> **W. W. Charles**
> (committee member)

Bob Bower's educational pilgrimage took him from his Detroit, Michigan, home to nearby Wayne [State] University for his B.S. degree (1943), then to the University of Chicago for the M.A. (1950) and Ph.D. degrees (1955), and Northern Baptist Theological Seminary for his B.D. (1953). His genealogy reflects his emphasis on education, rather than a primary affiliation with psychology. Bower was a "working" student, and from 1951 to 1955 served as professor of psychology and education at the California Baptist Theological Seminary (CBTS) and as advisor to the Baptist Theological College. He was ordained by the American Baptist Church USA in 1953, and from 1955 to 1958 served as minister of Christian education at the Sunnyside Baptist Church in Los Angeles, and as professor of Christian education at CBTS. At CBTS he also served as editor of the California Seminary Bulletin and as chair of the Christian Education Department.

Bower's career at Fuller went through several stages. When he was hired in 1958 he had been a featured speaker in many young people's conferences, leadership training schools, and parent-teacher meetings, and came as associate professor of Christian education. In this capacity he argued convincingly for the role of Christian education professionals in the church.[5] When he was promoted to professor in 1962, his inaugural address to his colleagues focused on "Non-Theological Factors Influencing the Church and its Educational Program." In 1965 his title was changed to professor of practical theology and pastoral counseling, a change which reflected his shift in focus from education to healing ministries, especially those related to marriage and the family.[6]

Threading together these various interests was a common commitment to what we now call "integration." Bob Bower actively encouraged integration, through participation in the character education movement arm in clinical pastoral education, his membership in the Academy of Religion and Mental Health, in the founding of the Graduate School of Psychology, the launching of the marriage and family counseling program, and his concern for the minister's family.[7] These concerns are reflected in the titles of his published books: *Administering Christian Education* (1964), *Solving Problems in Marriage* (1972), and *Biblical and Psychological Perspectives for Christian Counselors* (1974).

PAUL WAYNE CLEMENT (1967-1988)

Through his dissertation chair, Paul Clement's roots go back to Wundt through Titchener, the master of structuralism and introspection. It is perhaps ironic that Titchener's great-great-great-grandson should study "inter-animal attraction," defying the major rule of introspection that requires full self-consciousness and a trained consciousness. Clement describes his debt to Beier as follows:

Ernst Beier was director of clinical training in the Department of Psychology at the University of Utah during the years I did my doctoral studies (1962-65). He served as my dissertation chair and had an impact on my development as a clinical psychologist in many areas.

Beier endorsed a psychoanalytic theory of personality. He helped me to appreciate the relationship between conscious and unconscious processes. Although he based his understanding of human personality on psychoanalytic theory, he developed his own theory of psychotherapy, grounded in a communications model that focused on the therapeutic dyad of client and therapist. The essence of psychotherapy for Beier was the exploration of how the client attempts to influence the therapist through nonverbal communication. He taught me the distinction between manifest and latent content in a client's message and how to use my own feelings as the major clue for identifying the latent content. He provided a comprehensive description of his theory in his book, The Silent Language of Psychotherapy.[8]

A Faculty Genealogy for the Travis Years

Paul W. Clement
Ph.D. 1965, University of Utah
Factors Influencing Inter-Animal Attraction Among Whitetail Antelope Squirrels

Ernst G. Beier
Ph.D. 1949, Columbia University
The Effect of Induced Anxiety on Flexibility of Intellectual Functioning: A Study of the Relationship between Anxiety and Rigidity
(dissertation chair)

Laurance F. Shaffer
Ph.D. 1930, Columbia University
Children's Interpretation of Cartoons
(dissertation chair)

Harold Ordway Rugg
Ph.D. 1915, University of Illinois/Urbana Campaign
Descriptive Geometry and Mental Discipline
(dissertation chair)

William Chandler Bagley
Ph.D. 1900, Cornell University
The Apperception of Spoken Sentences
(dissertation chair)

Edward Bradford Titchener
Ph.D. 1892, University of Leipzig
Über binoculäre Wirküngen monocularer Reize
(dissertation chair)

Wilhelm Wundt
M.D. 1856, University of Heidelberg
(dissertation chair)

Although Beier didn't ask his students to believe in his theory, he did require them to learn the theory and to learn how to do psychotherapy within his system. In a fashion similar to a ball game hawker calling out "You gotta have a program!" Beier repeatedly challenged his students with the proposition, "You must have a theory of personality and of psychotherapy!" He left it to the students to make their own selections but encouraged them to be explicit about their major assumptions. His teaching and supervision encouraged the integration of psychodynamic theory, conjoint family therapy, communications theory, social learning theory, and direct interventions.

Beier invited me to participate in his research group early in my first year. I learned from him how a professor can run informal research meetings as a way to introduce research to clinical students. He also modeled how to relate research to problems faced in clinical practice.

He encouraged his students to read articles dealing with professional issues and concerns. He hosted a monthly clinical colloquium in which either the invited speaker or Beier himself would discuss issues related to the practice of clinical psychology. He was active in organized psychology and encouraged his students to be involved as well. Since graduating in 1965 I have been able to have regular contacts with Professor Beier at professional meetings. Many times I have turned to him for counsel on professional matters.

Finally, he played a key role in helping me to secure my first postdoctoral position. He called Ivan Mensh at UCLA and actively promoted me as a job candidate. Based on Beier's recommendation Dr. Mensh hired me without a face-to-face interview. Quite literally, Ernst Beier launched my career.

DONALD WILLARD COLE (1962-1969)

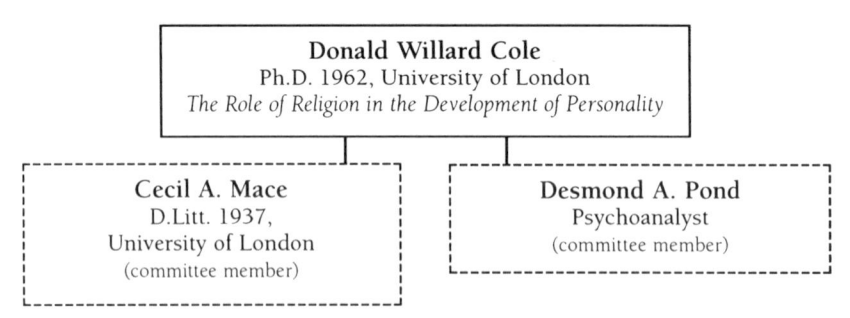

Donald Willard Cole
Ph.D. 1962, University of London
The Role of Religion in the Development of Personality

Cecil A. Mace
D.Litt. 1937,
University of London
(committee member)

Desmond A. Pond
Psychoanalyst
(committee member)

Don Cole also has a short lineage in the discipline of psychology, training under the philosopher/psychologist Cecil Alec Mace (who earned his doctorate in the 1920s) and the psychoanalyst

Desmond A. Pond. Dr. Cole died in 1991, shortly after he wrote the following reflections on his roots:

> My advisors, Desmond A. Pond and Cecil A. Mace, both encouraged me to pursue the whole area of psychology of personality. Pond was a psychoanalyst who served as professor of psychology at the London Hospital Medical College of the University of London, and author of Counselling in Religion and Psychiatry.[9] Mace was lecturer in philosophy and psychology at University College/Nottingham (1922-1925) and at the University of St. Andrews (1925-1932), reader in psychology at Bedford College/University of London (1932-1944), and professor of psychology at Birkbeck College/University of London from 1944 to 1961. He served as president of the British Psychological Society and the Aristotelian Society, and as editor of the Pelican Psychology series and Methuen's Manuals of Psychology. With G. F. Stout, he coauthored the article on "Psychology" in the 14th edition of the Encyclopaedia Britannica. In the festschrift published on the occasion of his retirement, his students described him as "charming, witty, 'extravagantly inquisitive,' deeply learned, and undogmatic on all things save the importance of man himself."[10]
>
> I was very inspired by Gordon W. Allport when he came to speak at our school. In 1964 or 1965 I was licensed by the state of California in clinical psychology. At Fuller Theological Seminary I served as the dean of students and professor of psychology. I left Fuller early in 1970 to pursue private practice. In 1973 I became the pastor of South Shores Baptist Church in Laguna Niguel, California, and am retiring this year. My first love continues to be psychology of personality.

Paul D. Fairweather (1961-1968)

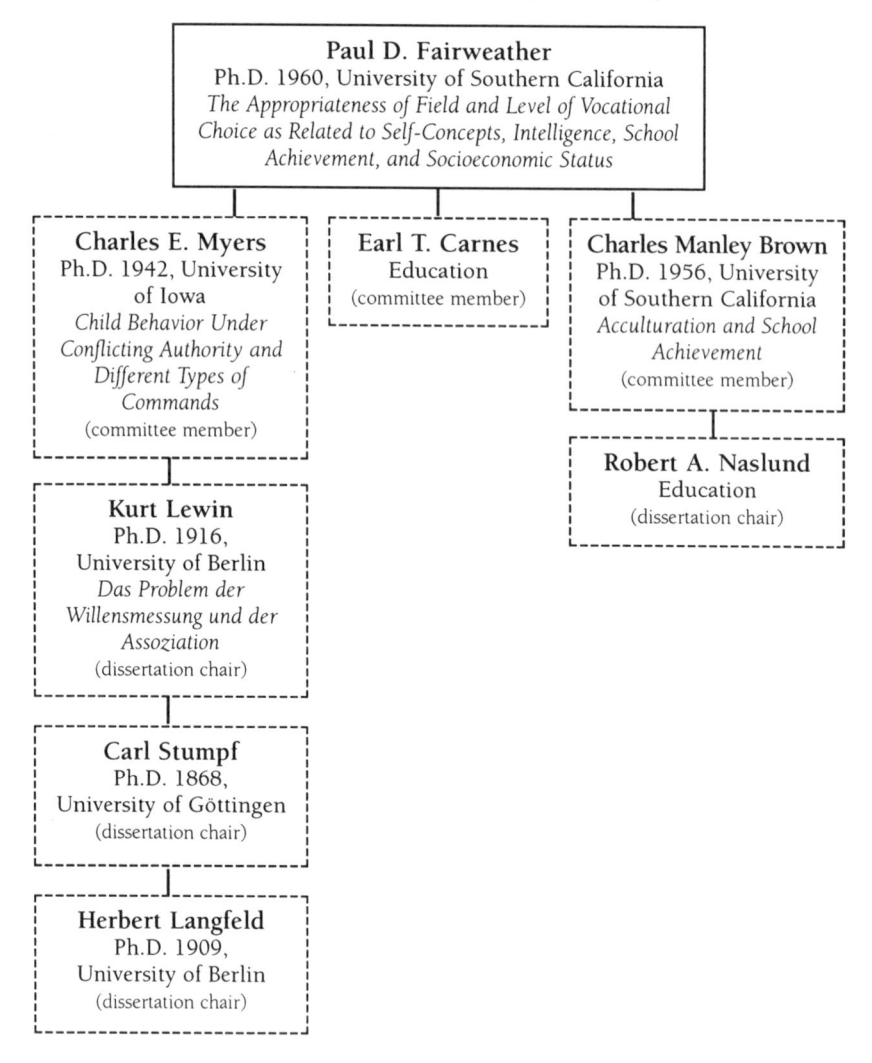

Paul D. Fairweather
Ph.D. 1960, University of Southern California
The Appropriateness of Field and Level of Vocational Choice as Related to Self-Concepts, Intelligence, School Achievement, and Socioeconomic Status

Charles E. Myers
Ph.D. 1942, University of Iowa
Child Behavior Under Conflicting Authority and Different Types of Commands
(committee member)

Earl T. Carnes
Education
(committee member)

Charles Manley Brown
Ph.D. 1956, University of Southern California
Acculturation and School Achievement
(committee member)

Robert A. Naslund
Education
(dissertation chair)

Kurt Lewin
Ph.D. 1916, University of Berlin
Das Problem der Willensmessung und der Assoziation
(dissertation chair)

Carl Stumpf
Ph.D. 1868, University of Göttingen
(dissertation chair)

Herbert Langfeld
Ph.D. 1909, University of Berlin
(dissertation chair)

Paul Fairweather earned a degree in education under Earl T. Carnes, and thus has another short lineage through his dissertation chair. But Charles Meyers, who served on his dissertation committee, was a student of both Kurt Lewin and Tamara Dembo, thus rooting him firmly in European Gestalt psychology and Lewinian field theory. Both Lewin and the Russian-born Dembo fled Berlin during the Nazi persecution. Lewin's teacher, Carl Stumpf, is well-known for his research on audition using the pieces of a tuning-fork piano as laboratory apparatus.

JOHN GEOFFREY FINCH (1964-1992)

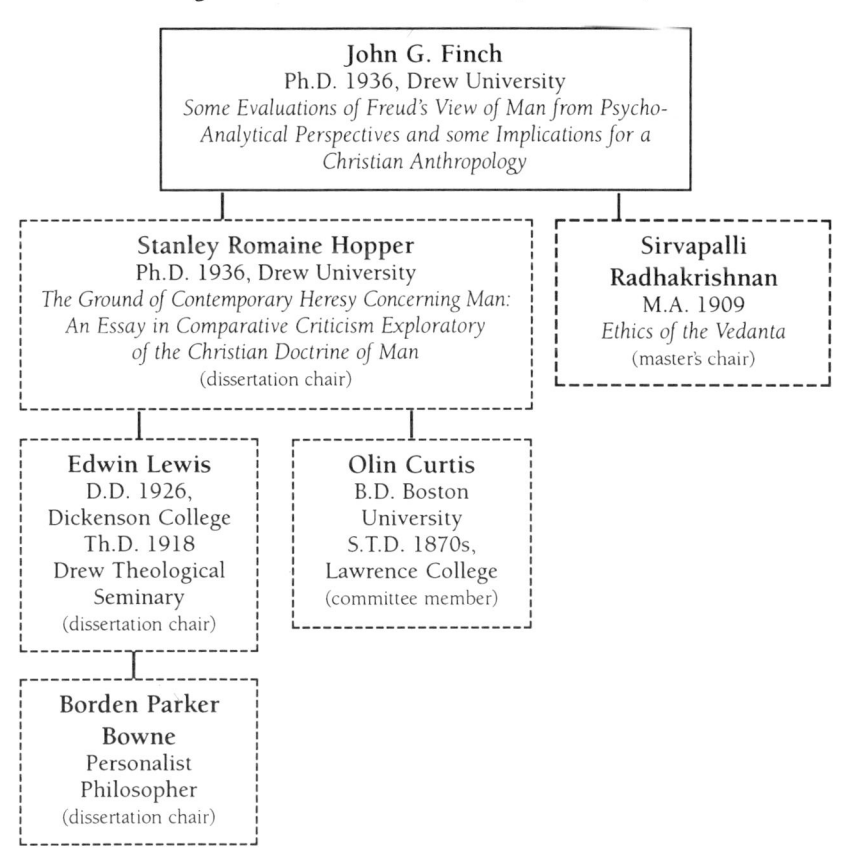

John G. Finch
Ph.D. 1936, Drew University
Some Evaluations of Freud's View of Man from Psycho-Analytical Perspectives and some Implications for a Christian Anthropology

Stanley Romaine Hopper
Ph.D. 1936, Drew University
The Ground of Contemporary Heresy Concerning Man: An Essay in Comparative Criticism Exploratory of the Christian Doctrine of Man
(dissertation chair)

Sirvapalli Radhakrishnan
M.A. 1909
Ethics of the Vedanta
(master's chair)

Edwin Lewis
D.D. 1926, Dickenson College
Th.D. 1918 Drew Theological Seminary
(dissertation chair)

Olin Curtis
B.D. Boston University
S.T.D. 1870s, Lawrence College
(committee member)

Borden Parker Bowne
Personalist Philosopher
(dissertation chair)

John Geoffrey Finch not only played a role in the founding of the Graduate School of Psychology, he also taught his philosophical psychology seminar on an annual basis as a prerequisite for his intensive therapy program. Finch's ideas on religion and psychology are best understood in the context of his childhood years in India and his later Indian education. His genealogical chart shows his master's thesis director as well as the dissertation chair, because his thesis director, Sarvapalli Radhakrishnan, played a central role not only in

Finch's development, but also in the wider community of scholars on comparative religion, and ultimately in world politics. We offer first a short biographical sketch of Radhakrishnan, written by Arthur Glasser of the School of World Mission, then Finch's recollections of Radhakrishnan, and finally Finch's reflections on his dissertation chair, Stanley Romaine Hopper.

Sarvapalli Radhakrishnan (1888-1975)
Review by Arthur Glasser

It was almost one hundred years ago that a remarkable event took place in Chicago: the Parliament of Religions of 1893. This event was so significant in its impact on the West that in 1990 plans were already afoot in the World Council of Churches circles to celebrate its centennial in 1993. On that earlier occasion a young Bengali electrified the assembly with an address that convinced many religious leaders in the West that there was something terribly wrong with their worldwide missionary enterprise. Many never recovered!

Few today can conceive of the intellectual ferment of those days among the educated elite of India. Hinduism had seemed moribund in sharpest contrast to the dynamism and power of the "Christian" West. Although a movement of renascent Hinduism had been gathering momentum for some years previously, the West knew virtually nothing about it. Christian missionaries had only reported on the bondage of caste, the inferior status of women, the preoccupation of Indians with the hopeless quest for release from worldly experience, and the spirit worship of its passive millions. But it was Swami Vivekanada who electrified the Chicago gathering with a myth created for the occasion. With great pride he announced that Hinduism was in dynamic renewal. It had long since reached the pinnacle of human development and concluded that all religions in their inmost essence are one. All are but cultural variations of the best in genuine human striving after God. All ultimately find their oneness in the supreme and universal Spirit. Then came the punch line: It is the East that is sublimely spiritual. The West is slipping into crass materialism.

In the years that followed, Mahatma Gandhi translated this new Hindu vision into political activity, and Dr. Finch's old professor, Sarvapalli Radhakrishnan, gave it intellectual validity. For 60 years, first at Madras Christian College and eventually at Oxford, this brilliant scholar and prolific writer was able to interject into world thought many of the themes that are dominant today in the debate on religious pluralism. Only late in life did he enter the political scene and become the president of India (1962-1967).

Radhakrishnan received his early education in mission schools. He had an amazing grasp of the Bible and of Christian theology, but was deeply offended by Christian apologists. Although always careful to maintain an attitude of generous tolerance, he was extremely critical of certain aspects of the Christian faith. The doctrine of sin offended him: "The natural desire of man is to be good and to seek truth." The need for reconciliation through atonement was absurd. Why should anyone regard the cross as an offense or stumbling block? "It only shows how love is rooted in self-sacrifice." All religious experience must be treasured, but creeds and dogmas, words and symbols must be resisted. They always lead to dogmatism, intolerance, exclusiveness, and the contention that the whole of truth can be confined to a single manifestation of the Eternal Spirit:

Hinduism has adapted itself with infinite grace to every human need, and it has not shrunk from the acceptance of every aspect of God conceived by man, and yet it has preserved its unity by interpreting all different historical forms as modes, emanations, or aspects of the Supreme.

One can visualize the young Finch—the only Christian in attendance—sitting at the feet of this utterly personable scholar, who without notes would lecture most persuasively on all aspects of religion. Radhakrishnan gloried in his vision of the excellence of Hinduism. He saw in religion neither psychological device nor escape mechanism, but rather an integral element of human nature. Perhaps we should ask Dr. Finch how he escaped being mesmerized by this brilliant man!

Reflections by John G. Finch

Sir Radhakrishnan was always impeccable. He was a lean, tall man who always wore a turban, which added to his height and stature. He was always dignified, almost to the point of pride. He was a philosophical lecturer. His scholarly acumen allowed him to remain a Hindu with supreme dignity. Most students approached him with hands folded together and addressed him with an attitude almost reflecting a feeling of godliness. But in his eyes we were merely students. The Indian students would put their hands together in a prayer gesture, quite typical behavior to express deepest respect. I did not follow this pattern entirely, but certainly did not keep my hands in my pocket!

There were 50 students in the class: one Muslim, one Christian (myself), and 48 Hindus or Buddhists. In class Radhakrishnan would sit in a chair, with little recognition of the class. He never used lecture notes, but would lean back in his chair and the lecture simply flowed forth like a stream. He never stopped to choose a word or backed up to repeat a word—his speech flowed. It was very difficult to take notes as he lectured. He was the class: He never recommended any outside reading. Students did not take notes—they were practically magnetized by his lecture. We were completely focussed on him: he was always brilliant. He would start the moment the bell rang and leave with the ending bell. There was no interaction through the entire period.

I started in English (Old English Literature) as a field of study as a basis for sermons. On one occasion I requested Radhakrishnan to sign a transfer to the Philosophy Department. This he did without any sense of personal contact. On another occasion I went to see him personally because I was seeking a scholarship. I was the only white person in the class, so there is no question of his recognizing me. When I asked if he would endorse the scholarship, he answered neither "yes" nor "no" but wordlessly signed the papers without any personal greeting or sign of recognition. When I presented the application, his reply was indifference. He signed, with no other response of any kind. He was impersonal. You might call it dignity or pride, but one always felt awed by him.

I had the feeling he was a man of deep prejudice. He was educated in a Christian missionary school that put down all other religions. This apparently left a painful scar on him. He himself was a Hindu, a Madrasi. He was a renowned scholar and was thoroughly familiar with the Bible as a book of wisdom. He drew from it freely and quoted Christian scripture to interpret Hinduism wherever necessary. And when Christian scripture offered new light, he would use it to explain Hindu scripture. I believe he was more Christian in his thought than he let on and melded the two traditions in a way that gave Hinduism greater priority. Wherever I traveled in India and Indians heard I'd been at Calcutta University, people would ask "When were you there?" I answered, "From 1939 to 1941." They would respond, with respect: "When Radhakrishnan was there." Because he had been my teacher, I would be given special treatment. The fact that I was his student was a privilege, especially since he was chairman of the Department of Philosophy. Later he was called to be chancellor of Benares Hindu University, a high calling that demonstrated India's recognition of him as the greatest of Hindu scholars. Other universities only had vice-chancellors, so that this also reflected the high regard in which he was held. He was a widely published scholar in comparative religions, and many volumes of his work can be found in McAlister Library.

Stanley Romaine Hopper
Recollections by John Finch

Hopper was the complete antithesis of Radhakrishnan as a teacher. He published only one book, *The Crisis of Faith*.[11] He didn't need to say anymore, because the essence of his ideas is all there, and the volume is a virtual encyclopedia. Like Radhakrishnan, he was lean and tall. Ulike Radhakrishnan, he was always late to class, tearing himself away from the radio baseball game! Students would ask, "What's the score?" and he would give it.

He always took a personal interest. When you came to see him, he didn't push you away. He was gentle, unobtrusive, and a beautiful person. His teaching method differed from Radhakrishnan's authoritarian lectures. He was socratic. We have remained friends, and a group of us visited him recently in Escondido. We were distressed to find him propped up in a wheel chair, suffering the effects of a serious accident. But none of this daunted him. He was pleased to see us, was very alert, and just as gentle as ever.

I deem it a great privilege to be permitted to reprint his book. This very undertaking is an expression of my profound respect for Dr. Hopper and his work. I am urging everyone to read it. It is a rather complete education in itself.

Archibald Daniel Hart (1973—)

> **Archibald D. Hart**
> Ph.D. 1970, University of Natal,
> Pietermartizburg, South Africa
> *The Preliminary Standardization of a South African Version of the Minnesota Multiphasic Personality Inventory and an Inquiry into its Diagnostic Validity*

> **P. A. Theron**
> (dissertation chair)

Dr. Hart offers the following comments:

Unfortunately, I have very little information about my Ph.D. mentor, P. A. Theron, head of the Department of Psychology of the University of Natal. He was a social psychologist by original training, but I don't know who his mentors were. He is now deceased. Another influential person was Dr. Peter Koen, the senior clinical psychologist at Fort Napier Mental Hospital in Pietermaritzburg. He was also a protégé of Professor Theron and helped me in the development of my research that focused on the preliminary standardization of a South African version of the Minnesota Multiphasic Personality Inventory.

Also, early in my training, I became very interested in electroencephalography and how the electrical responses of the brain were related to behavior. The work of A. C. Mundy-Castle, and a Dr. Nelson, both of the National Institute for Personnel Research of the South African Council for Scientific and Industrial Research, were influential, and this led me to my connection with Lee Travis. Both of these neuropsychologists had trained in England under people who, in turn, had their roots with Lee Travis' protégés.

My connection was peripheral, but I was familiar with Lee Travis' research in electroencephalography long before I knew he had any connection with Fuller.

A FACULTY GENEALOGY FOR THE TRAVIS YEARS

H. NEWTON MALONY (1969—)

H. Newton Malony
Ph.D. 1965, George Peabody College
Human Nature, Religious Beliefs and Pastoral Care

Nicholas Hobbs
Ph.D. 1946, Ohio State University
Psychological Research and Services in an Army Air Forces Convalescent Hospital
(dissertation chair)

Sidney Leavitt Pressey
Ph.D. 1917, Harvard University
The Influence of Color Upon Mental and Motor Efficiency
(dissertation chair)

E. B. Holt
Ph.D. 1901, Harvard University
The Motor Element in Vision
(committee member)

Herbert Langfeld
Ph.D. 1909, University of Berlin
(dissertation chair)

Robert M. Yerkes
Ph.D. 1902, Harvard University
The Psychic Processes of the Frog: A Study of the Instincts, Habits, and Reactions of the Frog by Reaction Time Methods
(dissertation chair)

Robert MacDougall
Ph.D. 1895, Harvard University
The Physical Coefficent of Certain Mental States
(committee member)

Carl Stumpf
Ph.D. 1868, University of Göttingen
(dissertation chair)

Hugo Münsterburg
Ph.D. 1885, University of Leipzig
Die Lehre von der natürlichen Anpassung in ihrer Entwickelung, Anwendung und Bedeutung
(dissertation chair)

Hugo Münsterburg
Ph.D. 1885, University of Leipzig
Die Lehre von der natürlichen Anpassung in ihrer Entwickelung, Anwendung und Bedeutung
(dissertation chair)

R. Hermann Lotze
M.D. 1838, University of Leipzig
(dissertation chair)

Wilhelm Wundt
M.D. 1856, University of Heidelberg
(dissertation chair)

Psychology and the Cross

My own reflections are as follows: At times the influences that determine one's scholarly bent are dependent on choice, at times on chance, and at times on crisis. The influence of my dissertation chair, Nicholas Hobbs, was one that began initially by chance but became an influence by choice. My decision to study under Hobbs at Peabody was unplanned. I was not admitted to graduate study in the Psychology Department of Vanderbilt, where I originally applied. Peabody was across the street. Hobbs admitted me as a special student, a status I retained until completion of my master's degree.

I had never heard of Nicholas Hobbs beforehand, and met him by chance. However, during this two-year trial period, I took one class with Hobbs and became aware of the aura surrounding his reputation. The class was Introduction to Counseling, and the text was Carl Rogers' Client-Centered Therapy,[12] for which Hobbs had written the chapter on "Group Therapy." He was a convinced espouser of this approach, both technically and philosophically. Most important to me, he exemplified empowerment by the way he related to persons outside of class. He always remembered your name and dignified you by expressing interest in your life. We students used to say we believed in "the Father, the Son, the Holy Ghost, and Nicholas Hobbs." I felt cherished by him and was sincerely privileged to be his student.

Hobbs was a true humanist who not only evidenced concern for graduate students but for disturbed and disadvantaged children. "Project Re-Ed," Tennessee's nationally known weekday residential treatment program for disturbed children, was his creation. Although he is deceased, the memory of his personhood continues to inspire me. No person other than Lee Travis has had quite as much personal influence on me as Nicholas Hobbs.

Actually, most of the thrust of my religio-psychological thinking was determined by a crisis which occurred over six years before I met Nicholas Hobbs. Although I had a minor in psychology, I had personally experienced few life traumas until the spring of my first year in seminary. A friend with whom I had attended Easter worship service in New York City jumped out of Riverside Church tower and killed himself. I became very anxious and suicidal. I began to doubt God as well as my calling to ministry. I tentatively planned to hang myself in the closet of my bedroom. No one knew of my travail, not even my roommate.

Concurrent with this experience, I was required by an instructor to read something written by a contemporary theologian of my choice. I selected Paul Tillich, and read his Terry lectures, "The Courage to Be."[13] That book changed my life. Next to the Bible I esteem this volume above all others. By affirming my basic anxiety and taking a leap of faith, I overcame my suicidal fears. These ideas have continued to provide a foundation for my thinking. Like Kant, I have "given up belief that I might have faith." I may find evidence for meaning and for God, but proof eludes me. Yet, while I could exist without faith, I cannot live without it. I have chosen to live. These ideas are foundational for my integration of psychology and theology.

The other influences on my thinking have been by "choice." The year after completing seminary, I evoked the influence of Sigmund Freud on my life by studying at the William Alanson White Institute for Psychiatry, Psychology, and Psychoanalysis. Here I was introduced to teachers like Rollo May and Clara Thompson—interpreters of Freud. I integrated this understanding of personality with Tillich's existential understanding of life crises.

Several years later I decided to return to graduate school. My dream was to prepare to teach pastoral counseling. By this time I had become aware of two persons who became models for what I wanted to do. One was James Dittes who, along with his seminary training, had received a doctorate in social psychology and was teaching at my alma mater, Yale Divinity School. The other was John Vayhinger, who was also seminary-trained but had a doctorate in clinical psychology. He taught at Garrett Biblical Seminary. I foresaw my study in psychology as leading to a career similar to theirs, applying clinical training to the work of ministry. I, too, wanted to do this.

Once in graduate school, two other persons influenced the direction of my scholarly bent. Gordon Allport's theorizing about "becoming" provided an umbrella that covered both Freud's determinism and Tillich's free decision-making. Allport's concept of "functional autonomy of motives," coupled with the importance of a central life philosophy (Allport's "proprium") became central coordinating themes for my integration, self-understanding, and counseling. I witnessed to the importance of Allport for my thinking by presenting a paper titled "The Contribution of Gordon Allport to the Psychology of Religion" on the first program of the newly formed division of Psychologists Interested in Religious Issues of the APA in the mid-1970s.

The influence of Paul Pruyser came somewhat later. He was a professor at the Menninger Foundation in Topeka, Kansas, where I took my predoctoral internship at the state hospital. In Pruyser I experienced a renaissance man. His knowledge about many things was broad and deep. He could lecture on brain damage in the morning and St. Augustine in the afternoon. Moreover, he was a professing and practicing Christian. He became my model for integration of my faith with my profession. I continue to remember his influence and, for the past decade, have been trying to develop measures of optimal religious functioning based on his theories. Most recently I have been engaged in editing and reevaluating his influence on the psychology of religion through a volume being published by Oxford University Press.[14]

In the essay I have sought to assess the influence on my scholarly life which has been concentrated on the integration of psychology and Christian theology in my personal life, professional counseling, and theorizing about guiding principles. As I said earlier, these persons became influential to be my crisis, by chance, and by choice. I remain unclear as to which of these three types of influence had has the greater impact. All were, and are, important.

JAMES A. OAKLAND (1970-1975)

James A. Oakland
Ph.D. 1976, University of Washington
The Performance of High School Students on the Edwards Personality Inventory and its Relationship to Overachievement and Underachievement

Allen E. Edwards
Ph.D. 1940, Northwestern University
Frames of Reference as a Factor Influencing Learning and Retention
(dissertation chair)

Adam R. Gilliland
Ph.D. 1922, University of Chicago
Experimental Studies of the Effect on Reading of Changes in Sensory Factors
(dissertation chair)

A Faculty Genealogy for the Travis Years

Dr. Oakland makes these comments:

Obtaining an adequate education in clinical psychology in the 1960s was not easy. Most psychology departments had a fairly strong bent toward basic (vs. applied) science with an experimental (or at least rigorously quantified) approach, modeled as much as possible on physics. It was seen as the best (and often only) antidote to a hopeless morass of speculation, the only sure way to gradually build a solid scientific structure in the field of psychology. I was skeptical but interested when I entered the graduate program at the University of Washington. By the end of my first year, I was quite sure that the promise was well beyond the reality of what experimental psychology had been or would be able to produce. Many (most?) of the questions of clinical psychology were receiving little or no attention; they were often in a "universe" ruled out ("mentalistic," etc.), or lost in preoccupation with attempting a rigorous methodology. It was depressing. I surveyed my options, chose to stay at Washington, finish the Ph.D. as rapidly as possible, and rely on clinical training elsewhere. My internship was something of a start; postdoctoral supervision helped more, but eventually I migrated to psychoanalytic training.

Allen Edwards, my dissertation supervisor, was a superb statistician who had interest and successes in "personality" measurement (from a decidedly empiricist direction). Using highly sophisticated statistical techniques, he was devising a new inventory (what became the Edwards Personal Preference Schedule)[15] which I thought was less distant from my research interests than other possibilities present. I proposed a research project to him which he accepted for my dissertation research. Our relationship was limited to the necessities of the project and was not extensive. Though I continued some research with the EPPS postdoctorally, I shortly moved to other things.

My first faculty position (University of Washington School of Medicine) left me little time to reflect on the methodological problems of psychology, yet these increasingly intrigued me. An invitation to join Fuller's Graduate School of Psychology provided the opportunity to think, read, and teach in areas from personality and measurement to philosophy of science, and I gradually evolved to the psychoanalytic world. I certainly did not find an "epistemological solution," only a community of people who had thought and were thinking about the same philosophy of science and psychological issues as I was and who had opted for a different course, and thereby accumulated a much more useful body of theory about human beings than I found in academic psychology. And I still find that true.

ADRIN CULVER SYLLING: 1965-1980

Adrin C. Sylling
D.Phil. 1973, University of South Africa
*The Creative Use of Conflict in Marriage:
A Social Casework Approach*

J. S. Theron
Chair, Department of Social Work
University of South Africa
(dissertation chair)

Dr. Sylling recollects:

Unfortunately, I know very little about J.S. Theron. He was the chair of the Department of Social Work in the Graduate School of Social Work at the University of South Africa. I know he was an esteemed academician and had good liaison with the Department of Psychology and with other European universities. The psychology department also evaluated my dissertation because it was deemed to be "highly psychological" in content and philosophy.

Maurice Connery was my U.S. advisor. He was the dean of the School of Social Work at UCLA, and I met with him on a number of occasions. He was a "wünderkind" out of the University of Minnesota. He was very bright, relaxed, and highly regarded in the profession of social work. After my first meeting with him, I came home and announced to Marion, "I can plainly see why he has a doctorate and I don't." He was very helpful, and when he wrote the University of South Africa to inform them he had approved my dissertation, Professor Theron responded with "He has made a good beginning."

My greatest mentor by far, however, was Lee Edward Travis, whom I still miss greatly. For many years, he was the dean and I was the director of the Pasadena Community Counseling Clinic, so we became very close.

A Faculty Genealogy for the Travis Years

Lee Edward Travis (1964-1987)

> **Lee Edward Travis**
> Ph.D. 1924, University of Iowa
> *A Test for Distinguishing between Schizophrenosis and Psychoneuroses: A Study in Abnormal Psychology*

> **Carl Emil Seashore**
> Ph.D. 1895, Yale University
> *Measurements of Illusions and Hallucinations in Normal Life*
> (dissertation chair)

> **Edward Wheeler Scripture**
> Ph.D. 1891, University of Leipzig
> *Über den associative Verlauf der Vorstellungen*
> (dissertation chair)

> **Wilhelm Wundt**
> M.D. 1856, University of Heidelberg
> (dissertation chair)

Much has already been written about the achievements of Lee Edward Travis. He was honored on his eightieth birthday by his Fuller colleagues with a *festschrift* that surveys his life's chief contributions to speech pathology, electroencephalography and neuropsychology, and integration, and celebrates his personal, spiritual, and artistic qualities.[16] After his death, he was honored with an obituary in *The American Psychologist*.[17] Travis was mentored by the Swedish-born Carl Seashore (formerly Sjöstrand), who headed the psychological laboratory at the University of Iowa and established the second psychological clinic in the United States. Seashore wrote several introductory psychology texts, contributed to the fields of educational psychology, speech and phonetics, and the measurement of musical talent. His best-known work was his *Psychology of Music*, published in 1938. Seashore's mentor was Edward W. Scripture, founder of the psychological laboratory at Yale, and George Trumbull Ladd, the great American psychology textbook writer who was also a well-known personalist philosopher-theologian and spent the latter part of his career teaching theology at Andover Theological Seminary. Fuller alumni/ae who remember our own George Ladd, the New Testament theologian, will find the pairing of Ladd and Scripture an amusing mnemonic tool. Scripture's mentor was Wilhelm Wundt, the great German physiological psychologist often credited with founding the science of psychology. Thus, Travis is the intellectual great-grandson of Wilhelm Wundt. In the sketch that follows, we see Lee Edward Travis through the eyes of Warren S. Brown, current Fuller professor, who is Lee's academic great-grandson:

Although most Ph.D. candidates get to know their dissertation chairperson and mentor fairly well, few have had the opportunity to become friends of their academic "grandfather" or "great-grandfather." The opportunity to know these gentlemen has been for me a valuable and enriching experience, particularly since both Lindsley and Travis are listed among the most famous psychologists in history.

My dissertation chair at USC, Gary Galbraith, was a student of Donald B. Lindsley (and thus Travis' "grandson"). Lindsley gained fame and notoriety for his work on the reticular activating system of the brain and its role in modulating tonic and phasic arousal and attention. For this work and other research on electrical activity of the brain, Lindsley has been given many of the most prestigious awards and honors in psychology, including election to the American and Soviet Academies of Science. It has been widely rumored that he was even considered for a Nobel Prize. From the laboratory and research of Donald B. Lindsley, I have inherited the concept of EEG as a reflection of the state of mental arousal, and the idea that human evoked EEG potentials can provide important measures of brain transactions in the processing of information.

My personal relationship with Don Lindsley began before we had even met, when he helped me obtain a UCLA Brain Research Institute postdoctoral fellowship. I soon came to know him as a very gracious and personable individual who was always glad to talk and exchange ideas. He had a "folksy" side which made him many friends in the scientific world. I remember twice hearing Don Lindsley give lectures on his research on the nervous system of the three-toed sloth. Into these lectures he quite naturally interwove slides and stories of his Amazon travels.

My academic "great-grandfather," Lindsley's mentor, was Lee Edward Travis. Via Lindsley and Galbraith, I inherited from Lee Travis a methodological commitment to measurement of physiological responses as a means of studying and understanding human cognitive and psychological functioning. It is particularly to Lee that I trace the idea that psychophysiological recordings can be relevant to the study and understanding of human clinical problems such as language disorders, developmental disabilities, abnormalities of hemispheric asymmetry, and other neurocognitive dysfunctions.

About the time I finished my degree and was bound for a UCLA postdoctorate, I made an academic pilgrimage to meet Lee Travis, then dean at Fuller. As he met me in the outer waiting area, I remember being impressed by his commanding physique and upright posture, remarkable for a man then well into his seventies. I also recall the picture of Jesus and a cross prominently displayed on his office wall. Most vividly, however, I remember how clearly he turned the tables on me. In our conversation, Lee succeeded in making me feel like I was the great and important person. I remember this experience well because it was repeated consistently in later conversations with him, even when we were faculty colleagues. The great Lee Edward Travis always made me feel like I was the great man of science.

DONALD F. TWEEDIE, JR. (1964-1976)

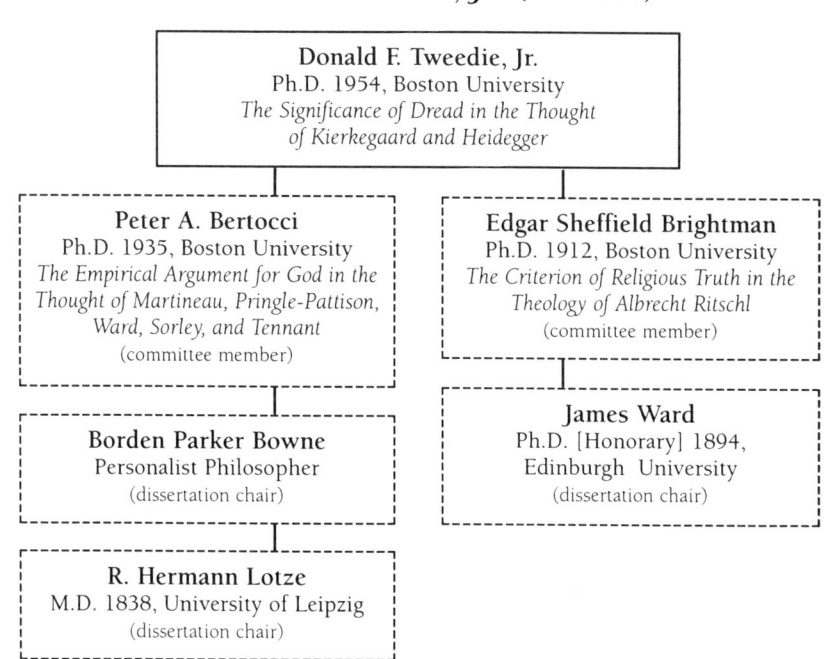

Donald F. Tweedie, Jr.
Ph.D. 1954, Boston University
The Significance of Dread in the Thought of Kierkegaard and Heidegger

Peter A. Bertocci
Ph.D. 1935, Boston University
The Empirical Argument for God in the Thought of Martineau, Pringle-Pattison, Ward, Sorley, and Tennant
(committee member)

Edgar Sheffield Brightman
Ph.D. 1912, Boston University
The Criterion of Religious Truth in the Theology of Albrecht Ritschl
(committee member)

Borden Parker Bowne
Personalist Philosopher
(dissertation chair)

James Ward
Ph.D. [Honorary] 1894, Edinburgh University
(dissertation chair)

R. Hermann Lotze
M.D. 1838, University of Leipzig
(dissertation chair)

Dr. Tweedie offers the following recollections:

I had only incidental influence from Peter Bertocci, who became my dissertation chair upon the death of E. S. Brightman. He had just arrived at Boston, having been chairman of both the Philosophy and Psychology Departments of Bates College, and allowed me to have dual majors in these two fields, doing qualifying exams in both. My chief dissertation influence was E. J. Carnell (Ph.D., Boston University, with a dissertation on "The Problem of Validation in Kierkegaard"). Heidegger's works were direct,, since none at that time were translated. Primary were Sein und Zeit, *and* Über den Humanismus *(which I translated for him).*[18]

My dissertation discussion of angst (dread), like Hume's "Principles"[19] *fell "dead-born"—a piece of exotic academic trivium—but was resurrected by the existential-phenomenological movement occasioned by the appearance of Rollo May's* Existence.[20] *Incidentally, Martin Luther King's dissertation significantly "piggy-backed" mine.*[21]

The chief influence upon me as a psychologist was Theodore Thass-Thienemann, a classical psycho-linguist who studied with Wundt. He taught me German, psychology, and linguistics, both as professor, and subsequently colleague. He was 30 years at the University of Budapest (several years as dean of the Faculty of Arts and Social Science). As a refugee from Communist oppression, he transitioned to the U.S. and taught here 35 more years! This grand old man of 95 years passed away in 1985.

Thienemann referred me to Frankl, in whose clinic (Psychotherapeutic Department of Vienna Polyclinic Hospital) I worked for a year. At that time only one of his 16 books was translated to English, so my Logotherapy[22] *was an effort to introduce these to the American public. I also translated* Homo Patiens *for Harper & Row.*[23] *My psycho-philosopho-anthropology was rather little influenced by him, although psychotherapeutic attitude and practice were, I felt, enhanced. The most significant personal impact upon me as a psychotherapist was made by Paul Tournier, whom I met indirectly through Frankl. I cherish the memories of personal interaction and correspondence with this loving and learned Christian man.*

An overview of my felt influence will be observed in an essay titled "My Heroes" upon which I work sporadically. The principals, in chrono-historical order, are Carnell, Ockenga, Gedney, Thass-

A Faculty Genealogy for the Travis Years

Thienemann, Frankl, Tournier,[24] Mowrer,[25] and Travis.

As an expsychologist, my 26 years as a professor, coupled with 35 years of psychotherapeutic practice, seem both pleasantly nostalgic and remote. More existential are my adventures of the '80s—climbing the sheerest cliff in North America (San Jacinto), flying to the Arctic Circle for lunch (with my psychologist son, D.F., as co-pilot), riding my motorcycle (Honda Silver Wing) 84,000 miles around the U.S., and sailing a 27-foot sloop 3,000 miles around the Caribbean. My plans are to start the 1990s with a circumnavigation of the globe in a 37-foot cutter-rigged sailboat. I'm not sure when the anniversary will be celebrated. (The first faculty was appointed June 15, 1964; the first function—Pasadena Community Counseling Center—October 2, 1964; the first class, September 1965, etc.) But I will be with you in spirit, being physically either in the Pacific or Indian Ocean, hoping for pleasant seas and a following wind for all of us.

Neil Clark Warren (1967-1982)

Neil C. Warren
Ph.D. 1968, University of Chicago
Structuring and Stabilizing of Psychotherapy for Low Prognosis Clients

Laura North Rice
Ph.D. 1955, University of Chicago
An Investigation of the Functioning of Concepts in a Perceptual Situation
(dissertation chair)

John M. Butler
Ph.D. 1950, University of Minnesota
Self-Evaluation of Personality in Adolescents
(dissertation chair)

C. Gilbert Wrenn
Ph.D. 1932, Stanford University
The Relationship of Intelligence to Certain Interests, Personality Traits, and Vocational Choices of College Students
(dissertation chair)

Walter Crosby Eells
Ph.D. 1927, Stanford University
A Plea for a Standard Definition of the Standard Deviation
(committee member)

Ernest Hilgard
Ph.D. 1930, Yale University
Conditioned Eyelid Reactions to a Light Stimulus Based on the Reflex Link to Sound
(dissertation chair)

Edward K. Strong, Jr.
Ph.D. 1911, Columbia University
Application of the "Order of Merit Method" to Advertising
(committee member)

Raymond Dodge
Ph.D. 1896, Halle-an-der Saale
Die Meterische Wertverstellungen
(dissertation chair)

Harry L. Hollingworth
Ph.D. 1909, Columbia University
The Inaccuracy of Movement
(committee member)

Benno Erdmann
Philosopher
(dissertation chair)

A Faculty Genealogy for the Travis Years

Dr. Warren recalls his early influences as follows:

My involvement with psychology began at Pepperdine University which had an outstanding Psychology Department in the early 1950s. Of the six full-time faculty members in the department, three had graduated from the University of Chicago. A fourth member, the department chairman, Everett Shostrom, had graduated from Stanford, but he had spent a summer or more at the University of Chicago and had been significantly influenced by Carl Rogers and his colleagues.

My brother-in-law, Dr. Richard Hogan, was a prominent member of that Pepperdine faculty, and he had worked closely with Carl Rogers in the development of Rogers' theoretical approach to the psychological defenses.

During my years at Princeton Theological Seminary in the mid-1950s, a new pastoral psychologist had been appointed to the faculty: Edward Golden, who adopted Carl Rogers' popular text, Client Centered Therapy, *as his principal approach to the teaching of pastoral counseling.*

It's not very surprising, then, that when I thought about graduate training in psychology, the University of Chicago was at the front of my mind. I wanted more than anything to study with the master himself, Carl Rogers. He was at the zenith of his popularity at that time. His research efforts in the area of psychotherapy had catapulted him to prominence in American psychology.

But when I arrived on the campus at Chicago, Rogers had just left for Wisconsin to begin his huge research project on therapeutic approaches to schizophrenia. Fortunately for me, all of his colleagues were still on the Chicago faculty, and the Counseling Center was extremely active in the areas of practice and research. I began immediately to work as a research assistant to John M. Butler and Laura North Rice. They had received a major research grant from the National Institute of Mental Health to investigate the relationship of process and outcome variables in psychotherapy.

Jack Butler was a major figure at Chicago during that period. He had a brilliant quantitative mind, and he developed all kinds of new models for investigating psychotherapy. Butler had received his doctorate at the University of Minnesota in 1950, and his training in measurement was outstanding. He, along with Donald Fiske, attracted outstanding students to the department and to this area of inquiry.

Butler was also the finest psychotherapist I have ever known. I listened to scores of his tapes, and was deeply influenced by him. He had an incredible ability to listen, and when he articulated what he had heard and experienced, his client nearly always seemed to move forward. His was a client-centered approach with a classic flavor, owing to his deep appreciation of literature. Butler needed someone to work with him who was as brilliant as he, but far more disciplined and productive. This person he found in his student, Laura North Rice. The two of them wrote numerous articles about the theoretical advances they had fashioned out of their active research program.

It was under Laura Rice that I studied most closely. She was an absolutely unselfish teacher, always willing to talk, always eager to help you develop your own ideas and to experience them fully, "clear to their edges," as she liked to say.

My research position under her direction involved listening to dozens of hours of therapy tapes every month. I sometimes imagined that I had heard more psychotherapy than any other person living. It was out of all this therapy listening that I became interested in the low-prognosis client, that person for whom therapy failure could be predicted from the very beginning. The real question was whether such a client could be taught to be more productive in the therapy hour. I developed and subsequently tested an approach designed to save this category of clients from inevitable disappointment and failure. Dr. Rice and I published an article on our findings which was reprinted in several edited books.[26]

Needless to say, my years at the University of Chicago were powerfully stimulating and formational. The genius of Carl Rogers for me involved his unique ability to link the best of theology, philosophy, and psychology—and then to place all of his ideas under the strictest form of empirical questioning. It was these emphases I attempted to share with my students and faculty colleagues when I arrived at Fuller in 1967.

A Faculty Genealogy for the Travis Years

ENDNOTES

1. The following history of psychology students participated in the portion of the research included here: Jeff Berryhill, Terry Brenneman, Deborah Cole, Nadine Cole, Peter Conrad, Tami Duran, Barbara Eurich-Rascoe, Indra Finch, Monica Guevara, Dariel Heinesh, Lu-lin Hom, Steve Hoskinson, Robert S. Kern, Stephen S. Meharg, Ruth Mills, Gail Murdock, Debra Neumann, Mary E. Palmquist, Doug O'Donnell, Lydia Strauch Glass, Richard M. Whited, and Peter Murray Young. Debra Neumann also served as research assistant, aiding my pursuit of elusive archival data. Additional secretarial and research assistance was provided by Freda Carver, Maryan Hinkel, Bert Jacklitch, Dan Palomino, Tracey Townsend, Carol Rush, and Pamela Williams.

2. The inspiration for this research came from two sources: Richard G. Weigel and James W. Gottfurch, "Faculty Genealogies: A Stimulus for Student Involvement in History and Systems," *American Psychologist*, October 1972, pp. 981-983; W. Scott Terry, "Tracing Psychologist's 'Roots': A Project for History and Systems Course," *Teaching of Psychology*, October 1980, pp. 176-177. The methodology was modified to focus on the use of historical resources and reference works and archival materials rather than personal interviews. Actual reference works and history of psychology texts consulted are too numerous to cite here, but can be provided for those who are interested.

3. I wish to thank the following persons for their assistance in locating archival data: Dagi Finch, for information on John G. Finch; Yvette Foster, the Office of University Alumni Affairs, for information on Robert K. Bower; Arthur F. Glasser of the School of World Mission at Fuller Theological Seminary, for his biographical sketch on Sarpavalli Radhakrishnan; Shieu-yu Hwang, McAlister Library, Fuller Theological Seminary, for general assistance; Penelope Krosch, archivist, Walter Library, University of Minnesota, Twin Cities, for information on John M. Butler; Haddon Klingberg, Jr., for information on Viktor Frankl; Richard L. Popp, archives assistant, the University of Chicago Library, for information on Ralph Tyler and Adam R. Gilliland; Patrick M. Quinn, university archivist, Northwestern University Library, for information on Allen L. Edwards; Mike Raines, curatorial assistant, Harvard University Library, for information on Robert MacDougall; Earl M. Rogers, curator of archives, The University of Iowa, for information on Charles E. Meyers; Stephen W. Rogers, reference librarian, William Oxley Thompson Memorial Library, Ohio State University, for information on Nicholas Hobbs and Sidney L. Pressey; Sandra Roscoe, assistant reference librarian, The University of Chicago Library, for information on Robert K. Bower and Laura North Rice; Kathleen S. Ryan, Elmer Holmes Bobst Library/New York University, for information on Dan William Dodson; Dennis Thomison, Doheny Reference Center of the University Library, University of Southern California, for information on Paul Fairweather and Charles Manley Brown.

4. The booklet eventually was incorporated into the book by Anna Freud, *The Ego and the Mechanisms of Defense*, translated by Cecil Baines (New York: International Universities Press, 1966).

5. Robert K. Bower, "Christian Education: A Vital Challenge for Today's Churches," *Bulletin of Fuller Theological Seminary*, Spring, 1959.
6. Robert K. Bower, "Doctor of Ministry and the Ministry of Marriage and Family Counseling," *Theology, News and Notes*, October 1977, 34-38.
7. Robert K. Bower, "The Minister's Attitude Toward Marriage," *Theology, News and Notes*, March 1968, 8-10.
8. This book is available in a 2nd edition by Ernst G. Beier and David M. Young, *The Silent Language of Psychotherapy: Social Reinforcement of Unconscious Processes* (New York: Aldine, 1984).
9. London: Oxford University Press, 1973. Dr. Pond delivered the 1971 Riddell Memorial Lectures, which form the text of this book, at the University of Newcastle upon Tyne.
10. Vida Carver, Ed., *C.A. Mace: A Symposium* (London: Methuen; Penguin, 1962).
11. Stanley Romaine Hopper, *The Crisis of Faith* (London: Hodder & Stoughton, 1947).
12. Carl Rogers, *Client-Centered Therapy: Its Current Practices, Implications, and Theory* (New York: Houghton Mifflin, 1951).
13. Paul Tillich, *The Courage to Be* (New Haven: Yale, 1952).
14. H. Newton Malony & Bernard Spilka, Eds., *Religion in Psychodynamic Perspective: The Contributions of Paul W. Pruyser* (New York: Oxford, 1991).
15. Edwards Personal Preference Schedule (New York: The Psychological Corporation, 1953). The EPPS assesses 15 needs postulated by Henry Murray and his colleagues, which are also measured by the Thematic Apperception Test and described in Henry A. Murray (and collaborators), *Explorations in Personality: A Clinical and Experimental Study of Fifty Men of College Age* (New York: Oxford, 1938).
16. Donald F. Tweedie, Jr. & Paul W. Clement, *Psychologist Pro Tem: In Honor of the Eightieth Birthday of Lee Edward Travis* (Los Angeles: University of Southern California, 1976).
17. Donald B. Lindsley, "Lee Edward Travis (1896-1987)," *The American Psychologist*, 1989, 44(11), 1414.
18. Martin Heidegger's Sein und Zeit (Halle, 1927) was translated by John Macquarrie & Edward Robinson as *Being and Time* (New York: Harper & Row, 1962); there is no published English translation of *Über den Humanismus* (Frankfurt: V. Klostermann, 1947).
19. Tweedie's reference here is not clear. He may be referring to the well-known "principles of association" (similarity, contiguity in place and time, and causality) articulated by David Hume in his *Treatise of Human Nature* (1739) and its later revision, *An Enquiry Concerning Human Understanding* (1758), or to Hume's extreme skepticism, which was the impetus for Kant's *Critique of Pure Reason* (1781), Critique of Practical Reason (1785), and *Critique of Judgment* (1790).
20. Rollo May, Ernest Angel & Henri Ellenberger, Eds., *Existence: A New Dimension in Psychiatry and Psychology* (New York: Basic Books, 1958)

21. Martin Luther King, "A Comparison of the Conceptions of God in the Thinking of Paul Tillich and Henry Nelson Wieman". Doctoral Dissertation, Boston University Graduate School, 1955. Abstracted in *Dissertation Abstracts International, 1966, 19/06*, p. 1458 (Order # AAC 0024708).
22. D.F. Tweedie, Jr., *Logotherapy and the Christian Faith: An Evaluation of Frankl's Existential Approach to Psychotherapy* (Grand Rapids, MI: Baker, 1961). Viktor E. Frankl, a Jewish psychiatrist and concentration-camp survivor, is the founder of logotherapy, an existential approach focused on the search for meaning in human existence. Frankl's *Man's Search for Meaning* (Boston: Beacon, 1963) has been published in 24 languages and named by the Library of Congress as one of the ten most influential books in America, and more than 120 books and nearly 140 dissertations (in 15 languages) have been written about logotherapy. These include Reuven Bulka's *The Quest for Ultimate Meaning: Principles and Applications of Logotherapy* (New York: Philosophical Library, 1979); R. C. Leslie's *Jesus and Logotherapy: The Ministry of Jesus as Interpreted through the Psychotherapy of Viktor Frankl* (New York: Abingdon, 1965); and A. J. Ungersma's *The Search for Meaning: A New Approach in Psychotherapy and Pastoral Psychology* (Philadelphia: Westminster, 1961).
23. Viktor Frankl, *Homo Patiens: Versuch einer Pathozidee* (Vienna: Verlag Franz Deuticke, 1950). There is no record of a published translation.
24. The works of Paul Tournier are well-known to Christian psychologists. Tournier, a Swiss psychiatrist, wrote in the tradition of personalist psychology, a legacy Tweedie inherited from Brightman and Bertocci. Personalism as a philosophical and theological movement gave rise to the earliest textbooks in personality theory, and it strongly influenced Gordon Allport's personality theory. Twenty-one books authored by Tournier have been translated into English. Perspectives on Tournier's life and work are offered by G. R. Collins' *The Christian Psychology of Paul Tournier* (Grand Rapids, MI: Baker, 1973); K. Houde's "The Christian Personality Theory of Paul Tournier," in *Dissertation Abstracts International*, 1990, 51-07B, 3603 (University Microfilms No. DEY-90-33-538); and M. Peaston's *Personal Living: An Introduction to Paul Tournier* (New York: Harper & Row, 1972).
25. O. Hobart Mowrer, the cofounder with Neal Miller of Social Learning Theory, was president-elect of the American Psychological Association when he suffered a psychotic break in the early 1950s. This personal experience led him to reflect on the role of religion. In *The Crisis in Psychiatry and Religion* (Princeton: Van Nostrand Insight Books, 1961) he challenged the Freudian notion that all guilt feelings have neurotic origin, focusing instead on real guilt. In *The New Group Therapy* (Princeton: Van Nostrand, 1964) he examined the role of reconciliation and confession, and noted the similarity of self-help groups to apostolic Christianity in their reinforcing of moral sanctions. These works inspired the later movements of "responsibility therapy" and "integrity therapy." Mowrer's personal experiences are further described in *Abnormal Reactions or Actions? (An Autobiographical Answer)* (Dubuque, Iowa: Wm. C. Brown Company, 1966).
26. Neil C. Warren & Laura North Rice, "Structure and Stabilizing of Psychotherapy for Low-Prognosis Clients." *Journal of Consulting and Clinical Psychology*, 1972, 39(2), 173-181.

SOUTH UNIVERSITY
709 MALL BLVD.
SAVANNAH, GA 31406